DANTE and MILTON

The *Commedia* and *Paradise Lost*

DANTE and MILTON

The *Commedia*
and *Paradise Lost*

IRENE SAMUEL

Hunter College

Cornell University Press

ITHACA, NEW YORK

Preface

TO encompass the universes created by Dante in his *Commedia* and Milton in *Paradise Lost* is beyond my intention as it is beyond my scope. My study takes its impulse from Milton's avowed admiration for Dante, an admiration so rare in seventeenth-century England that it ought to shed light on the resemblances between the two greatest narrative poems of the postclassical western world. Comparisons of the two have more often shed darkness. Thus T. S. Eliot writing of Dante could not avoid a glancing reference to Milton: "The vision of Satan [in *Inferno* 34] may seem grotesque, especially if we have fixed in our minds the curly-haired Byronic hero of Milton." Where in *Paradise Lost* Eliot found that curly hair on the scarred brow of Milton's Satan is a puzzle. With comparison so inevitable, we might hope that it would be carefully made. But scholars have been content to note parallels, and critics have indulged in the large, incautious, sometimes absurdly inappropriate, generality: either Dante must be better than Milton or worse.

My purpose has been simpler: to collect the evidence about Milton's interest in Dante and see what he may have learned from the *Commedia* that bears upon his writing of *Paradise Lost*. Where he learned chiefly that he differed from Dante I have not tried to minimize the difference, without, I trust, setting myself to judge between them. More often he evidently found in the *Commedia* matter and devices to his purpose. Where influence or divergence must remain conjectural, I have presented the substantial parallels without insisting that Milton must have had Dante in mind.

Since the reader will presumably follow my argument most easily if he has Dante's *Commedia* in English prose together with an Italian text, I have taken all my quotations from *The Divine Comedy* from the Temple Classics Edition, with English-Italian text, published by E. P. Dutton and Company, Inc. Quotations from the *Commedia* have been checked against the text of *Dante con l'espositione di M. Bernardino Daniello da Lucca*, printed in 1568, the only edition that Milton refers to, although he probably knew also the editions and commentaries of Landino and Vellutello, frequently reprinted during the sixteenth century. I have called the reader's attention to the one phrase quoted where Daniello's slightly different reading is significant. For the most part the differences are minor variants in punctuation, spelling, and elision, and the printer's inadvertent omission of *Purgatorio* 6.106–117, none of which bears on my argument.

The text of *Paradise Lost* cited throughout is the edition by Merritt Y. Hughes in *John Milton: Complete Poems and Major Prose*, copyright 1957 by The Odyssey Press, Inc. My debt to Professor Hughes's scholarship is considerably greater than any acknowledgment of my use of his editions of Milton can indicate. He has read my book in various stages of its composition and has generously given both advice and encouragement.

To Charles W. Jones of the University of California at Berkeley I am indebted for incisive comment on my manuscript in both earlier and final forms. It was my good fortune as a graduate student at Cornell University to study mediaeval literature with Professor Jones, and it has been my continued good fortune to have his wise counsel available. Professor James Hutton of Cornell University, who made valuable suggestions on several sections of the work, and Professor Walter MacKellar, who read and criticized the manuscript, have both saved me from a number of errors and infelicities.

I take this opportunity to thank President John J. Meng and Dean Mary L. Gambrell of Hunter College, who made it possible for me to arrange the academic leaves without which I could not have completed my work. The American Academy in Rome granted me residence privileges as well as use of its library from April through July in 1961 and again in 1963, thus enabling me to concentrate on two favorite poets in a favoring environment. Of the libraries that have facilitated my work, the Vatican Library, the Biblioteca Nazionale of Rome, the Magliabechiana in the Biblioteca Nazionale of Florence, the British Museum, the Cambridge University Library, and the Folger Shakespeare Library merit special thanks. I owe a very special debt to the Olin Library of Cornell University, which purchased from the Magliabechiana, at my request, microfilm of Benedetto Buommattei's commentaries on the *Commedia*, and made them available to me, with other virtually irreplaceable items from its Dante collection, both in Ithaca and through interlibrary loan.

Parts of this volume have previously appeared in somewhat different form: "*Purgatorio* and the Dream of Eve" (first read at a meeting of the Modern Language Association in Chicago in December 1963) was published in the *Journal of English and Germanic Philology* 63 (1964), 441–449; "Satan and the 'Diminisht' Stars" in *Modern Philology* 59 (1962), 239–247, published by The University of Chicago Press, copyright 1962 by The University of Chicago; "Higher Argument Remains," under the title "The Proems of the *Commedia* and *Paradise Lost*," in the *Bucknell Review* 12 (1964), 31–46; and "The

Preface

Valley of Serpents" in *PMLA* 78 (1963), 449–451, reprinted by permission of the Modern Language Association. All four publications have granted permission to reprint the material to which they hold copyright.

For assistance far beyond the typing and checking they were employed to do, I wish to thank my former students Daniel O'Connell and Marilyn Schauer, who cheerfully spent the summer of 1964 at their typewriters when they were not visiting the libraries of New York City in my behalf. It gives me pleasure to know that their labors did not discourage their commitment to careers of study and teaching.

A final word of thanks to the library of the American Academy in Rome, whose facilities are again available to me as I labor through galley proof.

And some final words of explanation. In place of a bibliography, I have listed in Appendix C significant comments on the relation of Milton's work to Dante's; but like all students of Milton, I am indebted in ways not easily acknowledged to the work of other scholars, notably Douglas Bush.

I had hoped when I completed my manuscript in August of 1964 that my book would appear during 1965, the seven hundredth anniversary of Dante's birth; but that was not to be. The Cornell University Press has generously supplied an index.

IRENE SAMUEL

Rome
July, 1965
New York City
November, 1965

Contents

Contents

DANTE and MILTON
The *Commedia* and *Paradise Lost*

I

Preliminaries

Purgatorio
and the Dream of Eve

SINCE prophetic dreams are common to epic and visionary poetry, their mere presence would hardly link *Paradise Lost* to Milton's interest in the *Commedia* of Dante. But the dream of Eve shares features with Dante's first dream on Mount Purgatory that genre alone cannot explain. In both sequences the dream has relation to something occurring at the time; the real incident is transmuted in the dream into other terms; the terms of both involve as their most striking feature the dreamer's being carried aloft above the earth; the dreamer awakens in terror, sees the reassuring presence of the familiar companion, is comforted with an explanation and a "Fear not," and quickly moves on afterward to break the dream-spell. The unfolding of both dreams is set in a superb dawn-passage; each follows the night-routing of a Satan-figure; each precedes extended instruction designed to remove possible motives for error and to confirm reason and will in right choice. A major difference distinguishes the two: the dream of Eve is a nightmare, whereas Dante's corresponds to a helpful reality. In structural importance, in what they point toward, the difference is no less marked. All the more surprising, then, is the impress of Dante's sequence on Milton's.

In Canto 7 of *Purgatorio*, Virgil and Dante have been led by

Sordello at evening into an Edenic dell where the negligent spend their nights until they can be admitted to Purgatory proper. In Canto 8 they see two angels clad in green descend to chase a symbolic serpent from the dell. As commentators have noted, the serpent, "perchance such as gave to Eve the bitter food" (8.99), moves like Milton's Satan in his reptilian progress toward Eve (*Purg.* 8.100–102 and *P.L.* IX.499–526). Clearly the scene in *Purgatorio* impressed Milton.

Shortly before the serpent appears, Dante admonishes his reader: "Aguzza qui, lettor, ben gli occhi al vero." The admonition sharpens attention to the scene itself, to Conrad's prophetic allusion in the following lines to Dante's coming exile from Florence, and in the next canto to Dante's prophetic dream.

In Canto 9 the poet, who in his own words has in himself "di quel d'Adamo," sinks to the grass conquered by sleep, and just before dawn, "when our mind, more of a wanderer from the flesh and less prisoned by thoughts, in its visions is almost prophetic," dreams that an eagle snatches him "up far as the fiery sphere."

> There it seemed that he and I did burn, and the
> visionary flame so scorched that needs was
> my slumber broken.   (31–33)

The dawn-setting vouches for the truth of the dream; its first element corresponds to what is happening in reality as Lucia carries Dante to the gates of Purgatory; the second element, which breaks his sleep, corresponds to what will happen much later, first when he passes through the painful fire of Canto 27, to be cleansed of the last stain before he may enter the Earthly Paradise, and second when he rises above the earth in *Paradiso* 1. The dream thus echoes well beyond the part of the poem in which it occurs.

Here in Canto 9, when the scorching of the "visionary

flame" awakens him, startled, he grows pale "come fa l'uom
che spaventato agghiaccia" ("even as a man who freezes with
terror"), but happily, beside him in the unexpected place he
finds Virgil, "solo il mio conforto." Told by Virgil that Lucia
has carried him here while he slept, he is reassured, less by
finding that the fire was only a dream than by Virgil's "Non
aver tema . . . fatti sicur (Have no fear . . . make thee
secure)." Thus comforted, he follows Virgil at once up toward
the height where a gate divides the wall of Purgatory, and
enters the specifically purgatorial process.

In *Paradise Lost* Eve's account of her dream follows the dis-
covery of Satan and his expulsion from the sheltered bower
by the two angels Ithuriel and Zephon. Caught in the form of
a toad, returned to his native form, led before Gabriel and the
rest of the angelic guard, Satan is ready to fight; but the sign
of the scales appears in the heavens, showing, as Gabriel
points out, that he will be defeated in any physical combat.
Thus, at the end of Book IV,

> The Fiend lookt up and knew
> His mounted scale aloft: nor more; but fled
> Murmuring, and with him fled the shades of night.

The phrase recalls the swift departure of the symbolic serpent
from the Edenic dell of Purgatory, where at the approach of
the two angels, "fuggì il serpente" (8.107).[1] There also two
angels of marked beauty were involved.

Book V opens with a dawn-piece before Adam awakens the
slumbering Eve, who then recounts her dream. Dante's prophetic dream occurred at dawn,

> At the hour when the swallow begins her sad
> lays nigh unto the morn.   (9.13–14)

---

[1] Cf. at the end of Dante's third dream, *Purg.* 27.112–113, "le tenebre
fuggian . . . / e il sonno mio con esse."

The dawn in Eden is marked by "the shrill Matin Song/ Of Birds on every bough" (V.7–8). Eve looks "with startl'd eye" at Adam, glad to find him beside her, whom she calls "Sole in whom my thoughts find all repose" (perhaps an echo of Dante's "solo il mio conforto" for Virgil). The dream is still so alarmingly real to her (as Dante's was to him: he *felt* the scorching of the fire) that she is uncertain whether it was a dream (30–32); its content has been entirely novel in her experience ("offense and trouble, which my mind/ Knew never till this irksome night"). In contrast Dante is astonished only on awaking to find himself removed from where he fell asleep. Indeed, the dreaming Dante can associate his eagle-bearer with the story of Ganymede; the dream-content suggests to him a customary procedure (22–27). The dreaming Eve also begins by attempting to associate the unfamiliar with the familiar: she thinks the voice at her ear Adam's, the shape before her eyes "one of those from Heav'n/ By us oft seen." Yet between her hearing the voice and seeing the shape at "the Tree/ Of interdicted Knowledge," some surprising things have been said: that the night is wasted unless she is awake to regard and—more important—to be regarded, that she is the object of all Nature's desire, the magnet of all vision.

None of this shakes the dreaming Eve, as the novel experience of being borne aloft by the eagle did not shake the dreaming Dante. The pain of the dreamed fire woke him. Eve's fear starts within her dream: after the seeming angel addressed the tree, "with vent'rous Arm/ He pluckt, he tasted." (The words will echo at the crisis in Book IX.781: "she pluck'd, she eat," just as the serpent there will elaborate his flattery of Eve's beauty and his insistence on the magical power of the tree.) Here, Eve reacts at once with astonished terror:

> . . . mee damp horror chill'd
> At such bold words vboucht with a deed so bold.

Preliminaries

(Her chilled horror, recalling Dante's "spaventato agghiaccia," will echo in Adam's "horror chill" at her bold words and deeds in Book IX.890.) Bolder words and deeds follow. Renewing his flattery of her and his praise of the magical tree ("be henceforth among the Gods/ Thyself a Goddess"), the figure puts the interdicted fruit to her lips so that, as she says, "I, methought,/ Could not but taste."

She does not taste the fruit. Rather, dream-fashion, the sequel leaps over the supposedly requisite preliminary: "Forthwith up to the Clouds/ With him I flew." No sooner is she offered the fruit than she is high above the earth, wondering at her "flight and change/ To this high exaltation" (89–90). Since wonder is not the same emotion as fear, Eve strikes some readers as accepting in her dream the supposedly unacceptable. Still, her distress returns when, just as suddenly, all again changes: her guide is gone (*we* know that Ithuriel and Zephon have gotten the toad away from her ear); she sinks down, seems to fall asleep, and wakes—"O how glad . . . / To find this but a dream!"

In *Purgatorio* 19.1–33 Dante has a second dream at dawn, whose truth is thus again vouched for, but this time with a nightmare element in the initial and final loathsomeness of the Siren. Again a sensation of physical distress, this time at the stench of the revealed witch, seems to rouse the dreamer, though in reality Virgil has just called three times to wake him (34–36), as Adam calls to Eve in Book V. The wakened Dante remains troubled (40–42,55–57) until Virgil guesses and explains the dream:

> "Sawest thou," he said, "that ancient witch be-
> cause of whom alone above us now they weep?
> Sawest thou how man frees him from her?
> Let that suffice thee . . "   (19.58–61)

In this second dream of Dante's a figure of evil, that for a time

7

at least appears delusively fair to the eye and ear (10–24), produces a less-than-right response in the dreamer: "I gazed upon her" (10); and "with difficulty should I have turned my attention from her" (17–18). Further, here the sleeper is roused at the same time by his companion and by his unpleasant sensation in the dream, and here his wise companion explains what he has dreamed. In substance Eve's nightmare is thus more like the second than the first of Dante's dreams. And here too the evil figure is routed by two benevolent ones: the "donna . . . santa e presta" and Virgil (25–32); but the routing occurs within the dream itself.

Dante's third dream at dawn, of the fair Leah gathering flowers and singing of herself and her sister, ends naturally as day breaks; it is not explained by Virgil, leaves no fear behind, and suggests almost nothing that appears in Milton's episode. For the fear in which Eve wakes is of importance. As she tells her dream she evidently relives its sensations. Adam has marked in her sleeping face signs of "unquiet rest," learns with distress "the trouble of [her] thoughts this night, . . . [her] uncouth dream," and thinks it "of evil sprung."

Virgil, at Dante's awakening from the first dream in *Purgatorio*, sees the startled terror, but rightly links it with Dante's shock at finding himself in the strange place; and if the familiar sight of him has not been assurance enough, he speedily explains what has happened. Lucia has come and borne the sleeper hither, shown Virgil the entrance to Purgatory-gate, and then departed. Dante has not recounted his dream, nor has Virgil set out to explain it. The conjunction of the two passages alone suggests to the reader the link between the external reality and the dream. Milton suggests a like relation by presenting first in Book IV the reality of Satan's attempt "to reach/ The Organs of [Eve's] Fancy," and then in Book V Eve's account of her nightmare. Neither Virgil nor Adam offers a prophetic explanation; in both poems, only later events do that. But Adam's immediate task of reassurance to the wakened dreamer is harder than Virgil's, since he does not know the reality that instigated the dream and he must reassure Eve not about a helpful fact but about the workings of her own mind. Adam must interpret Eve's dream for her, something that Virgil for all his tutorial role is not called on to do until Dante's second dream—and he must do it without knowing what the reader knows.

He does it successfully, and thereby removes a doubt. Was the dream produced by Satan or by Eve? If Adam can diagnose it correctly—as he does—however much it was *in*duced by Satan, it was *pro*duced by Eve's own mind. That Adam can suggest this and still reassure Eve is proof of the "contemplation and valor" in his nature. The calming words to the startled dreamer, a major similarity with the incident in Dante, constitute the climactic resolution of Milton's scene: "So cheer'd he his fair Spouse, and she was cheer'd." But Adam's assurance has not been facile. He has had to tackle a central issue of Milton's poem: "of evil sprung . . . / Yet evil whence?" And to answer that question he has had to explore faculty psychology, dream psychology, and—above all—a central problem of ethics, the origin of evil in a perfect world. The crucial lines of his explanation not only resolve the episode but state a main tenet of *Paradise Lost* as a whole:

> Evil into the mind of God or Man
> May come and go, so unapprov'd, and leave
> No spot or blame behind.   (V. 117–119)

Without some such episode as this of Eve's dream the reader could at some point be told, but would not be led himself to *see*, how little the evil that is not approved, not willed, not chosen, matters in the ethic of *Paradise Lost*.

The dream of Dante and its resolution have no comparable significance either in *Purgatorio* or in the *Commedia* as a whole. Those who truly desire Heaven get helped toward it, but first they must go through the purging fire. With that much made clear in advance, Dante is ready to enter the gate and begin his penitential climb. Expositions of psychology, of ethics, of issues crucial to the journey will come in abundance, but elsewhere. This dream, like the two others in *Purgatorio*, is a moment of high interest, a major link in the essential pattern of Dante's redemptive journey; but it is a link, not a turning point.

Why then should its sequence, its setting, its phrases recur thus in an episode alone of its kind, critical in its significance, essential to the structure of *Paradise Lost?* In spite of their differences, the common features of the two episodes are among the most striking in each: the removal of a Satan-figure from a divinely guarded Edenic dell by two angels, the swift flight of the intruder, a dawn passage, an account of a dream in which the dreamer is snatched aloft, a startled awakening in the chill of fear, the reassuring presence of the familiar companion, an explanation from that familiar wise companion which comforts the wakened dreamer and so resolves the episode, and a suggestion that it is time to move on to something else. Such resemblances do not come by chance, as a comparison with other notable dreams in narrative and dramatic poetry makes clear. Chaucer's parody of this very dream of Dante's in the *House of Fame*; the prophetic nightmares of Clytemnestra in Aeschylus' *Libation-Bearers*, or of Clarence in *Richard III*; the dream in Tasso's *Jerusalem Delivered*, XIV.1–19, which involves an angelic figure and a view of the earth below; Britomart's "wondrous vision" in the Temple of Isis—none of these suggests a pattern anything like the one that links Eve's dream with Cantos 7–9 of *Purgatorio*.

The impress of Dante on the one dream in *Paradise Lost*

may be explained by the very nature of the *Commedia*, particularly as it was debated in the Renaissance, and by the high value Milton assigned to the *Difesa della Comedia di Dante* by Iacopo Mazzoni. Since the *Commedia* is related to the dream-vision genre, the dream passages take on special importance: they indicate in some measure how the poem is to be read; they form a nexus linking widely separated parts of *Purgatorio*, they contrast with the sudden trances of *Inferno* and the continued waking clarity of *Paradiso*, they constitute notable features of the poem. Any reader is sure to mark them. A learned reader in the Renaissance could hardly have failed to. Much of the Cinquecento debate about the poetic value of the *Commedia* involved this very matter. Bellisario Bulgarini, for example, declared: a dream cannot have universal significance; Dante himself calls his work a dream; it therefore lacks both the universality and the credibility requisite to a poem; hence the *Commedia* is not properly a poem at all. To answering this argument Mazzoni devoted most of the first book of his *Difesa*. After showing that Dante called his poem a dream metaphorically, as poets commonly use metaphors, Mazzoni analyzed with scholastic fullness the origin and validity of dreams generally, arguing in Chapter 77 that dreams and poetic imaginings arise from the same faculty of the soul and hence have great likeness, and concluding that on every possible ground its relation to a dream does not bar the *Commedia* from poetic excellence.[2]

[2] On the *Commedia* as dream and poem, see especially Iacopo Mazzoni, *Della Difesa della Comedia di Dante*, Part I (Cesena, 1587), pp. 161–238, and Bellisario Bulgarini, *Annotazioni, ovvero Chiose Marginali sopra la prima Parte della Difesa* (Siena, 1608), pp. 37ff. Michele Barbi, *Della Fortuna di Dante nel Secolo XVI* (Pisa, 1890) summarizes the debate; and cf. Colomb De Batines, *Bibliografia Dantesca* (Prato, 1845), entries 249–294. Bernard Weinberg, *A History of Literary Criticism in the Italian Renaissance* (Chicago, 1961), II, 819–911, considers the debate as it bore on the development of critical theory.

Mazzoni's *Difesa* ranked high with Milton, high enough to win a place in *Of Education* among the five authorities on literary criticism,

that sublime art which in Aristotle's *Poetics*, in Horace, and the Italian commentaries of Castelvetro, Tasso, Mazzoni, and others, teaches what the laws are of a true epic poem, what of a dramatic, what of a lyric, what decorum is, which is the grand masterpiece to observe.

To give such importance to Mazzoni as a poetic theorist meant inevitably to give importance to the *Commedia:* Mazzoni produced his whole theory as a *Difesa*, to assert Dante's conformity to the principles established by Plato and Aristotle, his consequent invulnerability to such attacks as Bulgarini's, and indeed his absolute pre-eminence. Even the Introduction and Summary, in which Mazzoni presented his poetic theory before answering the attacks, takes repeated occasion to praise Dante as the greatest of poets. Thus in section 26, "In somma . . . sempre Dante narrando forma imagini, & Idoli meglio d'ogn' altro Poeta." Mazzoni's long argument defending the *Commedia* in its relation to dreams must surely have stamped Dante for Milton as the poet of the dream.[3] When he came to write a dream passage of his own, what could be more natural than to review the especially relevant parts of the *Commedia?* And among the three dreams in *Purgatorio* what could be more natural than that the one set in an Edenic dell should impress him most deeply?

Now Dante associates dreams specifically with the purgatorial process. And purgation for Dante involves specifically a reversal of feelings connected with motives formerly cherished and thus a reversal of the will to behavior formerly delighted in; it defines both a tendency to be repudiated and a new tendency to be confirmed. The Adam and Eve of *Paradise Lost* IV–V

[3] Milton presumably also knew Dante's comment on dreams, *Convivio* II.ix.

assuredly do not need what is commonly meant by purgation; but as the whole visit of Raphael in Books V–VIII will show, they do need to repudiate some tendencies and to confirm others before they meet the trial in Book IX. Specifically, Eve needs to turn from self-love and Adam to turn to responsibility for Eve. The dream of Eve provides an occasion for such turning. At no other point in the poem does Eve have an opportunity—and take it—so decisively to reject her mistaken impulse, or Adam both have an opportunity—and take it—so clearly to prove himself her "head." As prophecy of what is to come in Book IX, the dream sequence measures the fall through detailed contrasts both in Eve's response to the opportunity for self-aggrandizement and in Adam's ability to meet the problem with wisdom and courage. Some readers may find the Eve who dreamed that dream already fallen; Adam—and Milton—did not.

The pattern of Dante's first night in *Purgatorio* impressed itself on the sequence in *Paradise Lost*, despite their large differences in meaning, in structural importance, and in prophetic value. And the purgatorial association of dreams in Dante may clarify Milton's treatment. Between realms of chosen evil (Hell) and chosen good (Heaven), Adam and Eve are to prove themselves by their choices in "Another World . . . till by degrees of merit rais'd/ They open . . . at length the way/ Up . . . [to heaven,] under long obedience tri'd" (VII.155–159). The lines might stand as a summary of Dante's purgatorial process. The dream of Eve tests, chastens, and instructs; in advance of the later trial which she and Adam will fail, it marks prelapsarian Eden as a place designed for growth no less surely, though less painfully, than the postlapsarian world figured in the Purgatorial Mount of Dante.

Satan and the "Diminisht" Stars

Paradise Lost achieves its unusual degree of organic unity, among other methods, by repetition of themes with the significance varied to suit the developing action. One such theme is the question Eve puts to Adam at the end of her evening speech, in Book IV, about the stars at night:

> But wherefore all night long shine these, for whom
> This glorious sight, when sleep hath shut all eyes?
>
> (657–658)

The issue will recur at least twice later in the poem. At the moment, in its context, the question provides occasion for Adam's answer to establish his superior intelligence. He shows himself able to think in terms of the functions of things-in-themselves, apart from their relation to him and his wife; in terms of time beyond the present moment, the long future of mankind in "Nations yet unborn"; in terms of the vast universe of space beyond his home; and in terms of multitudes of other beings already in life, with their own mode of existence independent of his. The last element of his speech has been the chief concern of commentators since it can be taken as evidence of a strain of mysticism in Milton:

Preliminaries

> Millions of spiritual Creatures walk the Earth
> Unseen, both when we wake, and when we sleep.
>
> (677–678)

But whatever of mysticism the statement may reveal, in its context it serves to prove Eden the "Heav'n on earth" Milton calls it and Adam the gifted contemplator Milton calls him. Angels gladly visit here, moving freely between the Empyrean and this new outpost of the heavenly realm. Thus Adam and Eve have heard

> Celestial voices to the midnight air,
> Sole, or responsive each to other's note
> Singing thir great Creator.
>
> (682–684)

And Adam in his larger awareness has inferred, as Eve has not yet, that the universe outside them exists independent of them, in its own right, for purposes other than their importance.

The waking Eve accepts his explanation, but in her dream she reverts to her question, now hearing from another voice an answer more flattering to her self-esteem:

> Why sleep'st thou Eve? now is the pleasant time,
> The cool . . . ; now reigns
> Full Orb'd the Moon, and with more pleasing light
> Shadowy sets off the face of things; in vain,
> If none regard; Heav'n wakes with all his eyes,
> Whom to behold but thee, Nature's desire . . . ?
>
> (V.38–45)

The serenade has its effect: she takes the voice for Adam's and rises at his call. Her dream turns into a nightmare, and the theme of the stars at night lapses until Raphael in his account of the creation in Book VII suggests that the whole stellar universe was designed as a home for man. What else can be the significance of his saying as he draws his account to its climax,

> There wanted yet the Master work, the end
> Of all yet done; a Creature who . . . endu'd
> With Sanctity of Reason, might erect
> His Stature, and upright with Front serene
> Govern the rest, self-knowing, and from thence
> Magnanimous to correspond with Heav'n?
>
> (VII.505–511)

The expanded version of Genesis 1, fashioned to give Adam and Eve a due sense of their importance, that they may not lightheadedly toss away their happiness, raises a question for Adam: If this whole universe was specifically created with man as its end and aim, is there not some grave disproportion in Nature? The question rephrases Eve's, raising it to a contemplative level far beyond her simple "Why do the stars shine all night long when we are not awake to see them?" His question is rather, "How can man, little man on this little earth, be central to the infinite stellar universe?" For Raphael's account has seemed to imply that he is.

The discussion of possible astronomies that follows has, understandably enough, withdrawn attention from the way Milton transmutes Eve's earlier question into Adam's cosmic query, and Adam's earlier answer into Raphael's cosmic resolution of the problem. Man's importance is no less, and no more, whether sun or earth be center; size and brightness are not invariable indexes of worth; the universe can have been created as a home for man and yet have its own purpose to fulfill; its chief purpose as a home for man may indeed be "That Man may know he dwells not in his own" (VIII.103). For paradoxically, the best service this home designed for him can do man is to remind him that both he and it are parts of a cosmos that he can never fully grasp.

Raphael thus raises Adam's terms of the objective existence of the universe, of the enormous future stretching ahead, of the beings yet to be and the multitude of beings already in existence, to the level of all time, all space, all possible worlds and creatures and kinds of existence, as these derive from the Supreme Being who alone can know why and what they are. And there the theme of the stars at night seemingly rests.

But it had begun earlier than Eve's naïvely self-flattering question.

The first view of Heaven we are given in *Paradise Lost* involves a brief, but telling, star-image. After the invocation of light with which Book III opens, the narrative resumes with the incomparably radiant Father surrounded by the angels:

> About him all the Sanctities of Heaven
> Stood thick as Stars, and from his sight receiv'd
> Beatitude past utterance.   (III.60–62)

For anyone familiar with the *Commedia* of Dante, Milton's whole use of light and dark is bound to be reminiscent of the other great Christian poet's comparable system of symbols, and this particular passage reminiscent of a series of images in *Paradiso* where the inhabitants of heaven, starlike, draw the light of their bliss from the central and encompassing radiance of God. The starlike heavenly beings in *Paradiso* are the souls of the redeemed, not angels, and they never group themselves in loose clusters, but rather appear in ordered formations, ultimately in the supreme regularity of the great white rose of the Empyrean. The suggestion of spontaneity and easy diversity in Milton's image is alien to Dante's elaborately regulated Heaven. Perhaps that is why, though the parallel of their use of light has often been noted, little has been said of the striking parallels between the blessed spirits of *Paradiso* and the angels of *Paradise Lost*. Milton's angels have little in common with Dante's; they are much more like his human redeemed.

Here, once we put aside Milton's preference for an order that reveals itself in the wildest-seeming irregularity, and Dante's for an order that shows itself at every point in precisely patterned formations, it is clear that this star image for angels corresponds to Dante's many star images for the orders of the blessed, and that both Dante and Milton use the same involved equation: God is to the heavenly beings as the sun is to the stars; the beatific vision of the Supreme Light transmits radiance to the blessed as the sun gives light to the stars. Astronomically, Milton knew better; metaphorically, Dante's image struck him as right. And because he found it metaphorically right he was even willing to have Raphael use the astronomically wrong relation between the sun and the stars in his account of the fourth day of creation:

> Hither [to the sun] as to thir Fountain other Stars
> Repairing, in thir gold'n Urns draw Light,
> And hence the Morning Planet gilds her horns;
> By tincture or reflection they augment
> Thir small peculiar, though from human sight
> So far remote, with diminution seen.
>
> (VII.364–369)

Of the many variants scattered throughout the *Commedia*, the one that appears to have impressed Milton most forcibly occurs in *Paradiso* 20.1–6, without its usual associations with God and the redeemed, but in close conjunction with a passage to which Milton had attended for other reasons. *Paradiso* 20 is, as it happens, one of the few parts of the *Commedia* explicitly cited in Milton's published works. In *Of Reformation*, after translating *Inferno* 19.115–117 on the Gift of Constantine, he added: "So in his 20th Canto of Paradise, he makes the like complaint."

The complaint comes at lines 55–60, in a sequence that had much to interest Milton. Perhaps this particular version of the star-and-sun image impressed him especially because of his deep response to the whole context in which he found it.

In Canto 18 Dante had risen from the Heaven of the courageous, in the sphere of Mars, to the Heaven of the just, in the sphere of Jupiter. With a prayer for illumination to the "goddess Pegasean" that he may fittingly explain what he then saw, he proceeds to the striking image of the blessed spirits descending as lights to spell out the thirty-five letters of "Diligite justitiam qui judicatis terram," and then joined by other lights to turn the final *M* into the shape of an eagle. Since the Eagle of Jupiter symbolizes the divinely ordained justice of imperial Rome, Dante now prays that heavenly justice may take cognizance of the papal court with its buying and selling, its excommunications, its whole evil example of greed, which leads the church astray. The prolonged condemnation of papal avarice in these lines, 118–136, surely won Milton's sympathy.

In Canto 19, within the Eagle each of the blessed glows like a ruby in the sun; and from the beak proceeds a voice using the singular "I" for the "we" involved, since all the just consider themselves participants in a single Justice. Milton at the end of the angelic song of Book III uses the same device, with the same implication. The song ends with a skillful shift from the indirect discourse of lines 372–411 to direct discourse in the first person singular:

> Hail Son of God, Savior of Men, thy Name
> Shall be the copious matter of my Song
> Henceforth, and never shall my Harp thy praise
> Forget, nor from thy Father's praise disjoin.
>
> Thus they in Heav'n, above the starry Sphere,
> Thir happy hours in joy and hymning spent.
>
> (412–417)

The "my" is like the "I" and "my" of Dante's Eagle of Justice, the sign of complete "concord" in the "we" who speak.

In *Paradiso* 19, Dante prays the Eagle to resolve his unasked question: How can divine justice condemn pagans born without opportunity to become Christians? Now questions of divine justice surely interested Milton. And the first lines of the eagle's answer, "Colui che volse il sesto/ all' estremo del mondo" (19.40–41), probably re-enforced other sources when Milton wrote of the creation:

> He took the golden Compasses, prepar'd
> In God's Eternal store, to circumscribe
> This Universe, and all created things.
> (VII.225–227)

The Eagle proceeds:

> non potè suo valor sì fare impresso
> in tutto l'universo, che il suo verbo
> non rimanesse in infinito eccesso.
> ([God] could not so stamp his worth
> on all the universe but that his word
> remained in infinite excess.)
> (43–45)

Milton has Raphael give a slightly different emphasis to the necessary incommensurability of the creature with the Creator, but on what follows he agrees: Satan's fall is evidence that, in spite of the Creator's goodness, evil somehow entered the created universe:

> . . . il primo superbo,
> che fu la somma d'ogni creatura,
> per non aspettar lume, cadde acerbo.
> (that first proud Being,
> who was the summit of all creation, because
> he would not wait for light, [fell] unripe.)
> (46–48)

With Satan as "la somma d'ogni creatura" Raphael's account, coming from the same tradition, naturally enough accords:

> . . . he of the first,
> If not the first Arch-Angel; (V.659–660)

but Dante's general explanation of the Satanic pride is useless to Milton's Raphael, who gives a specific occasion for Satan's rebellion:

> fraught
> With envy against the Son of God, that day
> Honor'd by his great Father, and proclaim'd
> Messiah King anointed, [he] could not bear
> Through pride that sight, and thought himself impair'd.
> (V.661–665)

Still, Dante's metaphor, "per non aspettar lume," may have suggested to Milton that Satan's relation to light would be somehow abnormal and symptomatic of his whole perverse relation to the universe.

The Eagle of Jupiter uses the example of Satan's fall only to illustrate the inability of the creature to fathom divine justice, and thus to reveal the absurdity of Dante's unasked question. For who is Dante, who cannot at this point even understand the Eagle's mystic song—who is Dante to judge the ways of God? Yet the Eagle then explains as much as can be explained. Just so in Book VIII of *Paradise Lost* Raphael, after chiding Adam for his question about Nature's dispro-portion, then proceeds to answer. Raphael too makes the point of the creature's inability to fathom the ways of the Creator:

> God to remove his ways from human sense,
> Plac'd Heav'n from Earth so far, that earthly sight,
> If it presume, might err in things too high,
> And no advantage gain. (VIII.119–122)

In both Dante and Milton, be it noted, it is created being speaking to created being of the Creator, not the Creator himself forbidding the creature knowledge. And Raphael too then proceeds to answer the question as best he, another created being, can. Like Dante, Milton apparently chose to mark the possible presumption in a certain kind of question, to note the impossibility of a final answer, and yet to suggest a tentative answer. Here the Eagle asserts that no one ever did rise to Heaven without belief in Christ, though the world cannot know who does or did believe. For many who profess belief shall find themselves condemned in the Book of Judgment. There follows a passage of remarkable emphasis through repetition: Three times the Eagle asserts, "Lì si vedrà," and three times "Vedrassi," in six tercets condemning the kings of the time for their injustice; and the wholesale condemnation continues with a thrice repeated "E" to the end of the canto. The anti-monarchist Milton must surely have read that vehement passage with satisfaction.

In Canto 20 the Eagle brings to Dante's attention the six pre-eminently just men who form its eye, among them two supposed pagans who were in fact believers in Christ. Concerning each of the six the Eagle speaks two tercets, naming, with an emphatically repeated "ora conosce," something the just man had not known in his mortal life, that yet concerns the workings of divine justice. Constantine is one of the six. The lines on him read:

> The next who followeth . . . with good in-
> tention that bore evil fruit, to give place to
> the pastor, made himself a Greek;
> now knoweth he that the ill deduced from his
> good deed hurteth not him though the world
> be destroyed thereby. (55–60)

22

Why, in *Of Reformation*, Milton should merely have cited this passage instead of translating it along with *Inferno* 19.115–117, is self-evident. But he remembered it as important; presumably he saw its importance not only to arguments against ecclesiastical ownership of secular realms. At any rate, the statement that a good deed may lead to evil without involving guilt in the doer, though the world be destroyed in consequence, might summarize an incident in Milton's own *Paradise Lost:* Uriel's gracious directions to the disguised Satan help him find his way to Eden, without involving Uriel in any slightest guilt for the subsequent destruction of the world.

In the context, the Eagle details how the two pagans came to be Christians, the one after, the other even before the vicarious atonement of Christ, and in connection with the latter exclaims:

> O predestination, how far withdrawn is thy
> root from such vision as sees not the first
> cause entire!   (130–132)

Predestination is, of course, one of Milton's great questions; for him, too, God makes salvation possible to all, while specially favoring some chosen few, whose identity, however, mortals cannot distinguish. He would thus surely have agreed with the tercet that follows:

> And ye mortals, hold yourselves straitly
> back from judging; for we who see God,
> know not as yet all the elect.   (133–135)

The condemnation of unjust monarchs, the contempt for a church that seeks worldly gain, the blamelessness of one whose good deed has evil consequences, the availability of salvation generally, the special predestination of some to grace, the inscrutability of God's ways, the ignorance of men about the salvation of others—on all these matters Dante's opinions in *Paradiso* 18–20 are also Milton's, though Milton did not necessarily draw his opinions on them from Dante. But clearly he was glad to have the support of *Paradiso* 20 on the Gift of Constantine; he did use the "I" for "we" of *Paradiso* 19 in the angelic song of *Paradise Lost* III; he did have Raphael, like the Eagle, first note the absurdity of a question and then answer it; and with the compass delimiting the universe and the emergence of evil in the highest of created beings the precedent of Dante probably helped to guide his writing.

In this sequence, filled with matter so congenial to Milton's thought, comes one of Dante's most remarkable similes of the sun and the stars. *Paradiso* 20 opens:

> When he who doth illumine all the world descendeth
>   so from our hemisphere that day on every side is
>   done away,
> the heaven which before is kindled by him only, now
>   straightway maketh itself reappear by many lights
>   wherein the one re-gloweth.   (1–6)

The image came to Dante's mind because as the Eagle was silent the other living lights were heard singing other songs; but like most readers Milton was apparently impressed more by the visual image than by its auditory import. The one commentary on the *Commedia* that we can be certain he knew does little more than paraphrase and summarize most of Canto 20; but on this image of the sun and the stars Bernardino Daniello da Lucca is expansive:

Then he describes the season of the day: when the sun, which with his light illumines and makes clear all the world, descends from our hemisphere to the opposite, and day is ended and begins to be missing from every part, the sky which was before lighted by *Lui*, that is by the sun, suddenly remakes itself, shows itself, and lets itself be seen by means of many *Luci*, by many stars, in which *Una*, that is one light which is that of the sun, shines forth. All the stars have their glow from the sun, and since it is one sole light, it shines in all the stars, which by day cannot be seen because of the sovereign splendor of the sun; and therefore it happens that by day the beauties of the sky cannot be contemplated as at night, when the stars, not submerged and extinguished by the sun's rays, show themselves.

(p. 625)

Though Daniello's phrasing is awkward, his understanding of the importance of the simile is much like that of William Warren Vernon in *Readings on the Paradiso* (1900), II, 96. Interestingly enough, though Dante explicitly says, and both Daniello and Vernon explain him as saying, that the stars shine by light reflected from the sun, both Daniello and Vernon suggest—as Dante does not—that the stars have been obscured by the sun during the day so that their beauty can be seen only at night. That suggestion has no relevance here, and Vernon at least should have been kept from any least hint of it by his recognition that the lines repeat an idea used elsewhere and often by Dante. Dante is emphatic and explicit on the matter: the sun gives the stars their light. Yet a reader of the latter sixteenth century, and another at the end of the nineteenth, could both intrude here, with like irrelevance, that the sun obscures the stars by day.

If the observation intruded itself into Milton's reading of *Paradiso* 20.1–6, he at least knew what to do with it: he assigned it to Satan, making it a symptom of perversity. Perhaps the line on Satan in the preceding canto, "per non aspettar lume, cadde acerbo," suggested the symptom to Milton. In any event, the famous address to the sun with which Satan begins his first soliloquy, when he alights on earth, reads as though along with

25

Daniello he had been misconstruing *Paradiso* 20:

> O thou that with surpassing Glory crown'd,
> Look'st from thy sole Dominion like the God
> Of this new World; at whose sight all the Stars
> Hide thir diminisht heads; to thee I call,
> But with no friendly voice, and add thy name
> O Sun, to tell thee how I hate thy beams . . .
>
> (IV.32–37)

Satan at once perceives the right analogy: the sun is to the stars as God to the angels, as in Book III, lines 60–62; his perverse inference shows his alienation from the divinely created universe. The normal inference, for Milton as for Dante, is that the star-angels derive their light from the sun-God with the normal response of loving joy—much as normal people, we might say, rejoice to bask in sunlight. Dante had made a point of that normal pleasure in his phrase for the perversely sullen spirits in *Inferno* 7.121–122: "Tristi fummo/ nell' aer dolce che dal sol s'allegra."

If for Satan the superior glory of the sun serves only to extinguish the light of the stars, the radiant Godhead similarly serves only to outshine and thus extinguish the glory of every other being. Inevitably, then, far from rejoicing in the light he derives from God, he hates the superior brilliance which diminishes and hides his rival glow. As it happens, Satan has *seen* the other heavenly bodies in his flight to the sun; it is only now, from his new position on earth, that his sight is unable to distinguish them in sunlight. But where Satan is is indeed Hell: relations of which he has himself been aware lose their validity for him the moment his own vantage point obscures them. Astronomically, of course, the whole analogy is false; metaphorically, in terms of all the meanings that attached themselves to the sun–God analogy, and of Dante's elaboration of it into the sun to the stars as God to the blessed, Satan's perverse inference proves him dead wrong. The specific perversity in Satan's words shows him unable to understand generosity: for him, glory is something snatched from others, not something given others to enjoy. For him the sun, far from being the giver of light to other heavenly bodies, is their extinguisher; God, far from giving life to other heavenly beings, diminishes them. His natural home is thus inevitably with those who never see the sun—or the stars.

But Milton is not Dante: the image does not as he uses it turn into a symbol, but only emerges now and again for a moment to enrich the meaning it suggests. The stars provide no refrain in *Paradise Lost*—no patterned notation for leaving Hell "a riveder le stelle," for purging the soul into a state "puro e disposto a salire alle stelle," for arriving at the blessedness in which the individual will moves with "l' amor che move il sole e l' altre stelle."

Nevertheless, Milton too employs three chief images of sun and stars. For the angelic beings in Heaven, God transmits radiance as the sun transmits light to the stars. For Eve and Adam in Eden, there is doubt as to what purpose the stars in their beauty serve. For Satan, carrying his Hell-making mind with him to the edge of Eden, the sun "with surpassing Glory crown'd" and thus looking "like the God/ Of this new World" makes "all the Stars/ Hide thir diminisht heads." The three themes—of the sun giving light to the stars, of the beauty of the stars at night, of the starlight extinguished in daytime by the superior radiance of the sun—never appear together in either Dante or Milton. Interestingly enough, however, Daniello links them closely:

All the stars have their glow from the sun, and . . . it shines in all the stars, which by day cannot be seen because of the sovereign splendor of the sun; and therefore it happens that by day the beauties of the sky cannot be contemplated as at night, when the stars, not submerged and extinguished by the sun's rays, show themselves.

Thus Daniello may even have been the medium through which, for Milton, the passage in *Paradiso* 20 on the stars at night gathered to itself the symbolism of the sun and stars in the *Commedia*, and refracted it into the subtly linked sun-and-star imagery of *Paradise Lost*.

II

Milton's Reading of Dante

TO review comparisons of Dante and Milton from the eighteenth century to the present is largely to survey shifts in literary taste. Apart from those scholars who have noted parallels of phrasing, chiefly between the *Commedia* and *Paradise Lost*, critics have generally preferred to exalt the one poet or poem at the expense of the other. In the nineteenth century this became a popular critical sport: Chateaubriand, Coleridge, Hazlitt, Carlyle, Hallam, Macaulay, Ruskin, John Addington Symonds—to list only the best known—all indulged in it. Apparently it began in the eighteenth century when Antonio Conti briefly compared the two in order to show Dante's superiority—and Dorothy Sayers played it to the same purpose as recently as her *Further Papers on Dante*, published in 1957. Nor is it likely to end, in spite of John M. Steadman's recent dictum that the game ought never to have been played at all, since the *Commedia* and *Paradise Lost*, being of unlike literary genres, are not comparable. E. E. Kellett, in *Reconsiderations* (1928), rightly noted that the same taste seldom favors both Milton and Dante (p. 134), though without offering any reason. Probably the most obvious explanation holds: readers who take Dante as the great Catholic poet and Milton as the great Protestant poet enlarge upon the differences between the two to justify extraliterary predilections. Certainly it would surprise us to find T. S. Eliot preferring Milton, or the young Macaulay Dante. Even readers aware of how tags like Catholic and Protestant, monarchist and republican, medieval and humanistic, necessarily oversimplify the many-sidedness of either poet, cannot entirely forget those tags. And few are likely to respond with equal enthusiasm to the seeming immediacy of Dante's narrative and tone and to the seeming detachment of Milton's.[1]

Such personal biases are every critic's right. Voltaire and Landor naturally found Milton more to their taste; Lamennais and Carlyle as naturally preferred Dante. And when Ruskin asserts that we can know Milton's opinions as we cannot know Dante's because Dante is the more various and inclusive poet (*Sesame and Lilies, Works*, XVIII, p. 77), or that Milton "hews his gods out to his own fancy, and then believes in them," whereas Dante always subordinates his art "to the true vision" (*Fors Clavigera, Works*, XXIX, p. 459), or even that Milton in *Paradise Lost* I.224ff. suggests the nature of fire less effectively than Dante in *Purgatorio* 26.4ff., we must remember that for Ruskin Dante was "the greatest poet of that or perhaps of any other age" (V, 37). Conversely, if Arthur Henry Hallam thought Milton had the advantages natural to "a Protestant and English position" (*Remains* [1863], p. 140), and if J. B. Broadbent more recently contrasted the "torture-chamber" of Dante's Hell with "the natural abode of the irredeemably damned" imagined by Milton ("Milton's Hell," *ELH* 21 [1954], 165), the ground of judgment is self-evident. But the use—and sometimes the misreading—of one poet to show the superiority of another is not likely to tell much about the relation between the two.

[1] See Appendix C for comments, listed under the year of publication. Cf. John M. Steadman, "Milton and Mazzoni: the Genre of the *Divina Commedia*," *HLQ* 23 (1960), 107–122.

Milton's Reading of Dante

There was a relation: Milton chose to study Dante. Commentators have enjoyed arguing that he could not have read Dante sympathetically, because of either Dante's defects or his own. Thus C. H. Herford (1924) pronounced: "Certainly, the *Inferno*, with its savagery and ugliness, . . . must have repelled him; as the mystic and transcendent metaphysics of the *Paradiso* must have left him cold" (p. 198). And Dorothy Sayers, divining that "Milton was a Dante deprived of Beatrice" (p. 151), got the impression that "whenever Milton feels Dante's influence he deliberately goes out of his way to repudiate it" (p. 167). Although Miss Sayers admitted that "it is no more than an impression," neither she nor many others have troubled to start from ascertainable fact: Milton knew Dante's work intimately, and that knowledge in itself was phenomenal in seventeenth-century England. After the endless argument on what he must have thought of Dante, and why he is and had to be Dante's inferior or superior, it is refreshing to find Ettore Allodoli (1907) asserting, "Milton conobbe e ammirò il poema di Dante" (p. 79), or Kenneth C. M. Sills (1905–1906), "Milton took almost a scholar's interest in his study of Dante" (p. 11). Milton did indeed know and admire the *Commedia* and its author. The evidence has never been obscure.

Some questions concerning his knowledge are likely to remain unanswerable—its precise beginning, the extent to which it was influenced by his Italian friends in England and re-enforced by his visit to Italy, whether indeed he knew all Dante's extant works. But the fact of his knowledge and admiration is as plain as it is extraordinary. Dante enjoyed little favor, even in Italy, during the seventeenth century. Whereas the Cinquecento had argued violently about him, the Seicento largely ignored him, and outside Italy he was scarcely named. Thus Milton's interest was exceptional. Though Toynbee may have been inaccurate in saying that Milton was the first recorded owner of a copy of *Convivio* in England, that he made the earliest known mention of Boccaccio's *Vita de Dante*, and that he was the first English writer to cite Dante's *Monarchia* by name, the sheer paucity of references by others underscores the frequency of those made by Milton. His nephew and pupil Edward Phillips was one of the few other writers of the century to make any mention of Dante.[2]

From explicit citations, disregarding for the present all presumed echoes, we can affirm that Milton knew the *Commedia*, *Monarchia, Convivio* IV or at least the *canzone*, "Le dolci rime d'amor," on which it is a commentary, and something of Boccaccio's *Life of Dante*; and further that it is fairly sure he knew also the *Vita Nuova*, and perhaps the treatise *De Vulgari Eloquentia* and Dante's epistles. His interest was chiefly in the *Commedia*, and external evidence suggests that he knew it well. In *Of Reformation* (1641) he refers explicitly to *Inferno* 19.115–117 and to *Paradiso* 20.55, and in his sonnet to Lawes (?1646) he refers to the Casella episode of *Purgatorio* 2.76–119. He cites the *Commedia* six times in his *Commonplace Book*, once adding the remarks of Bernardino Daniello da Lucca, whose edition with commentary he knew. All eight citations are admiring; so too are his single references to the *Monarchia* and to *Convivio* IV. In addition, he elsewhere names Dante three times as a model or study, probably with the *Commedia* in mind, but possibly with other works too: once in a letter to Benedetto Buommattei dated 1638, again in the *Apology for Smectymnuus* of 1642, and again in a letter to Carlo Roberto Dati of 1647.

[2] See Paget Toynbee, *Britain's Tribute to Dante*, pp. ix, x, 13; and *Dante in English Literature* I, pp. xxv–xxvii. H. F. Fletcher, *The Intellectual Development of John Milton* II, pp. 301f., questions whether the copy of *Convivio* was Milton's. See Ruth Mohl, ed., Milton's *Commonplace Book*, Yale *Milton's Prose* I, p. 438, n. 4; and F. P. Wilson, *A Supplement to Toynbee*, p. 50, on related matters.

Milton's Reading of Dante

The reference in the *Apology for Smectymnuus* tells all that we can know with certainty of when and how he first read Dante. He came to him young, soon after his reading of "the smooth elegiac poets," and took him to be a great love-poet like Petrarch:

Above them [the amorous poets] all, [I] preferred the two famous renowners of Beatrice and Laura, who never write but honor of them to whom they devote their verse, displaying sublime and pure thoughts, without transgression. And long it was not after, when I was confirmed in this opinion that he who would not be frustrate of his hope to write well hereafter in laudable things, ought himself to be a true poem, that is, a composition and pattern of the best and honorablest things—not presuming to sing high praises of heroic men or famous cities, unless he have in himself the experience and the practice of all that which is praiseworthy.

Perhaps Dante has no part in the sentence that follows the reference to him, though the opinion Milton was confirmed in fits Dante's career. Perhaps it is only the *Vita Nuova* that Milton has in mind as celebrating Beatrice, though by the time he wrote the *Apology for Smectymnuus* he was certainly more interested in the *Commedia*. The passage can be taken as positively asserting only that, while still in his youth, Milton read Dante with great admiration.

Echoes and analogues in his early poems, which of themselves might mean little in a poet of Milton's unusual verbal memory and quick responsiveness to literature, bear out the assertion.[3] Fletcher concludes that he studied Italian before 1625 and read Dante along with other Italian writers, thanks to the influence of the Diodati circle, both before and during his Cambridge years (I, 293–294; II, 300–307, 513). Ruth Mohl, working with evidence related to his *Commonplace Book*,

[3] See Appendix A.

concludes that he was reading "Dante, Petrarch, and Ariosto in the Horton period" (Yale I, 366, n. 2).

The one certainty is that he knew Dante well by the time he went to Italy. In the one extant letter to Buommattei in 1638 he writes:

possum tamen nonnumquam ad illum Dantem, & Petrarcham aliosque vestros complusculos, libenter & cupide commessatum ire.

(I . . . can yet sometimes willingly and eagerly go for a feast to that Dante of yours, and to Petrarch, and a good few more.)

(tr. Masson)

The passage confirms what the internal evidence of *Lycidas* suggests, that by the time Milton contributed his poem to the memorial volume for Edward King, printed in 1638, he had been profoundly impressed by Dante. Beyond verbal echoes like those in his earlier work, *Lycidas* contains indications, in the speech of St. Peter, that he had begun to take Dante as an ally in his protest against a church greedy for earthly realms and power. The "famous renowner of Beatrice" was also the famous denouncer of a corrupt clergy. Perhaps Milton did not know then of the attack on Dante's *Monarchia* to which he refers in his *Commonplace Book*, fol. 182. But he was certainly aware from his own study that the *Commedia* opposes the fusion of church and state as corrupting both. He may not have known the whole tale of Dante as a target of the counter-Reformation, though the English Diodatis were likely to have provided him with just such fuel for Protestant indignation; but he apparently took impetus from *Paradiso* 27 and 29 in using *Lycidas* as occasion to "foretell the ruin of our corrupted Clergy then in their height."

The whole idea of having St. Peter himself denounce those in the pastoral office as usurpers and predict the vengeance soon to overtake them points to Dante's influence. The episode in *Paradiso* 27 is of a kind to impress a reader, and especially a reader who himself felt strongly on the subject; and the theme recurs in *Paradiso* 29, with Beatrice adding that a self-seeking clergy beyond degrading their high function leave the sheep unfed, when instead of sound doctrine they offer empty trivialities. The issue, part of the central meaning of the *Commedia*, plainly impressed Milton. *Lycidas* is the product of much more than his reading of Dante, but Paul Elmer More surely was not fatuous to suggest (*On Being Human*, p. 200) that it has something like "the mighty structure of Dante's *Paradiso*." Its inner movement—rising from desolation through a growing assurance to the climactic assertion that Lycidas is of the company of the blessed, gathering to itself along the way such themes as the ultimate reward of noble effort and the coming destruction of an ignoble clergy, and ending with the singer's return from his vision to the pursuits of the morrow—encompasses a range far beyond the usual scope of pastoral elegy. It asks, like the *Commedia*, the great question: What kind of world is it in which the good are afflicted, die young, win no reward, while the evil flourish, and flourish in places of power, within the very institution that should guide men to their salvation, but which instead encourages every kind of folly and degeneracy? And like the *Commedia* it nonetheless goes on to affirm that despite all such evidences, the universe is just and, though it seemingly delays, does not neglect either due reward or due retribution. Even the mysterious instrument of vengeance, "that two-handed engine at the door," has a close counterpart in the coming vengeance threatened throughout the *Commedia* and summed up in St. Peter's "Ma l' alta provvidenza . . ./ soccorrà tosto, sì com' io concipio" (*Par.* 27.61–63) and in Beatrice's "Ma tale uccel nel becchetto s'annida,/ che, se il vulgo il vedesse, vederebbe/ la perdonanza di che si confida" (*Par.* 29.118–120). Without external evidence, that there had been such an impress of pattern and theme might be doubted, all the verbal resemblances notwithstanding; but here internal and external evidence agree.

By the time Milton met the literati of Florence, his knowledge of Dante was able to provide a bond between himself and them. His extant correspondence includes only one letter apiece to Buommattei and Dati, each of which makes significant mention of Dante. The reference in the earlier letter is the more important because of Buommattei's position as the great Dante scholar of the age. The letter as a whole concerns his work on the Tuscan language, urges him to add a section on pronunciation for foreigners, and asks his advice on further reading in Italian literature. Milton addresses him as a highly distinguished scholar whose literary judgments he respects, and shows himself aware of the place Dante held in Buommattei's esteem. His phrase, *illum Dantem*, "that Dante of yours," was appropriate in addressing the man who, in an age that largely ignored the *Commedia*, had made it his lifelong study. As public lecturer in the perpetual commentary on the *Commedia* he delivered his inaugural address on December 13, 1632, and he continued his "lezioni," with some interruptions, during his active life. When he died after a long illness on January 27, 1647, he had reached *Purgatorio* 18; he was almost certainly lecturing on *Inferno* while Milton was in Florence. He had published the first seven parts of his *Della Lingua Toscana* in 1623, and reissued it with two additional parts in 1626. That work too bears witness to his enthusiasm for Dante, from whom he drew more examples than from any other writer. On the occasion of the 1623 publication, Buommattei had spoken "Delle Lodi della Lingua Toscana" before the Florentine Academy, and in the course of enumerating the glories of the language had delivered a eulogy of Dante. In 1638, the year of Milton's letter, he published an analytical table designed to help students of *Inferno*, in 1640 he published another for *Purgatorio*, and at his death he left notes for a similar table for *Paradiso*.[4]

Although Buommattei was the leading scholar as well as the leading Dante enthusiast among Milton's Florentine friends, he was not the only one. Agostino Coltellini and Dati at least, of those named by Milton in his *Second Defense* (1654), became Danteans under Buommattei's teaching. Coltellini took charge of the notes that Buommattei left on *Paradiso*, and turned them over to Francesco Cionacci. And Carlo Roberto Dati, Milton's closest friend in the group, wrote a brief *Difesa di Dante* (MS. Magliabechiana VII, 468; printed in *Scelta di Prose di Dati*, Venice, 1826, pp. 117–136), in which he emphasizes his difference from the common seventeenth-century view of the *Commedia:*

Many blame Dante's poem because few read it, and very few understand it because very few read it as much as and in the way that it must be read to be properly understood. (p. 119)

He names as the great models, for both their novelty and their sublimity, Dante in poetry and Michelangelo in design (p. 120). He praises Buommattei as the "Dotato," the gifted scholar who has penetrated more deeply than any other into the mysteries of the divine Dante's poem (p. 121). Milton was aware of the interest of Dati and the others, for in his letter of 1647 to Dati he asks his Florentine friends to grant him indulgence for his

harsh sayings against the Pope of Rome, . . . the indulgence you were wont to give, I say not to your own Dante and Petrarch in the same case, but with singular politeness to my own former freedom of speech among you. (tr. Masson)

Perhaps the Florentine group, defenders of Dante and friends

[4] See Appendix B.

of Galileo,[5] were in his mind when he spoke in *Areopagitica* (1644) of having in Italy

sat among their learned men . . . and . . . been counted happy to be born in such a place of philosophic freedom as they supposed England was, while themselves did nothing but bemoan the servile condition into which learning amongst them was brought; that this was it which had damped the glory of Italian wits; that nothing had been written now these many years but flattery and fustian.

Like Milton himself, the literati he met in Florence were clearly not bound by the tastes and fashions of their time. Their particular influence on his continued reading of the *Commedia* can hardly be identified, especially since the entries in his *Commonplace Book* cannot be precisely dated; but their enthusiasm for Dante must surely have encouraged his.

At any rate, the references in *Of Reformation*, *The Apology for Smectymnuus*, and the sonnet to Lawes show the continuity of Milton's interest. So too the high place he accords Mazzoni in his tractate *Of Education* (1644), when he prescribes a course in poetics to deal with

that sublime art which in Aristotle's poetics, in Horace, and the Italian commentaries of Castelvetro, Tasso, Mazzoni, and others, teaches what the laws are of a true epic poem, what of a dramatic, what of a lyric, what decorum is, which is the grand masterpiece to observe.

The three Italian critics named differ from each other no less

[5] See Galileo's two lectures on *Inferno*, *Le Opere di Galileo* (Florence, 1933) IX, pp. 31–57, and the comments on pp. 7–8; for evidence of his relations with Chimentelli and Buommattei, see XIX, pp. 444, 520. Dati, who had been a student of his, writes of the wrong done to Galileo, in a letter to N. N., July 2, 1673; see Dati's *Lettere* (Florence, 1825), p. 160. On Iacopo Mazzoni, whose *Difesa della Comedia* Buommattei, Dati, and Milton all admired, as Galileo's teacher, see Enrico Mestica, Introduction, Galileo, *Scritti di Critica Letteraria* (Turin, 1889), p. xx.

than Aristotle does from Horace, but they all admired Dante. The naming of Castelvetro and Tasso in Milton's list is easily explained: Castelvetro, the chief Renaissance commentator on Aristotle's *Poetics*, was the great name in Renaissance criticism; and Tasso's own *Jerusalem Delivered* was for Milton a model of epic poetry. He may have been unaware of the views of either commentator on Dante. But the naming of Mazzoni, who produced all his literary theory as a defense of Dante's poem, points unmistakably to Milton's own admiration of the *Commedia*.

Perhaps Milton knew that Mazzoni had been the friend of Tasso and the teacher of Galileo; perhaps it was Buommattei and Dati who first called Mazzoni's work to his attention. Doubtless he knew the importance of the *Difesa* in the Cinquecento controversy over Dante, at a time when, just as his views on church and state made Dante suspect to a clergy bent on counteracting the Reformation, a self-conscious new humanism was entertaining serious doubts of the *Commedia*'s literary worth. Was Dante a greater poet than Petrarch? was he a great poet at all? was he not rather an extraordinary barbarian, with at best a talent for satire, ignorant of the classics and hence inevitably a victim of the most grotesque errors of taste? had he even done much good with his vaunted efforts to make Tuscan available as a literary language? had he not defied the canons of poetic decorum, the laws of logic, and even plain common sense? To answer such attacks Mazzoni had first written a brief *Discorso in Difesa della Commedia*, praising poetry generally as a species of moral philosophy, and Dante's poem in particular as greater even than Homer's. As the war of words continued, Mazzoni undertook his more elaborate *Difesa della Commedia*, the first part of which, published in 1587, Milton knew.

Even in the *Discorso* Mazzoni had exalted the *Commedia* as the greatest of poems in its moral teaching; in the *Difesa* he set forth the ground of that exaltation in more detail. Since poetry is an imitative art, whose objects exist only by and in imitation, he argued (Introduction, section 10), therefore invention is the chief poetic talent; and Dante is thus the greatest, because the most inventive, of poets. Though the immediate purpose of poetry is delight (29–30), instruction is its more important purpose; in both Dante is supreme, a civic teacher in the *Commedia* no less than in his prose (works). Better than any other poet, Dante fulfills Plato's as well as Aristotle's requirements for poetry, so much so that if Plato could have read the *Paradiso* he would have regarded his own treatment of the afterworld in *Phaedrus* as inferior (52). This is high praise indeed. For the Platonist Milton, who was also concerned with the doctrinal and exemplary in poetry, the Platonist Mazzoni's esteem for Dante would have had great significance.

True, Milton may not have taken the *Commedia* as an epic poem, though Mazzoni and Buommattei both found epic features in it. And Milton may not have agreed that the poem is called a comedy chiefly to distinguish it not from epic poetry but from tragedy, though Daniello and other Renaissance commentators made like assertions. But Steadman begs the question when he concludes from Mazzoni's argument on genre that it is impossible that "Milton could have regarded the *Commedia* as a potential *model*" for *Paradise Lost* (p. 119, n. 62). Tasso, whom Milton cites along with Mazzoni, did think the *Commedia* one of the four great models of epic poetry;[6] and Mazzoni regarded it as superior to the *Iliad*, *Odyssey*, and *Aeneid* both as poetry and as doctrine. At any rate, in writing *Paradise Lost* Milton used much that he did not regard as epic poetry, notably Genesis 1–3 and Ovid's *Metamorphoses*. Since

[6] "Tasso's Account of the Allegory of the Poem," appended to the translation of *Jerusalem Delivered* by Edward Fairfax, which Milton knew.

Dante was for Mazzoni and Buommattei the greatest of all poets on every ground of style, invention, fable, philosophic instruction, and organization, Milton would hardly have listed Mazzoni as a major critic, or have consulted Buommattei on what to read, unless he too thought highly of the *Commedia*. He nowhere names the *Commedia* as a model, but his promise in the *Reason of Church-Government* (1642) to undertake some great literary work has a marked similarity, as Kuhns noted (1898, p. 4), to the promise at the end of the *Vita Nuova*, especially in conjunction with his praise of Dante in the *Apology for Smectymnuus* of the same year. He never regarded Dante as less than a great poet and an important thinker. Under the influence of Protestant and counter-Reformation views alike, he gave special attention to Dante's attacks on the Roman church; but from the first he attended to more than the protest in Dante. His earliest interest had been in the love-poet. Only three of his citations in the *Commonplace Book* concern issues of church and state; the other five deal with such diverse matters as suicide, liberal studies, true nobility, the indisposition to either good or evil, and usury. The reference in his sonnet to Lawes is to the Dante who shared his own delight in music. Perhaps his address to Cromwell on liberty in the *Second Defense* (1654) owes something to Dante's Seventh Epistle, with its plea to the Emperor Henry VII, as Herford suggests (1924, p. 213); and probably the reference to Constantine in the *Means to Remove Hirelings* (1659) harks back to his earlier interest in *Inferno* 19 and *Paradiso* 20. Doubtless Dante also expresses many views that Milton did not share, but to these Milton nowhere refers. All his citations show agreement: Dante writes most understandingly on one matter (*Commonplace Book*, fol. 16), speaks admirably of another (ibid., 191), provides a feast (letter to Buommattei) and an example (*Ap. Smect.*).

Dante and Milton

If he read the whole of Boccaccio's *Vita di Dante*, and not only the section he cites—that on the condemnation by Cardinal Poggietto of the *Monarchia* (*Commonplace Book*, fol. 182)—he would have found resemblances to his own tastes, talents, and habits, and ultimately to his own experiences.[7] The studiousness of the young Dante, his early attempts to imitate the great Latin poets, his faith in the high office of poetry, the disappointments of his marriage and political career, the continuity of his studies and writing, his perseverance in creating his great poem through every adversity—here was a man like himself, a poet involved in the crises of his time, who loved music and inveighed against abuses in the church, who preferred books to politics and yet saw it as his duty to enter political life, who incurred exile with its attendant hardships but nevertheless produced his great work. But we need not argue from inferred community of spirit what explicit references demonstrate: Milton admired what he knew of Dante, and he knew Dante well.

He was still turning to the *Commedia* after the onset of his blindness, for the entry from *Purgatorio* 16 on folio 197 of his *Commonplace Book* is in the hand of an amanuensis. Indeed if Hanford ("Chronology" [1921], pp. 284, 303–305) is right in assigning it to the same Amanuensis D who transcribed the extant manuscript of *Paradise Lost* Book I, Milton was rereading Dante at the very time he was composing his epic poem. According to his anonymous biographer, during its composition he used to spend the evenings "reading some choice poets, by way of refreshment after the day's toil, and to store his fancy

---

[7] Probably too he knew the brief account of Dante in Giovanni Villani's *Croniche*, IX, 136. He quotes VI, 61, just after citing *Inferno* 7 in his *Commonplace Book*, fol. 12. Villani calls Dante "a consummate poet and philosopher . . . with the most polished and beautiful style" and praises the *Commedia* for its "polished verse, . . . great and subtle arguments, . . . new and beautiful figures" (tr. Napier).

against morning." The many parallels to the *Commedia* in *Paradise Lost* may all be due to chance or a long memory, but there is no reason to suppose they are. We need not assert with Michele Renzulli that Milton was "one of the most fervid worshipers and admirers of Dante, whose influence is conspicuous in almost all his literary work" (1925, p. 45), but there is good reason to argue that the poet who thought Spenser a better teacher than Aquinas, and who wished to write what would be "doctrinal to a nation," also found Dante a better teacher than Calvin and far more helpful in the composition of *Paradise Lost*.

Milton was apparently the first English poet to get at the heart of the *Commedia*, to recognize its large meanings, as he was the first to adapt its techniques of instruction through narrative to his own purposes. His references do not of themselves prove Dante to have been a major influence on him but they do prove what was in itself unusual, that he read Dante with sympathy. Together with all the echoes, analogues, and parallels in the poem itself, they leave no doubt of the importance of the *Commedia* in the writing of *Paradise Lost*.

III

"Higher Argument Remains"

WHATEVER it may have been that turned Milton from the kind of subject for epic poetry proposed in his verses to *Manso* (80–84), in the *Epitaph for Damon* (162–168), and in the Trinity manuscript, it was surely not distaste for Tasso or Spenser, any more than for Homer and Virgil. The impress of all four on *Paradise Lost* is evident. Yet the detailed rejection of familiar epic matter in the proem to Book IX suggests something more than the intention of soaring "above th' Aonian Mount" announced at the opening of the poem. There he may have been asserting only the Renaissance commonplace on the superiority of Christian to pagan themes, as again in the Proem to Book VII, lines 3–4. Here he declares not merely that his argument is "more Heroic" than that of the *Iliad, Aeneid,* or *Odyssey,* but that compared with his subject the common stuff of Renaissance epic, "hitherto the only Argument/ Heroic deem'd," is common stuff indeed:

> . . . fabl'd Knights
> In Battles feign'd . . . ,
> . . . Races and Games,
> Or tilting Furniture, emblazon'd Shields,
> Impreses quaint, Caparisons and Steeds;
> Bases and tinsel Trappings, gorgeous Knights
> At Joust and Tournament; then marshall'd Feast

Serv'd up in Hall with Sewers, and Seneschals;
The skill of Artifice or Office mean,
Not that which justly gives Heroic name
To Person or to Poem.   (30–41)

The topics are recognizably those of Boiardo, Ariosto,
Spenser, and Tasso, as well as lesser poets of the Renaissance,
and recognizably, too, quite alien to the subject of Book IX.
Why then does Milton go out of his way to name them? In
Book VI he had demonstrated that he could feign a battle in
high Homeric fashion. In Book II he had written a brilliant,
if brief, passage describing races and games. He was later, in
Paradise Regained, to describe a "marshall'd Feast" (II.337–367)
with no mean skill, and in quick surveys of the Parthian and
Roman might (III.310–344; IV.25–85) sketch the furniture
and trappings of great armies and the wealth and luxury of a
great empire as well. Evidently he was both skilled and studious
enough in the very matters he was determined to repudiate at
the opening of Book IX.

The rhetorical device of exalting a chosen subject by dis-
paraging others was, of course, not Milton's invention. Yet
that alone would hardly account for the insistence of these
lines, with their deliberate emphasis on the *heroic* quality of
his chosen subject. No doubt the continued discussion during
the Renaissance of the matter proper to epic and other kinds
of poetry had its influence. Milton's list of the topics he chooses
to avoid has a counterpart, for example, in Giraldi Cintio's
Discorso on the composing of romances, which praises the
romance precisely because it can include such matter and thus
gain variety with its "unexpected incidents, . . . victories,
triumphs, single combats, jousts, tournaments, . . . and other
similar things" (p. 26). But Milton's inversion of the argument
into exaltation of his own subject has a closer counterpart.

Benedetto Buommattei had exploited just such a contrast in

order to exalt the *Commedia* of Dante in his 1623 oration *In Praise of the Tuscan Language*. After enumerating the resources of the language itself, Buommattei climactically asserted:

Nor has our tongue lacked its Homer or its Virgil. It has had its Dante, who is as much greater than they (let us not let ourselves be blinded by envy) as the conception he expounds is greater, as Heaven is nobler than earth, as things eternal and invisible are more prized than the temporal and visible. He could, following the ancients, have woven his poem out of some famous action of important persons, and imitating them acquired a name neither obscure nor lowly. But he scorned the narrow confines of the epic because to that sublime soul no bound was prescribed. He left behind every familiar path and with the sharpness of his profound genius penetrated the most hidden mysteries of the high mind of God, learnedly figuring for us the active and contemplative lives, *not by means of furious loves, unreasonable wraths, bloody battles, cruel spectacles, and vain, improbable fictions and chimeras,* but by representing to us those three states which by the just judgment of God are assigned to each one after death according to his merits, a thing to astonish art, make nature marvel, and cause poetic imitation itself to admit itself vanquished. He indeed had the right to take pride in himself and to protest himself the first who dared sail a sea so measureless; and well might he sing:

> L' acqua, ch' io prendo, giammai non si corse,
> Minerva spira, e conducemi Apollo,
> E nuove Muse mi dimostran l' Orse.
>   (II, pp. 553–554; italics mine)

Whether or not Milton knew the passage, or even its substance, it is significant that Dante's subject could be praised on the same grounds as his own: that this higher argument surpasses common epic matter as it involves the just judgment of God and the merits of men—in short, the realities of Christian doctrine as opposed to mere fictions.

Dante's own declaration in the lines from *Paradiso* 2 on the novelty of his subject, which Buommattei cites as fully justified by his achievement, provides a direct link with *Paradise Lost.* When Milton declares at the opening of his poem that it will pursue "things unattempted yet in prose or rhyme," the phrase recalls, according to Todd, like assertions by Lucretius, Homer, Virgil, Spenser, and Cowley, and even like words in Boiardo, Ariosto, Skelton, and Davies; but the meaning recalls Dante. The second canto of *Paradiso* opens with the warning,

> O ye who in your little skiff, longing to hear,
>   have followed on my keel that singeth on its
>   way,
> turn to revisit your own shores; commit you
>   not to the open sea; for perchance, losing me,
>   ye would be left astray.
> The water which I take was never coursed
>   before; Minerva bloweth, Apollo guideth
>   me, and the nine Muses point me to the Bears.
>   (1–9)

The proper readers will be "Ye other few (Voi altri pochi)." Since Milton too dismisses improper readers at a major turning point of his poem, in Book VII, Dante's passage presumably had an influence upon the proems to both Book VII and Book I. And since a vein like Dante's has long been recognized in the proem to Book III with its invocation of light, may it not be that the same precedent is partly responsible for the emphasis at the opening of Book IX?

At any rate, a like structural function may be discerned in the exordia of the *Commedia* and of *Paradise Lost.* Doubtless Renaissance commentators exaggerated the importance of Dante's opening cantos in each cantica. But in a critical tradition that regularly named proposition, invocation, and narration as the quantitative divisions of a poem, especially an epic poem, the exaggeration was inevitable, especially in the thick of a dispute over both the genre and the merits of the *Commedia*. In the letter to Can Grande della Scala, if indeed it is his, Dante himself gave the precedent:

The part in question, then, that is, this third cantica which is called *Paradise*, falls by its main division into two parts, namely the prologue, and the executive part; which second part begins:

Surge ai mortali per diverse foci.

As regards the first part, it should be noted that although in common parlance it might be termed an exordium, yet, properly speaking, it can only be termed a prologue; as the Philosopher seems to indicate in the third book of his *Rhetoric*, where he says that "the proem in a rhetorical oration answers to the prologue in poetry, and to the prelude in flute-playing." It must further be observed that this preamble . . . is one thing in the hands of a poet, and another in those of an orator. For orators are wont to give a forecast of what they are about to say, in order to gain the attention of their hearers. Now poets not only do this, but in addition they make use of some sort of invocation afterwards. And this is fitting in their case, for they have need of invocation in a large measure, inasmuch as they have to petition the superior beings for something beyond the ordinary range of human powers, something almost in the nature of a divine gift. Therefore the present prologue is divided into two parts: in the first is given a forecast of what is to follow; in the second is an invocation to Apollo; which second part begins:

O buono Apollo, all' ultimo lavoro, &c.

With reference to the first part it must be observed that to make a good exordium three things are requisite, as Tully says in his *New Rhetoric;* that the hearer, namely, should be rendered favorably disposed, attentive, and willing to learn; and this is especially needful in the case of a subject which is out of the common, as Tully himself remarks. Inasmuch, then, as the subject dealt with in the present work is out of the common, it is the aim of the first part of the exordium or prologue to bring about the above-mentioned three results with regard to this out-of-the-way subject.   (tr. Toynbee)

The emphatic conjoining of the exordium with the novel subject suggests a direct line connecting Dante with Milton: if rhetorical tradition stresses the need of exordia in treating such subjects, the use of an exordium may itself suggest that the novelty of the subject undertaken be stressed. Dante makes the point clear in *Convivio* II.vii.59: "The most potent persuasion to render the hearer attentive is the promise to tell novel and imposing things" (tr. Wicksteed).

The particular functions of prologues named in the letter to Can Grande, and the division into a forecast and an invocation, both coincide with critical pronouncements of the Renaissance. Naturally enough, editors and defenders of the *Commedia* made much of them. Daniello, for example, notes that Dante's poem as a proper comedy is divided into three acts, each with a prologue of its own after the initial prologue to the work as a whole. In his comments on *Inferno* 1 and 2, *Purgatorio* 1, and *Paradiso* 1, he echoes what the letter says on the structural function of the prologues, distinguishing the statement of subject, the invocation, and the beginning of the narration. Thus on *Purgatorio* 1 he writes:

The poet does not depart in this second cantica, any more than in the first or third, from the order kept and observed by all other poets in their works, stating the subject, invoking aid, and narrating, the statement coming in verses 1–6, the invocation in 7–12, the narration beginning with "Dolce color."   (p. 231)

Mazzoni gave like importance to the proems, and Buommattei's Tavole stress them for the eye, dividing all the matter of each cantica into Proemio and Narrazione. Like most Renaissance editors, Buommattei not only marks the invocation as part of each proem, but neatly assigns the proems: *Inferno* 1 for the *Commedia* as a whole, *Inferno* 2 for *Inferno* itself, *Purgatorio* 1 for the whole second division, and *Paradiso* 1–2 for the final cantica.

Now Dante does not, in fact, use his exordia so strictly as his Renaissance commentators and defenders would suggest. He renews his invocations at various critical moments in his narrative when he consciously changes style, turning to address his readers in his own person as narrator when it suits him, and commenting at need on the stage at which his poem has arrived. Still, for all their exaggeration, his defenders were thus far right: the opening cantos of each part of the *Commedia* do mark out the new realm now opening and the new experience to be gained there. They point to an elaborately conceived architecture. And in this they furnish a structural precedent for Milton.

Both Dante and Milton had, of course, other precedents for calling attention to a new division, notably Virgil's pointer for the second half of the *Aeneid:*

> Maior rerum mihi nascitur ordo,
> maius opus moveo.   (VII.44–45)

Milton also had as a possible model the proems of Spenser to the various completed books of *The Faerie Queene*. But like those of Dante, and unlike other possible models, Milton's proems are part of the structure. He uses them, as Dante did the opening cantos of the *Commedia*, to mark his structural divisions. The first proem introduces *Paradise Lost* as a whole, Books I–VI more particularly, and Books I–II more particularly still. Renewed invocations and statements of subject begin Books III, VII, and IX—the proem to Book III introducing Books III–VI and marking the shift from Hell and Chaos to

Heaven; that to Book VII introducing the second half of the poem, but more particularly Books VII–VIII with their shift from supraterrestrial to terrestrial concerns; and the last introducing Books IX–XII, the remainder of the work, but more particularly the tragic central episode, the loss of Paradise. The structural function of Milton's proems is thus multiple: even more elaborately than those of Dante, they mark shifts from realm to realm, from theme to theme; and even more intricately, they link and distribute the tensions of the whole narrative pattern. Though Milton elaborates it, the device is Dante's.

More remarkably, the closest thematic parallels to Milton's four proems are to be found in Dante. But here the parallels are furnished by the invocations and exordial matter interjected at critical moments of the *Commedia*, as well as by the proems proper. For example, Dante and Milton each comments on the amount of his life that has gone into the making of his poem. Perhaps Statius gave the precedent, speaking in the *Achilleid* I.18–19 of "the theme whereat with long nor yet confident preparation" he was laboring, and in the *Thebaid* XII.810ff., addressing his work, "O my *Thebaid*, for twelve years object of my wakeful toil." But Dante specifically connects this theme with another that Milton uses in his prologues, namely the ills, largely of political origin, with which he has been beset. He opens *Paradiso* 25 with the poignant lines:

> Should it e'er come to pass that the sacred poem
>   to which both heaven and earth so have set hand,
>   that it hath made me lean through many a year,
> should overcome the cruelty which doth bar me forth
>   from the fair sheepfold wherein I used to sleep, a
>   lamb, foe to the wolves which war upon it;
> with changed voice now, and with changed fleece
>   shall I return, a poet, and at the font of my baptism
>   shall I assume the chaplet.   (1–9)

Milton speaks in the proem to Book IX of his "long choosing and beginning late," and in the proem to Book VII, where "Half yet remains unsung," comments on arriving at a part that can be sung

> . . . with mortal voice, unchang'd
> To hoarse or mute, though fall'n on evil days,
> On evil days though fall'n, and evil tongues;
> In darkness, and with dangers compast round,
> And solitude.   (24–28)

The "voice *un*chang'd" inverts Dante's "altra voce," as the sense of danger and solitude echoes Dante's "guerra" against his wolvish enemies. Since Milton here proceeds to ask the Muse for "fit audience . . . though few," as Dante had warned off all but "pochi" among his readers, several exordial passages in the *Commedia* may be presumed to have influenced Milton here.

For Dante scatters such exordial themes as Milton confines to the proems that begin *Paradise Lost* I, III, VII, and IX. Thus invocations occur in *Inferno* 2.7–9; 32.1–12; *Purgatorio* 1.1–12; 29.37–42; *Paradiso* 1.13–27; 18.82–87; 22.112–123; 30.97–99; 33.67–72. But comparable matter occurs also in *Inferno* 20.1–3; 21.1–2; 26.19–24; 34.22–24; *Purgatorio* 8.19–21; 9.70–72; 32.61–70; 33.136–141; *Paradiso* 2.1–15; 10.22–27; 23.55–69; 24.25; 25.1–9; 30.28–33. Indeed, between the two groups of passages the difference is so slight that calling upon an inspiring power would shift most of the second group into the first. Lists of line numbers can mean little, and to detail the thematic resemblances would involve tedious repetition. Often several passages in Milton recall one in Dante, as we have noted with *Paradiso* 25.1–9. Conversely, one passage in Milton may recall several in Dante, as we have observed of the proem to Book

VII. The appended table shows many overlappings, as well as many themes that have analogues elsewhere, some that are commonplaces, and some where Milton's phrasing is closer to that of another poet. Ariosto, Virgil, and Statius are among his likely sources. But no other model for Milton's proems shows the same concentration of resemblances as the *Commedia*. (See Appendix D.)

Needless to say, not every theme in Milton's prologues has its parallel in Dante. Dante had not gone blind, he had not lost the delights of the seasons returning or the human face divine, he did not speak of selecting after long deliberation the subject of his poem, he was not concerned to rise above Homer and Virgil in their own genre, he did not change his notes to tragic, nor was he afraid of the effect of a northern climate on his verse. And there are many themes in Dante which are not echoed in Milton's prologues. Milton had no longing to be crowned with laurel in a city from which he had been exiled, nor did he regard himself as commanded by heavenly powers to write his poem; he never compared any part of *Paradise Lost* to a ship large or small, did not attribute his poetic gift to favoring stars, never called on the reader to sharpen his wits or to supply an ineffable experience for himself, and was not concerned that others after him should write even better in the same vein; he would not have invoked the Apollo who caused Marsyas to be flayed; he never told his reader that a given section must end because he had reached a self-imposed limit. The list of such disparities can easily be expanded.

But the likenesses are more important. Like Dante, Milton at once indicates that he works from a conscious plan and asserts that his verse is dictated by an inspiring power. Dante calls himself "one who, when Love inspires me take note, and go setting it forth after the fashion which he dictates within me" (*Purg.* 24.52–54); Milton speaks of his

"Higher Argument Remains"

> Celestial Patroness, who deigns
> Her nightly visitation unimplor'd,
> And dictates to me slumb'ring, or inspires
> Easy my unpremeditated Verse.
>
> (IX.21–24)

Both thus emphasize the spontaneity of their composition—Dante in the "dolce stil nuovo" which records what the "dittator" Love bids, Milton in the "unpremeditated Verse" dictated by his nightly visitant. And yet each just as emphatically underscores the careful working out of his poem. Each, for example, deliberately calls attention to its consciously divided parts (*Inf.* 20.1–3; *Purg.* 1.4; 33.139–141; *Par.* 1.10–12; *P.L.* III.13–21, VII.21–23; IX.5–6). Again like Dante, Milton renews his invocations to mark such divisions, and varies the power he invokes to mark the change or heightening of his theme. The procedure is so clearly deliberate that to take all his invocations as addressed to one theological person under a mere confusion of names would be to miss the purpose of the variations. No doubt the "Muse" and the "Spirit" of the first invocation address the same creative power under a pagan and a Biblical name; no doubt the invoking of Urania and the rejecting of Calliope in Book VII is Milton's way of insisting on the heavenly inspiration of his account of the creation; and no doubt calling Urania own sister to Wisdom is his way of removing her pagan family ties. But why trouble to invoke the *heavenly* Muse, Urania, in a poem professedly *epic?* And why deliberately associate a pagan muse not only with the inspiration of Biblical Moses and David, but with the Spirit that prefers "Before all Temples th' upright heart and pure"? Why shift to Holy Light as the power invoked at the opening of Book III, and return to Urania at the opening of Book VII, only to urge that she is not one of the pagan nine at all and never dwelt on Olympus like the hollow fictions of the ancients? Clearly

Milton intends the variants to guide as well as startle his reader. In just such a fashion Dante calls upon the Muses, together with genius and memory, to aid him at his approach to Inferno (2.7–10); just so, he asserts his special need of them to describe the final scene there (32.1–12), renews his appeal to dead Poesy itself, as well as to the "sante Muse" generally and to Calliope in particular at the opening of *Purgatorio* (1.7–9), later re-invokes the "sacrosante Vergini," and Urania particularly, that Helicon may stream forth for his description of the pageant in the Earthly Paradise (29.37–42); just so, he calls upon Apollo himself, declaring his need of both peaks of Parnassus for the undertaking of *Paradiso* (1.13–27), asks the "goddess Pegasean" to aid him (18.82), beseeches the stars and light itself for power to treat of highest Heaven (22.112–114, 121–123), and declares that Polyhymnia and all her sisters could not provide adequate inspiration to speak its glory (23.55–63); just so, he finally implores the "luce eterna," the Triune God, the ultimate source of all inspiration, to help him at least indicate his final blinding vision (33.124).

Again like Dante, Milton speaks of his relation to his poem and to chosen prototypes. Dante had shown throughout the *Commedia*, but especially in his exordia, how such self-revelation could support the persuasiveness of the speaker; Milton too worked the familiar rhetorical device. Dante had used exordia to guide the reader's understanding of his aims; Milton elaborated the design. Dante had taken his unjust suffering as more than recompensed by his poetic power and as giving him a special right to speak; Milton makes a like assertion. There may have been no deliberate imitation; verbal reminiscences are few. But certainly the conscious artist in Milton attended with special interest to the conscious artist in Dante, absorbing from the *Commedia* not a few devices of structure and imagery for the exordia of *Paradise Lost*. Perhaps some resemblances come from likeness of context. Thus if Milton's lines on the relief he feels as he turns from Hell and Chaos to the realm of light, at the beginning of Book III, recall *Purgatorio* 1, it may be simply that Dante too had left behind the darkness of Inferno so that naturally enough

> Sweet hue of orient sapphire . . .
> to mine eyes restored delight, soon as I issued
>   forth from the dead air which had afflicted
>   eyes and heart.   (*Purg.* 1.13–18)

But Dante's words at that comparable point in his poem may have underscored for Milton his own affliction; for he takes the occasion to speak of his blindness as he addresses light:

> . . . thee I revisit safe,
> And feel thy sovran vital Lamp; but thou
> Revisit'st not these eyes, that roll in vain
> To find thy piercing ray, and find no dawn.
>   (III.21–24)

And then, just as Dante asserted a few lines earlier, "O sante Muse, poichè vostro sono," Milton continues:

> Yet not the more
> Cease I to wander where the Muses haunt
> Clear Spring, or shady Grove, or Sunny Hill,
> Smit with the love of sacred Song.
>   (26–29)

Although his phrase both translates Virgil's in the Second *Georgic* 475–476, and sums up a long tradition of the Biblical epic as "sacred Song," Milton is closer to Dante (*Par.* 25.1) in dedicating *himself* to the sanctifying Muse. So too the conscious shift of tone when he changes his "notes to tragic," in the proem to Book IX, may have its parallel in Dante's need to change style as he changes subject (*Purg.* 1.7–9; *Par.* 1.13–27; 23.55–63), simply because both poets inherit a common rhetoric that sets a high value on stylistic decorum. But their similar association of a possible change of voice with the injustices they have suffered (*Par.* 25.4–8; *P.L.* VII.24–28) is not likely to have come by chance.

Virtually the only important theme in the proems to *Paradise Lost* that has no parallel in the *Commedia* is the explicit rejection in Book IX of the matter of earlier epic verse. Yet it may be just here that the impress of Dante is deepest. For what chiefly emerges from a scrutiny of the thematic parallels between the proems of *Paradise Lost* and the relevant parts of the *Commedia* is that for each poet his subject is the very highest, so high that only with the help of the divine creative power itself can he hope to sing it worthily. And each insists that it is his subject and the inspiring power, not he, that makes the poem. Thus Dante, in the invocation for his climactic third canticle, writes:

> O divine Virtue, if thou dost so far lend thyself
> to me, that I make manifest the shadow of
> the blessed realm imprinted on my brain,
> thou shalt see me come to thy chosen tree and
> crown me, then, with the leaves of which *the
> matter and thou shalt make me worthy.*
>
> (*Par.* 1.22–27)

And Milton, when he comes to the climactic proem of Book IX, declares:

> . . . *higher Argument*
> *Remains, sufficient of itself to raise*
> *That name* [Heroic], *unless* an age too late, or cold
> Climate, or Years damp my intended wing
> Deprest; and much they may, if *all be mine,*
> *Not Hers who brings it nightly to my Ear.*
>
> (42–47)

Milton speaks more of his relation to the chosen subject and the inspiring power, doubtless because he is entirely the narrator of his poem, not its main agent as well. Inevitably too he shows more consciousness of his relation to the poetic tradition. Whereas Dante can feel that he is inaugurating a tradition (*Par.* 1.34–36), Milton implies how much his work has inherited from the "Aonian Mount" as well as "Sion Hill" and "Siloa's Brook." To stress the novelty, difficulty, and importance of his undertaking he must therefore say more than Dante said: he must note, for example, that he both does and does not write in a vein familiar to the reader of Homer, Virgil, Tasso, or Spenser.

And he is naturally most aware of the need to stress the distinction of his poem when he reaches its most distinctive part, the crisis in Book IX. Dante too, at the climactic moment of his vision, near the end of *Paradiso*, speaks a climactic prayer for unusual inspiration:

> O light supreme, who so far dost uplift thee o'er
> mortal thoughts, re-lend unto my mind a little
> of what then thou didst seem,
> and give my tongue such power that it may leave
> only a single sparkle of thy glory unto the folk
> to come.   (*Par.* 33.67–72)

As we observed earlier, Milton similarly invokes light before he ventures, in Book III, into highest Heaven, but for his poem that step is neither the grand climax nor even the most difficult part. Significantly, he notes the danger of his theme when he turns to earthly matters in Book VII(15–20). Now when he comes to the human action of the fall in Book IX he stresses its uniqueness among epic subjects (5–41).

A comparison of the proems of Milton with Dante's illuminates Milton's central aim: the distinctive concern of *Paradise*

Lost is not to offer instruction in or justification of God's ways. What Raphael says to Adam, Milton's whole poem says to the reader:

> Heav'n is for thee too high
> To know what passes there; be lowly wise:
> Think only what concerns thee and thy being;
> Dream not of other Worlds, what Creatures there
> Live, in what state, condition or degree,
> Contented that thus far hath been reveal'd
> Not of Earth only but of highest Heav'n.
>
> (VIII.172–178)

Thus easily Milton puts aside matter essential to Dante's *Paradiso* and focuses his poem on the human scene. To Virgil he was no doubt indebted for the phrasing of "higher argument remains"; but a sense of how to insist on his own special purpose Milton owed to Dante.

His purpose being to clarify the human lot, it is strange to find the last lines of his opening invocation constantly misread. Grammatically, logically, and in the light of his handling of every other part of the poem, the lines

> That to the highth of this great Argument
> I may assert Eternal Providence,
> And justify the ways of God to men,
>
> (I.24–26)

signify not the purpose of *Paradise Lost*, but the level at which Milton hopes to deal with his subject, a level consistent with the provident justice of the universe man inhabits. Milton was under no illusion that God had been waiting through the centuries for John Milton to be born and elucidate the whole question of the divine providence; on the contrary he was intensely aware of the dangers inherent in the subject he had chosen. To write of the fall of man meant encountering issues which, improperly handled, might indeed risk impugning divine providence and justice. So many readers have thought the poem fails on that very ground that the danger needs no further discussion. And certainly Milton knew how very much the issues of human happiness and misery must depend on the kind of universe man believes himself to inhabit—whether he finds it benevolent, malevolent, or merely indifferent. But that it is a supremely benevolent universe is for Milton virtually all that man needs to have revealed in order to lead his life rightly.

God, therefore, the very climax of Dante's poem, remains offstage at the great crisis of *Paradise Lost*, and not only because Book IX is tragic and *Paradiso* joyful. The tragedy of Book IX is tempered before the poem ends. But even in its resolution, where the final providence and justice of God are essential, *Paradise Lost* gives the center of the stage to humanity.

That is to say, in brief, that Milton's concern—with man's life as it succeeds or fails of happiness—is not the same as Dante's with man's life as it leads him toward or away from God. Yet even if we do not add that Dante equates human happiness and misery with the movement toward and away from God, and that Milton equates obedience to God's will with man's happiness, and disobedience with the initiation of man's misery, the relevance of Dante's subject to Milton's is clear. In the light of the passages in the *Commedia* comparable to the proems through which Milton directs his readers' understanding of *Paradise Lost*, the importance of Dante's precedent becomes clearer. That precedent may indeed help to explain why Milton, in the invocation to Book IX, explicitly rejected the familiar themes and trappings of epic poetry: the "higher Argument" of his choice, although not the same subject as Dante's, was much influenced by his reading of the *Commedia*.

Milton's deliberate use of "tragic" for the substance of Books

IX–XII, the last third of his epic poem, recalls Dante's deliberate use of "commedia" twice over for his narrative in contrast to Virgil's "tragic" poem (*Inf.* 16.128; 21.1). Thus Dante may even have marked for Milton the tonal resemblance between the *Aeneid* and *Paradise Lost*. More important, when Milton chose Virgil as one of his epic models, he had the precedent of Dante in putting the model to the use of his own "sacred song" and then going beyond it. Dante too soars above the mount up which the ancient poet guides him, and his flight may have encouraged Milton to renounce his earlier Spenserian and Tassonian projects. A poem not less but more heroic than the familiar matter of epic poetry could be written on the essential human theme of the loss and restoration of one man's happiness, especially if that man were clearly a type of every man, experiencing as participant or witness the whole range of human woe and joy.

IV

Hell and Its Populace

PARALLELS of phrase have more often been noted between Books I and II of *Paradise Lost* and the first cantica of the *Commedia* than between other parts of the two poems.[1] The assumption has generally been that such echoes are Milton's chief debt to Dante. But analogues can in fact be found between most analogous parts: if details of scenes in Hell recall *Inferno*, details of scenes in Heaven recall *Paradiso*, and details of scenes on earth, both in Eden and in Michael's presentation of man's future, recall *Purgatorio*. But echoes in themselves count for little with Milton, who poetized less with separate words than with whole phrases assimilated from a vast range of literature. Moreover, both he and Dante had an extraordinary familiarity with many of the same books: Virgil, Ovid, Statius, the Psalms, the Gospels, the Book of Revelation were absorbed into the very workings of their minds. And both had probed the church fathers—notably Augustine, but Aquinas too for Milton as well as Dante—for help in fusing their treasured classical reading to their Christian commitment. Both regarded themselves as

[1] The most important parallels, in Todd's notes to *The Poetical Works of John Milton* (1801) and Oscar Kuhns, "Dante's Influence on Milton," *MLN* 13 (1898), 1–12, are collected in Paget Toynbee, *Dante in English Literature* I (1909), pp. 127–128, 587–598. See also E. H. Plumptre's comments in *The Commedia and Canzionere of Dante* (1886) and E. E. Kellett, *Reconsiderations* (1928), pp. 128–146.

heirs of one intermingled tradition, with two roots in Greece and Palestine. If Greek sources were directly available to Milton, Dante managed to know a good deal of and about them through Roman and medieval intermediaries.

Thus some of the labor expended on collecting parallels is bound to be futile. Only where supposed echoes are evidence of a controlling concept can they show how Milton used the *Commedia*. And *Inferno*, we may observe at once, was not the section of Dante's poem that he chiefly used, though he obviously read it with care. It happens to be the part he had most occasion to cite in his *Commonplace Book* and from which he quoted a passage in *Of Reformation*, but it was not his preferred part of the *Commedia* any more than it was Dante's. His five explicit references cannot even tell the full impression that *Inferno* made on him.

They do tell something. All five concern the human inhabitants of Hell, and the fact has significance. Though Milton also took features of demonic appearance and of landscape from *Inferno*, he concentrated his interest on Dante's treatment of human error. The particular passages he cites in his *Commonplace Book* concern those condemned to the anteroom of Hell in *Inferno* 3, the avaricious clergy in Canto 7, the analysis of usury in Canto 11, and the punishment of suicides in Canto 13. From *Inferno* 19 he translated, in *Of Reformation*, the lament on the Gift of Constantine. In context, of course, these passages involve much more; they occur linked with ideas central to *Inferno*. Thus Canto 3 contains the inscription over the gate of Hell and the first evidence that the damned now have what they had chiefly desired. Canto 7 notes the great number—greater than elsewhere—of those whom concern with money has vitiated; it discusses the error of reviling Fortune for redistributing "li ben vani," and implies the relation of wrath and sullenness. Canto 11 explains the great divisions of Hell into the realms of incontinence that lie outside, and those of violence and fraud that lie within, the City of Dis, marking fraud as the evil at once peculiar to man, most alien to his humanity, and therefore most damnable. And Cantos 13 and 19 offer two striking examples of the relation between a crime and the penalty divine justice assigns it in the suicides transformed to blasted trees, never to re-invest the bodies of which they have divested themselves, and in the simonists fixed head downward in their perversity, to be pressed ever deeper by the successors to whom they showed the way.

To turn from these citations to what commentators have made of the contrast between Milton's Hell and Dante's is to lose one's way at once. Milton uses the vast and vague in contrast to Dante's limited and detailed realism (Kuhns, 1898, p. 7); whereas Dante classifies crimes to create a medieval-philosophical Inferno, Milton creates a place of "promiscuous punishment, comparative gaiety, and crude theological discussion" that blurs Dante's grand concept (Gurteen, 1896, pp. 367, 376); Dante's Hell, Purgatory, and Paradise are all precisely related to each other and to earth, whereas Milton, having centered his poem on earth, works out his cosmic map as he moves back and forth (Watkins, 1955, pp. 48–49). Macaulay, as so often, made the point best, as well as first, in all its wrongness: "The exact details of Dante" are "the illustrations of a traveller"; "the dim intimations of Milton" have their value less in "what they directly represent" than in "what they remotely suggest." On the two Satans Macaulay is equally striking and equally misleading: "The English poet has never thought of taking the measure of Satan," and again on the devils of the two Hells: Dante's are mere "spiteful ugly executioners," whereas Milton's have in their characters, as in their forms, "a certain dim resemblance to . . . men, but exaggerated to gigantic dimensions, and veiled in mysterious

71

gloom." Chateaubriand, Coleridge, Lamartine, and Henry Hallam alike belabor Dante's Lucifer for being, in contrast to Milton's Prince of Darkness, "a mere odious monster." Symonds reverses the process to belabor Milton: whereas Dante rejoiced in the concrete, Milton takes off into the indefinite and descends to detail only to lose his power (pp. 232–234); Dante's sublimity is moral, his concern is with the human, but Milton prefers the grandiosely titanic and superhuman (p. 239). Gurteen defends Dante's devil as "powerless, speechless, hopeless" because he is intended as the symbol of impotent hate (p. 366), and objects that Milton hardly even assigns Satan a punishment distinct from his followers, or sees, as Dante did, the inwardness of Hell (pp. 379–381). Pember at least justifies the difference: whereas Dante's Lucifer is the archetypal transgressor, permanently and fittingly imprisoned in the lowest pit, "silent, inactive, impassive," with none of his former beauty, Milton's Satan is "the original and present transmitter of sin and misery" to mankind, using his energies freely within only the limits fixed by Omnipotence (pp. 78–82).[2]

But surely the first thing to be said of the two Hells is that Milton grasped the meaning of Dante's and found it relevant to his own concept. The two Hells have in common the same primary purpose: to set forth in the figures of an imagined alien scene the poet's insights into what has gone wrong in the world we know, what traits in humanity lead it to make earth a hell. On these issues the two agree, no matter how many critics may prefer to contrast Dante's grotesque demons with Milton's heroic fallen angels, or the geographic particularity of Dante's Inferno with the vagueness of Milton's. True, Dante's Hell is in the bowels of the earth, Milton's beyond geography. True, Dante's Hell is hereafter as well as here, peopled by familiar

[2] See Appendix C.

figures who once did walk this earth—and to be peopled by some now on it—whereas Milton's, removed in both time and place from humanity, as yet contains only superhuman inhabitants. But Milton's devils are men writ large: if they have little in common with the demons of *Inferno*, they constantly remind us of its human damned. The types of evil for which Dante ransacked history, legend, and his own era, Milton created in his fallen angels. The repeated critical contrasts of Dante's Lucifer with Milton's Satan, or of the specialized and constricted rungs of Dante's Hell with Milton's vast nether world, simply miss the point. The Lucifer of *Inferno* is an experience, brief though climactic, for the traveler through his realm; the Satan of *Paradise Lost* is himself a main agent engaged in a representative action. The difference is less in the way Dante and Milton view him than in the role Satan plays in either poem. Not surprisingly, the two poems are not the same, though many critics appear to have thought they should be.

Milton's devils enact in sequence the variety of evils that Dante's condemned souls perpetually re-enact fixed in their several rungs. What Dante conveys through an ever-changing scene with ever-new personae, Milton conveys through dramatic consequence. But on what to convey they markedly agree, and not simply because they are heirs of a common tradition. Impressed by Dante's *Inferno*, Milton adopted its concepts as well as its details.

The details usually relate to the concepts. Among the commonly noted analogues to *Inferno* are the rivers of Hell, its walled city, its torments of darkness, fire, ice, and foul stench, the towering size of its worst devils, the grotesque forms of its guardians—all that Milton summed up in the lines,

> . . . many a Frozen, many a Fiery Alp,
> Rocks, Caves, Lakes, Fens, Bogs, Dens, and shades of death, . . .
> Created evil, for evil only good,

Where all life dies, death lives, and Nature breeds,
Perverse, all monstrous, all prodigious things,
Abominable, inutterable, and worse
Than Fables yet have feign'd, or fear conceiv'd,
Gorgons and Hydras, and Chimeras dire.   (II.620–628)

The phrasing would serve as well to summarize Dante's infernal scene and monsters. Such matters Milton adapts from a variety of sources and prefers to summarize; they do not bear upon the developing action of his poem as they do on the *Commedia*. But when Dante's phrases concern human error, Milton uses them more elaborately, freely applying to his fallen angels what Dante wrote of the human damned. The application begins with his earliest lines on Hell:

Regions of sorrow, doleful shades, where peace
And rest can never dwell, hope never comes
That comes to all; but torture without end
Still urges, and a fiery Deluge, fed
With ever-burning Sulphur unconsum'd:
Such place Eternal Justice had prepar'd
For those rebellious . . .   (I.65–71)

The passage obviously recalls the famous inscription over the entrance to Inferno:

"Through me is the way into the doleful city;
    through me the way into the eternal pain; through
    me the way among the people lost.
Justice moved my High Maker; Divine Power made
    me, Wisdom Supreme, and Primal Love.
Before me were no things created, but eternal;
    and eternal I endure: leave all hope, ye that
    enter."   (3.1–9)

It recalls too the echo of that inscription for the lost souls of the first circle within: "No hope ever comforts them, not of

74

rest but even of less pain" (5.44–45). And it assimilates the fiery deluge of the realm below, where the violent rebels against God, notably the arrogant Capaneus, are confined:

> Over all the great sand, falling slowly, rained
> dilated flakes of fire, like those of snow in
> Alps without a wind.
> As the flames which Alexander, in those hot
> regions of India, saw fall upon his host,
> entire to the ground;
> whereat he with his legions took care to tramp
> the soil, for the fire was more easily ex-
> tinguished while alone:
> so fell the eternal heat, by which the sand was
> kindled, like tinder under flint and steel,
> redoubling the pain.   (14.28–39)

Milton does not exploit the "torture without end"; he has the sulphurous hail cease at once (I.171ff.), and permits his devils to break their confines. But when Satan, no longer chained to the burning lake, makes for the burning strand, he repeats the Dantean theme:

>   . . . on dry Land
> He lights, if it were Land that ever burn'd
> With solid, as the Lake with liquid fire
> And such appear'd in hue; as when the force
> Of subterranean wind transports a Hill
> Torn from Pelorus, or the shatter'd side
> Of thund'ring Aetna, whose combustible
> And fuell'd entrails thence conceiving Fire,
> Sublim'd with Mineral fury, aid the Winds,
> And leave a singed bottom all involv'd
> With stench and smoke: Such resting found the sole
> Of unblest feet.   (I.227–238)

Just before that, Satan's flight recalls a phrase from *Inferno:* "the dusky Air/ . . . felt unusual weight" (226–227) much as the stones under Dante's feet, when he first entered the realms of violence, moved "per lo nuovo carco" (12.30). The shift of phrase from the human newcomer visiting Hell to the arch-fiend newly damned is a recognition by Milton of Dante's power in creating the appropriate detail for his invented scene. The decorum of Dante's inventions evidently impressed him as it had Mazzoni; presumably he was aware that Dante used them to give verisimilitude to his imaginary journey.

When Milton uses the familiar Homeric comparison of the generations of men to leaves, like Shelley he recognizes what Dante had done with the *Aeneid* VI.309 in his image for the damned casting themselves into Charon's boat:

> As the leaves of autumn fall off one after the
> other, till the branch sees all its spoils upon
> the ground:
> so one by one the evil seed of Adam cast
> themselves from that shore . . .
>
> (3.112–116)

Dante, as Ruskin commented, "gives the most perfect image possible of their utter lightness, feebleness, passiveness, and scattering agony of despair" (*Modern Painters, Works* V, p. 206). Milton, in turn, makes the figure convey the sodden devitalized rotting of Satan's clustered legions: they

> lay intrans't
> Thick as Autumnal Leaves that strow the Brooks
> In Vallombrosa, where th' Etrurian shades
> High overarch't imbow'r.   (I.301–304)

Presumably the simile concerns only the great number of the fallen angels and offers a distraction in the beauty of the natural scene; in fact it concentrates, as Dante's does, on suggesting added meanings. Critics have often remarked that Milton's epic similes differ from Homer's on precisely that score. Since this, his most famous, shares the feature with Dante's most famous simile, he may well have learned the device from the *Commedia*, where it is so strikingly used.

Dante's elaborate similes imply, as do Milton's, a whole range of similarities between the objects compared. In the *Commedia* they occur with increasing frequency from *Purgatorio* 30 onward; in *Paradise Lost* their frequency diminishes after Book IV.[3] As Dante leaves the recognizable behind, he has more need to illuminate the unfamiliar with the familiar; Milton, as he shifts his scene to earth, has less. We have already had occasion to note how the simile in *Paradiso* 20.1–6 may have shaped Satan's perverse view that the sun diminishes the stars; and other similes of Dante's may have given Milton other matter. But more important, Dante's characteristic use of the simile to amplify comment apparently helped Milton to evolve his kind of epic simile.

For Milton is full of echoes that show how strong an impression Dante's diction and imagery made upon him. Two students of Virgil would naturally agree in calling the way up from Hell "long and hard" (*Aen.* VI.126; *Inf.* 34.95; *P.L.* II.432–433). But when Satan, voyaging through Chaos, "With head, hands, wings, or feet pursues his way;/ And swims, or sinks, or wades, or creeps, or flies" (II.949–950), the words recall a phrase from *Purgatorio* on Dante's difficult ascent of the mountain which needs "swift wings . . . , and . . . both feet and hands" (*Purg.* 4.28–33), and the meter recalls the adulterers

---

[3] See, for example, *Purg.* 30.85–93; 31.64–67, 70–73; *Par.* 4.1–6; 5.100–104; 8.22–27; 15.13–20; 20.19–27,73–77,142–147; 22.1–6,55–57; 23.1–9; 24.13–18; 25.64–66,118–121; 30.1–9; 31.31–36,43–45,103–105,118–120, 124–126; 33.58–60,64–66,133–135.

storm-tossed by the winds "di qua, di là, di giù, di su" (*Inf.*
5.43). Milton's placing of the metrical effect may suggest that
he understood the scene better than most readers: the emotions
of a Francesca, not to say a Semiramis, produce motions appropriate to Chaos. Again, the powerful line when Dante treads
on the face of Bocca degli Abbati, "se voler fu, o destino,
o fortuna" (32.76), suggests Satan impugning God's supremacy
"Whether upheld by strength, or Chance, or Fate" (I.133).

Dante's impressive phrases sometimes recur more than once
in Milton, transferred to unlike contexts. For example, the
words used by Virgil of the noble heathen, "che senza speme
vivemo in disio" (4.42), echo both in Satan's contrast of his
own lot with that of Adam and Eve ("while I to Hell am
thrust,/ Where neither joy nor love, but fierce desire,/ Among
our other torments not the least,/ Still unfulfill'd with pain of
longing pines," IV.508–511), and in Eve's proposal of suicide
rather than "with desire to languish without hope" (X.995).
And Dante's tribute to Virgil, "Tu se' lo mio maestro e il mio
autore" (1.85), re-enforced by repetition in "Tu duca, tu
signore, e tu maestro" (2.140), suggests Sin's words to Satan,
"Thou art my Father, thou my Author" (II.864) and again
"Thou art thir Author and prime Architect" (X.356).

The shift of context is sometimes as striking as the verbal
parallel itself. Thus Virgil's assurance to Dante at a critical
moment in their passage through Hell, "io non ti lascerò nel
mondo basso" (8.108), becomes the sign of the Son's perfect
trust in the Father—"Thou wilt not leave me in the loathsome
grave" (III.247)—at the most critical moment of the Council
in Heaven. Like any good reader of poetry, Milton responded
to perfection of phrase. Find the impressive passages in the
Commedia, and Milton will generally be found impressed by
them too. For instance, echoes of *Inferno* 3, the best known of
Dante's hundred cantos, occur not only in the passages already

noted, and not in Milton's Hell alone. The confused babble of the crowd just past the gate of Hell reminds Dante of wind-tossed sand:

> Here sighs, plaints, and deep wailings resounded
>   through the starless air: it made me weep at
>   first.
> Strange tongues, horrible outcries, words of pain,
>   tones of anger, voices deep and hoarse, and
>   sounds of hands amongst them,
> made a tumult, which turns itself unceasing in
>   that air for ever dyed, as sand when it eddies
>   in a whirlwind.   (3.22–30)

Milton uses the comparison for the confusion of his illimitable Chaos. As Dante's "trimmers" (to use Wicksteed's word) rush after "an ensign, which whirling ran so quickly that it seemed to scorn all pause" (3.52–54), Milton's

> embryon Atoms . . . around the flag
> Of each his Faction . . .
> Swarm populous, unnumber'd as the Sands . . .
> Levied to side with warring Winds . . .
>   (II.900–905)

And Satan, standing on the brink, "Pondering his Voyage" through Chaos, hears a babble of sound:

> Nor was his ear less peal'd
> With noises loud and ruinous . . .
>   (II.920–921)

Perhaps Charon's words to the damned in *Inferno*, "I come to lead you to the other shore; into the eternal darkness; into fire and into ice" (3.86–87), are not the source of the insistent darkness of Milton's Hell with its region where "cold performs th' effect of Fire" and the damned are to "feel by turns the bitter change/ Of fierce extremes, . . . / From Beds of raging Fire to starve in Ice" (II.595–600). But Milton completes the description with what seems a recollection of Dante's frozen pit in the phrase "there to pine/ Immovable, infixt, and frozen round" (601–602). A reference to the ferrying of the damned across a river just afterward in *Paradise Lost* (II.604) may once again recall Charon's ferry, in Canto 3 (83). Other Hells than Dante's surely gave features to Milton's; but Dante had most fully explored the realm, and Canto 3 seems to have struck Milton with unusual force. It is, after all, impressive even to far less responsive readers.

Thus when Sin tells how at the name of Death "Hell trembl'd . . . and sigh'd/ From all her Caves" (II.788–789), it is again Canto 3 that comes to mind. There, as the new group entered Charon's boat, "the dusky champaign trembled. . . . The tearful ground gave out wind" (130–133). This extraordinary phenomenon, at which Dante falls into his first swoon (135–136), presumably stayed with Milton as a way of emphasizing the terrible consequences of evil.[4]

The behavior of those who enter Charon's boat is striking too. When they hear Virgil tell Charon that Dante's passage "is willed there, where what is willed can be done," in their powerlessness to frustrate the divine will, they curse it:

> They blasphemed God and their parents; the human
> kind; the place, the time, and origin of their seed,
> and of their birth.   (3.103–105)

---

[4] Milton invites a comparison between the birth of Death from Sin in Hell and the introduction of death-from-sin into Eden, when he echoes the phrase as first Eve and then Adam breaks the bond of Eden with Heaven (*P.L.* IX.782–784, 1000–1004). Similarly, Dante had invited a contrast between the tremor of Hell as its new inhabitants enter Charon's boat, and the tremor of the Purgatorial Mount each time a soul is released from one of its rounds (*Purg.* 20.127–132; 21.34–72).

Their impotent rage has its counterpart in that of Satan's followers: "highly they rag'd/ Against the Highest" (I.666–667). And their blasphemy has its counterpart in Satan's at the climactic turn in his first soliloquy, when he finds himself unable either to pursue self-condemnation to its logical end in repentance or even to satisfy himself with his attempted self-exoneration. Powerless against the divine justice, love, and wisdom, he concludes, "Be then his Love accurst, since love or hate,/ To me alike it deals eternal woe" (IV.69–70). But what Milton owed to Dante for the concept of Satan, that supposedly heroic figure, is a large question.

Evidently Milton's Satan and his followers are as unable to blame themselves as a Francesca or a Guido da Montefeltro; to hate the universe in which the will "Chose freely what it now so justly rues" (IV.71–72) is the posture most common in either Hell. To scorn it is less common.

As Galimberti noted (p. 63), Satan in his arrogance is partly Farinata degli Uberti, partly Capaneus—though somewhat more the latter, we may amend. His behavior at the end of Book IV recalls Farinata rising in the tomb among the heretics, "as if he entertained great scorn of Hell," to demand of Dante, "almost contemptuously . . . : 'Who were thy ancestors?'" (10.35–42), as though the living man were an intruder, not he the convicted prisoner of Hell. A similar contempt marks Satan surprised in the bower of Eden by the youthful Ithuriel and Zephon, and made to resume his proper shape. To their question about his identity and purpose he answers with an arrogant counter-demand, as from his old superior station:

> Know ye not then said Satan, fill'd with scorn,
> Know ye not mee? ye knew me once no mate
> For you, there sitting where ye durst not soar;
> Not to know mee argues yourselves unknown,
> The lowest of your throng.   (IV.827–831)

Dante and Milton

The aggressive trick of assuming superiority before a reasonable query underscores the pride of both heresiarchs. Satan continues the scene by demanding to see their chief:

> If I must contend, . . .
> Best with the best, the Sender not the sent.
>
> (IV.851–852)

And overcome with rage when he must then go before "the Sender," he moves

> like a proud Steed rein'd, . . . haughty . . . ,
> Champing his iron curb.   (858–859)

It is significant that Gabriel recognizes him not by his face but "by his gait/ And fierce demeanor" (870–871), just as Farinata's posture reveals him.

An even greater arrogance links Satan with Capaneus, the violent rebel against God. Dante, as soon as he beholds him, asks of Virgil,

> who is that great spirit, who seems to care not for
> the fire, and lies disdainful and contorted, so
> that the rain seems not to ripen him?
>
> (14.46–48)

And Capaneus hearing him cries, "Qual io fui vivo, tal son morto" (51). Satan shares his unconquerable defiance, as Kuhns has observed (p. 8). For Capaneus declares that his conqueror may weary himself with penalties and yet will not "thereby have joyful vengeance" (52–60). Defying Jove's whole armory of thunderbolts, he resembles Satan repeatedly attributing God's victory to his chance possession of the "Thunder" that is his superior weapon, (I.92–93,328,641–645; II.28), and assuring his followers that God will learn from their continued resistance that

who overcomes
By force, hath overcome but half his foe.
(I.648–649)

Even his first speech in Hell reveals Satan's kinship to Capaneus, whom neither death nor Hell can change. He too is of the "fixt mind/ And high disdain" (I.97–98) that admits no defeat lest the victor rejoice, and he too declares that he is what he was (I.106–111). To recognize the nature of Capaneus in him from the beginning would disabuse those readers who mistakenly accept the Satan of the first two books at his own appraisal. Blake and Shelley were only the most eminent students of Dante and Milton who, thus duped, were certain that Milton was "of the Devil's party" with or without knowing it. An animosity like theirs toward the injustice prevalent in the world convinces Quasimodo that Dante's poetry is all in *Inferno*. But in fact it is Blake and Shelley who are of Milton's party, without knowing it; and Quasimodo is probably of Dante's. Their error, which is that of the romantics generally, and which would allow every established power to claim God's sanction for its own injustice, encourages them thereby to see every rebel as a champion of liberty. Camus knew better the course of most rebellion, though he too, we may suggest, confused power with authority. The taste of a Farinata for divisiveness and self-assertion, and the more deadly taste of a Capaneus for forcible dominance over others and violent enmity to all law that proscribes such dominance—this is the taste, not of Milton's God or Dante's Heaven, but of Satan and the damned. Indeed Capaneus' speech is so characteristic of evil that in *Paradise Regained* Milton again gives similar words to Satan:

The Son of God I also am, or was,
And if I was, I am.
(*P.R.* IV.518–519)

83

Neither his inner death nor his inner Hell has, to Satan's mind, altered him; like Capaneus, he boasts his inability to learn from any experience, and denies his degeneration, as though denial could efface the fact.

If Milton thus saw Dante's implications, verbal reminiscences alone—and we have by no means exhausted the possibilities— can tell little of his response to *Inferno*. Their frequency and range show the extent of his familiarity, their transfer to unlike contexts his freedom in using Dante; but they cannot show how thoughtfully he read the poem.

With Dante, Milton holds that great numbers of men are bound for neither Heaven nor Hell, but doomed to an eternity of mere futile restlessness; that no violence is so evil as fraud, which begins with deceiving others and ends with deceiving itself; that the origin of evil, necessarily mysterious in a world created wholly good, is in the act of an evil will; that Highest Wisdom permits and indeed compels the Hell-making habit to enact and re-enact itself endlessly; and that evil finally reduces itself to immobility. These doctrines are naturally not of the same importance in the two poems. For Milton, concerned with beginnings, the origin of evil demands expository fullness; for Dante, looking toward eternity, the origin of evil is subordinate to its end. Milton, with a single continuous action to recount, can only indicate the relentless compulsiveness of the evil will; Dante, with all the circles of Hell to explore, can elaborate the variety of willed evil in its endless re-enactments. We cannot expect the same emphasis by the two poets upon the doctrines they share; the narrative context that presents the doctrine determines the emphasis for each. But all the more remarkable is their agreement.

"The Sport of Winds"

Canto 3 of *Inferno* made a lasting impression on Milton. In his *Commonplace Book* (fol. 70), under the heading "Ignavia," he observed:

The punishment, in the infernal regions, of the slothful who have done nothing in this life well, nor anything which is notably evil, is described by Dante of Florence; they are agitated in vain by perpetual disquiet and by a certain gad-fly. Dante Inferno. cant: 3.

As we have seen, the striking phrases of the canto contributed to his account not only of Hell, but of Chaos too. The particular section his *Commonplace Book* remarks on contributed to yet another part of his cosmic scheme—Limbo, the Paradise of Fools. But here a disparity between the comment and the use suggests two separate readings.

The term "Ignavia" points to Milton's acceptance, at the time he made the entry, of Renaissance interpretations, for he reads the passage as Landino, Vellutello, and Daniello read it. Daniello took the group, whom Wicksteed calls the "trimmers," as undergoing "punishments contrary to their dead life," and explained that "having been lazy and slow while they lived, here they are prompt and rapid" (p. 21). Landino and Vellutello had taken the passage similarly, Landino calling the group "the ignorant" and defining their error as

> the vice of *viltà*, which hinders man, whom God created either to work in the active or to meditate in the contemplative life, and he gets lazy through not having in him any generosity of soul, so that he abandons every honorable and excellent enterprise . . . and lives in such laziness that he comes to despise himself.

Vellutello too thought that the group erred by doing nothing, even anything mediocre, and that their punishment is the opposite of their lives. And Milton when he made the entry in his *Commonplace Book* accepted the common view: laziness is the vice punished just inside the gate of Hell.

Here Voltaire's witticism in his article on Dante in the *Philosophical Dictionary* seems justified: "He has commentators, which is perhaps another reason for his not being understood." For laziness is a vice prompted by motives vastly unlike those that send the group in *Inferno* 3 whirling after their shifting ensign. To call them slow or shiftless makes their penalty contravene the common—though perhaps not uniform—principle of Inferno, that its inhabitants go on doing what they have formed the habit of doing in their lives. It is further to miss the importance of their numbers and of their being the first group encountered. Yet that is still a common interpretation. Scartazzini, for example, in his notes on the passage also labels them "Ignavi" and insists on their laziness:

> Indolent, incapable of evil as of good, because so sluggish, inert, slothful, cowardly, good for nought, they want only to enjoy themselves in the world, taking as their idol the *dolce far niente* . . . . The banner is unfixed, and they who would like above every other thing to enjoy quiet must run after it.   (4th edition, 1903)

Inevitably Scartazzini too makes nothing of their number or

their place. Centuries pass, and commentators can still keep poets from being understood.

But Milton for his Limbo in Book III, the Paradise of Fools, created a group whose penalty, place, and number point to his independent rereading of *Inferno*. Commentators generally derive his Paradise of Fools from Ariosto, since the enumeration of follies recalls the catalogue of vanities that Astolpho saw in the moon (*Orl. Fur.* XXXIV. 73-85). But Milton's Limbo is no mere enumeration of vanities, and the impulse to invent it derives from Dante.

When Satan in *Paradise Lost* III has made his way through Chaos, he alights on the "firm opacous Globe" that separates the newly created universe from that anarchic realm. Here he walks "in spacious field" on a "boundless Continent/ Dark, waste, and wild, . . ./ Starless . . . [with] ever-threat'ning storms/ Of Chaos blust'ring round" and no light "Save on that side which from the wall of Heav'n,/ . . . some small reflection gains/ Of glimmering air." The anteroom of Dante's Hell is no boundless continent suspended over the void, but it too is a dark field ("buia campagna"), its air starless ("l' aer senza stelle"), with only a glimmering light entering from the ordered universe above, noisy with blustering storm ("un tumulto . . . / come la rena quando a turbo spira"). Since Dante's description suggested features of Milton's Chaos, it naturally suggested features too of this outpost of Chaos, and among them the chief feature, the kind and quantity of its future inhabitants:

> other Creature in this place
> Living or lifeless to be found was none,
> None yet, but store hereafter from the earth
> Up hither like Aereal vapors flew
> Of all things transitory and vain, when Sin

With vanity had fill'd the works of men:
Both all things vain, and all who in vain things
Built thir fond hopes of Glory or lasting fame,
Or happiness in this or th' other life;
All who have thir reward on Earth, the fruits
Of painful Superstition and blind Zeal,
Naught seeking but the praise of men, here find
Fit retribution, empty as their deeds.

                                    (III.442–454)

Then Milton proceeds, like Ariosto, to exploit the possible types of "painful Superstition and blind Zeal." But the passage is Dantean in that the essential failing it describes is emptiness; it hammers at the words "vain," "vanity," "empty," as Dante in describing the same thing hammers at negatives: "*senza* infamia e *senza* lodo," "*non* furon ribelli, *nè* fur fedeli," "Cacciarli i ciel per *non* esser men belli, *nè* lo profondo inferno gli riceve," "*non* hanno speranza di morte," "Fama di loro il mondo esser *non* lassa," "*non* ragionam di lor"—passing finally to the most famous negator of all, the one "who from cowardice [viltate] made the great refusal," and summing up the group as those "who *never* were alive" (3.34–64). Milton links his group with "th' unaccomplisht works of Nature's hand,/ Abortive" (455–456), and puts among them the "builders of Babel," who if they could would build "New Babels" (466–468), as though recalling the "diverse lingue, orribili favelle" of Dante's trimmers and the "tumulto" they make.

In Milton's version the group at death expect to enter Heaven, when

              . . . lo
        A violent cross wind from either Coast
        Blows them transverse ten thousand Leagues awry
        Into the devious Air . . . ,
        The sport of Winds: all these upwhirl'd aloft

Fly o'er the backside of the World far off
Into a Limbo large and broad, since call'd
The Paradise of Fools, to few unknown
Long after.   (III.486–497)

In short, this limbo, "now unpeopl'd and untrod," will ultimately house the bulk of mankind. The ironic inversion, "to few unknown/ Long after," has the ring of Dante's phrase in *Purgatorio* (12.94) on the small number of the saved: "vengon molti radi" in Daniello's text; it signifies the same grim fact as the comment in *Inferno* 3: behind the standard

> . . . came so long a train of people
> that I should never have believed death had
> undone so many.   (55–57)

Milton was as aware as T. S. Eliot of the dire meaning behind the laconic phrasing. And thus he, like Dante, disposes of most men—by removing them from Hell and Heaven alike. Ultimately, of course, the idea comes from Revelation 3.16: "So then because thou art lukewarm, and neither cold nor hot, I will spue thee out of my mouth." And Milton may have known Machiavelli's epigram:

> The night that Peter Soderini died
> He at the mouth of Hell himself presented.
> "What, you come into Hell? poor ghost demented,
> Go to the babies' Limbo!" Pluto cried.

Machiavelli, as Longfellow remarks in his note on *Inferno* 3.42, from which I quote the translation, evidently had Dante's anteroom of Hell in mind. His identification of it with Limbo perhaps suggested Milton's; but Milton is closer to recognizing the main point about Dante's throng, that self-seeking is the clue to their nature, number, place, and penalty.

The passages in Dante and Milton are not entirely alike. Whereas Dante mingles the lost human souls with "that caitiff choir of the angels, who were not rebellious, nor were faithful to God; but were for themselves" (37–39), Milton takes only men as capable of such vacuous self-seeking, and equates that error with "Naught seeking but the praise of men." Dante has Virgil say that these worthless folk "lived without blame and without praise," praise being the least disreputable motive of those properly in Hell; Milton, taking another view of possible kinds of fame, equates "all who in vain things/ Built thir fond hopes of Glory" with "All who have thir reward on Earth." Needless to say, Dante would not indiscriminately condemn to their ranks "Cowls, Hoods and Habits"; but his emphasis on the meanness of their blind mode of life (47) may have suggested Milton's "blind Zeal" as the mark of their emptiness. Dante specifies that they "have no hope of death" and "are envious of every other lot" (46–48); Milton, seeing annihilation as proper to those whose lives went for nothing, appoints them their habitat "Till final dissolution."

But these very changes emphasize the Dantean impulse behind the passage as a whole: to create a fit penalty and a fit place for those too empty to play any part in the cosmic scheme. Like Dante he makes them the playthings of the winds. Dante uses characteristically translatable symbols for their penalty when he has them rush about after the shifting standard, veering with every wind, stung by the meanest insects, feeding worms with their tears: they take their direction wholly from without, prompted by the most trivial of motives, and achieve neither happiness nor misery. Milton, with a characteristically sweeping image, has them, just as they think to approach St. Peter's "wicket" (a grim bit of word-play in itself), blown "ten thousand Leagues awry" into Limbo: devoted to nothingness, they end nowhere, swept to a place as remote from Heaven as their misconceived purposes were from realities. The group in *Inferno* whirl "come la rena quando a turbo spira"; Milton's are "the sport of Winds, . . . upwhirl'd aloft/ . . . o'er the backside of the World" (493–494).

Redemptive mercy and punitive justice alike scorn them in *Inferno* (3.50); they have excluded themselves from the cosmos through sheer fatuousness according to *Paradise Lost*. Mere self-seekers, indifferent alike to good and evil, according to Dante they must be left behind on the shores of Acheron lest they give the very damned reason to feel proud of themselves (3.34–42). Milton interprets Dante rightly. The "viltà" of this group could never have been inertia. They are repeating in eternity the senselessness of their former lives: they must always have rushed about ready to turn with the wind, with no direction but what chance circumstance bestowed, scarcely with a nature of their own, wanting only what the world from moment to moment told them to want. They are thus hardly worth talking of even in the mass, and scarcely worth naming (46–51). Milton only names Empedocles and Cleombrotus to underscore their senseless kind of zeal, and dismisses the "many more too long" en masse. Evidently he agreed with Virgil's dictum on them.

Probably a purposeful rereading of the passage was at work, a sense of its relevance to the universe he was creating in *Paradise Lost*. But possibly the interpretation of Buommattei guided his rereading. We cannot know that Milton was aware of Buommattei's view, but it comes closer to his own than does the common Renaissance interpretation. Although in his table for *Inferno*, published in the year of Milton's visit to Florence, Buommattei conventionally names the vice involved "Viltà o Pigrizia," his commentary raises the question why, if laziness is their vice, Dante did not put the group in Limbo or among the slothful. In the course of his answer, although he never rescinds the label "pigrizia," he illuminates the meaning of their "viltà":

These . . . never resolved to do any good, and if by chance they ever so resolved, they did not put the thought into effect, and so came to death without having done well or ill. (II.IV.131, p. 343)

He comments that the devices on men's banners stand for their inclinations, but that these have none (p. 346). They run in a circle, because

such persons never have any determined goal. . . . Never resolving to think about any thing, lest it frighten and disturb them . . . , they run from one thought to another and thus go whirling their brains and never have repose. . . . They are punished with a race at high speed but . . . with no determined goal. (v. 346)

Buommattei, like other Renaissance commentators, takes their punishment as the opposite of their former habit, those who were unwilling to move at all now being made to move perpetually (v. 346); but he recognizes that their motive in life and in the afterlife is the same, a *mental* laziness that makes them purposeless, a lack of resolution in any direction that now displays itself in their perpetual motion in any and all directions. And he remarks of "him who made the great refusal" that Dante does not name him because he ought not to be identified, the point being not that he is Esau or Diocletian or Pope Celestine V, as most commentators argue, but that he himself chose to be nameless (p. 347). None of those found in this anteroom of Hell should be identified since the meaning of their being here is that they willingly lost their identity. Thus Buommattei alone among Renaissance commentators, to my knowledge, recognizes that Dante imagined a penalty which itself somehow represents the crime. Buommatei's independent reading and insight may have stirred Milton to a like independence in pursuing Dante's meaning.

With or without the precedent of Buommattei, Milton did come to understand the passage. The "viltà" of those in the anteroom of Hell is the emptiness of the mass of men, who belong with neither the saved nor the damned. Yet as constituting the bulk of humanity, they in a sense actually constitute the entrance to Hell. As Dante puts them just within its gates, Milton puts them at the juncture of Chaos and the cosmos, just where Sin and Death, following in Satan's tracks, will link their giant causeway from Hell to the fallen world (X.314–318). Marked in both Milton and Dante by their mass-identity, by their susceptibility to external commotion, by their wild shifts of front, they remain outside the order of values, at the passage to the inverted order below. As their fit retribution the universe ignores them; they are inevitably the mere "sport of winds."

"O con Forza o con Frode"

If Milton knew Buommattei's Tavola for *Inferno* he could have seen at a glance how Dante divided the City of Dis into the realms of force and of fraud. But he need hardly have looked beyond the canto he himself cites (in his *Commonplace Book*, fol. 160) on usury, to know with what emphasis Dante marked the division.

> Of all malice, which gains hatred in Heaven, the
>   end is injury; and every such end, either by force
>   or by fraud, aggrieveth others.
> But because fraud is a vice peculiar to man, it more
>   displeases God; and therefore the fraudulent are
>   placed beneath, and more pain assails them.
>
> (Inf. 11.22–27)

Whereas the mass of humanity finds itself eternally outside the cosmos, evil has its own purpose and character. We may define it as mere negation, just as cold may be defined as absence of heat; but in act it produces not an absence of form but deformity. For both Dante and Milton, its origins and its outcome are a perversion of the natural. Neither poet begins, however, by more than suggesting the ultimate truth about his subject. To begin with we confront what seems only all-too-human—desire gone astray or self-assertion gone a step too far: at first reading Francesca's story wins sympathy, and Satan's postures may inspire admiration. Except for some advance warning phrases ("the wretched people, who have lost the good of the intellect" in *Inferno* 3.17–18; the "baleful eyes . . . obdurate pride and steadfast hate" of Satan in *Paradise Lost* I.56–58), it is only later, looking back from words of unimpeachable authority (Virgil's explanation in Canto 11, Raphael's narrative in Books V–VI) that we properly estimate what we first encountered in Hell. The two revelations have unlike effects: in *Inferno* the incontinence punished outside the City of Dis is indeed less offensive, less born of malice, than what is yet to be traversed; in *Paradise Lost* the determined malice has already revealed itself in Satan and his fallen angels, however much the Satanic magniloquence has disguised it. Raphael's version of the War in Heaven is so unlike the references of Satan, Beelzebub, and Moloch that placed beside their earlier assertions it shows up the deliberate distortion as well as the inadvertent self-delusion of Hell. Virgil's analysis of evil shows up only the delusive self-pity and self-exoneration in Francesca's romanticized story.

For in Milton's Hell we are from the outset, with no prelude of mere tolerable weakness, well inside Dante's City of Dis—though we are not likely to know at once where we are. In *Paradise Lost* we witness, as it were, the founding of the city whose developed state we see in *Inferno*. The two views can illuminate each other.

In Canto 11 Virgil explains, while he and Dante pause to brace themselves for the stench of the City of Dis, that within they will find two realms, the first housing doers of violence of various kinds, the second workers of all manner of fraud. Outside the city wall and separated from it by the Stygian marsh, they have left behind the merely incontinent. Now they will meet the true citizens of Hell. Dante's source is doubtless the passage in Cicero's *De Officiis* on the evils of force and fraud:

Cum autem duobus modis, id est aut vi aut fraude, fiat iniuria, fraus quasi vulpeculae, vis leonis videtur; utrumque homine alienissimum, sed fraus odio digna maiore. (I.13.41)

But Dante adds considerable emphasis to Cicero's brief distinction, and his commentators call attention to it as a main structural feature of *Inferno*. Daniello deals with it at length; and in Mazzoni's *Difesa* as Milton knew it, the passage is discussed prominently at the end of the argument, on the last page before the analytical table that completes the volume. All make much of Dante's assertion that fraud is the evil peculiar to man and therefore most hateful to God. Daniello keeps close to Dante in explaining:

But because fraud is an evil peculiar to man, whom God endowed with intellect and reason so that he might use it in good works, . . . it follows that the fraudulent are much more displeasing to the divine majesty. (p. 74)

Mazzoni adds:

Now fraud being peculiar and violence foreign to man, it can consequently be said that when man sins by fraud he sins by a thing peculiarly his, and sins thus more often than by violence, which is strange and adventitious in him. One can then say just this, that he who injures others through fraud, most times in order to be hidden and unknown, can cause greater damage than he who injures through violence, which is always open and obvious. (p. 738)

And he argues that, though homicide and the like may seem graver evils than flattery and theft, the sins of fraud, being far more common than those of violence, are more dangerous, and so justify Dante's arrangement.

Even without the emphasis of Daniello or Mazzoni, the importance of the passage in Dante's scheme is obvious. The frequency with which Milton uses the phrase "force or fraud" in *Paradise Lost* suggests that in his reading he gave it a like emphasis.

Dante defines degrees of evil geographically; incontinence in the upper, outermost circles of Hell; violence within the walled city; fraudulence far below in Malebolge. Indeed, such gulfs separate the three parts that the first must be crossed in the bark of Phlegyas, the second on the back of Geryon. There will be yet one other extraordinary descent, when the giant Antaeus must lift Virgil and Dante down to the central pit of ultimate treachery (*Inf.* 31). The first gulf is peopled by the habitually angry and sullen, drowned in mud, whose error is worse than incontinence but less disastrous than violence; the second is a yawning cavity so far below the circles of violence that only the monstrous Geryon can cross it. The cleavages thus marked by the geography of *Inferno* bear upon the developing action of *Paradise Lost*. The sequence from Satan's displeasure at the elevation of the Son, to his commencement of the war in Heaven, to his plotting to seduce mankind, traverses a deepening of evil like the shifts from realm to realm in *Inferno*. Milton concerns himself chiefly with the last realm, the Satan we meet in Book I having already passed the deep gulf that separates fraud from force.[1]

His very first speech in Hell assures Beelzebub that theirs will be an endless war against Heaven either "by force or guile" (I.121), though he has surely already determined that it must be by guile. In his address to his reassembled armies he shifts from the possibility of open war to insinuate a new scheme:

[1] Milton's imagery for the leap may recall *Purg.* 25.116–117 with its choice between the fire and the cliff's edge.

> . . . our better part remains
> To work in close design, *by fraud or guile*
> What force effected not.   (I.645–647)

Then he summons his council to decide "Whether of open War or covert guile" (II.41). The way of fraud, proposed by Beelzebub as Satan's spokesman, is chosen; and Heaven, beholding Satan en route to earth, predicts his course:

> . . . to assay
> If [man] by force he can destroy, or worse,
> By some false guile pervert.
>
>   (III.90–92)

Again, God sending Raphael to forewarn Adam observes that Satan

> is plotting now
> The fall of others from like state of bliss;
> By violence, no, for that shall be withstood,
> But by deceit and lies.   (V.240–243)

The God of *Paradise Lost*, we note, will intervene only to prevent violence. So at the close of Book IV the Scales appear in Heaven to forestall imminent combat between Gabriel and Satan (IV.995–1015). So too God had halted the war in Heaven (VI.695–703). The reason is evident: moral issues are not settled by force. But for Milton, as for Dante, force can in fact do less damage in the world than fraud. Violence is naïve in the possibilities of evil.

How Milton followed the subtleties of Dante in these matters we may gauge from the speech of Moloch, representative of the resort to brute force, at the Council in Book II. Dante distinguishes violence as directed against God, against oneself, or against others, recognizing the common root of all three in brutishness ("la matta bestialitade," *Inf.* 11.82–83). Moloch, to whom, as a heathen god, infants will be sacrificed (*P.L.* I.392–405), speaks for the open use of force in a renewed war. Milton introduces his counsel with its motive: "rather than be less" than military victor, he "Car'd not to be at all" (II.47–48). He is the Farinata of Milton's Hell. At worst, he argues, in open war they will "be quite abolisht and expire"—a happier fate, in his view, than to languish in defeat. At very least they will disturb Heaven, "Which if not Victory is yet Revenge." The moral coarseness of Moloch is matched by his coarseness of speech, as well as by his naïveté of mind. He really supposes that his fellows can convert their torments into arms, and that he can win his hearers with his argument. In his habit of violence he cares little whether that violence turns on God, Heaven, Hell, or himself. The only desirable alternative he sees to effecting his combative will is annihilation. Thus Milton links the impulses of murder and self-destruction and sees the roots of both in the aggressive need of brute force to dominate its world in order to feel adequate. Dante traces the destructive impulse first as it turns against others, then as it turns on itself, and finally as it turns against God, whether in himself, in the universe he created, or in art. Milton links all these varieties in the "matta bestialitade" of Moloch.

From Moloch's speech at the council to those of Belial and Mammon is a sharp descent. For Moloch is still clinging to the way of force, which the rebels have already tried, but Belial and Mammon are forward-looking, willing to make Hell their home and even to exploit it. Moloch has learned nothing from the lost war; they have learned the wrong things—Belial to adjust to Hell, and Mammon to assert that it can be made every bit as good as the Heaven they have lost. But even Belial and Mammon cannot represent the total shift from force to fraud. That is left for Satan through his henchman Beelzebub.

The Satan who started the war in Heaven had already begun to use lies. Still, the war itself with its open violence took place before his irreversible leap into the abyss. On three days he and his followers had the opportunity to see the irrationality as well as the futility of their attempt, time enough for them to change their minds. When in Book VI the Son, sent by God to end the contest of violence, confronts them, they still have a choice. But to Satan the only issue is how to continue the war "by force or fraud" (*P.L.* VI.794). He and his followers with him choose the abyss. The shift from the war in Heaven to the regathering of forces in Hell thus narrates a moral gap like that represented by the gulf between the violent and the fraudulent in Dante's City of Dis. To stress the enormity of the gap, Milton creates in Sin a figure as clearly allegorical as Dante's Geryon. Like Geryon half human and half reptile, she bears in her own person the double character that symbolizes fraud.[2]

We shall have occasion in dealing with the origin and end of evil as treated by Dante and Milton to note Milton's use of infernal grotesques similar to Dante's, and the allegory of Sin and Death is more fittingly treated there. Here we may note the parallel between the figure that crosses the gulf from violence to fraudulence in *Inferno* and the wardress of Hell-gate who enables Satan to start on his fraud-bent journey in *Paradise Lost*. Virgil calls Geryon "that uncleanly image of Fraud," and the description bears him out:

> His face was the face of a just man, so mild an
> aspect had it outwardly; and the rest was all
> a reptile's body.   (17.10–12)

Milton's "formidable shape" of Sin resembles Ovid's Scylla and Spenser's Error with their dreadful brood; she too

---

[2] Buommattei's comment on Geryon is pertinent: "La frode disumana gli huomini, e gli rende fiere crudeli" (II.IV.132, p. 300).

Hell and Its Populace

> . . . seem'd Woman to the waist, and fair,
> But ended foul in many a scaly fold
> Voluminous and vast, a Serpent arm'd
> With mortal sting.   (II.650–653)

But the inward gnawing of her hell-brood recalls the phrase in *Inferno*, "Fraud, which gnaws every conscience" (11.52), and what Virgil says of Geryon bears on her role in *Paradise Lost:*

> Behold the savage beast with the pointed tail, that
> passes mountains, and breaks through walls
> and weapons; behold him that pollutes the whole
> world.   (17.1–3)

In the realm of which such a figure is wardress we may expect Satan to use every sort of deceit as his preferred weapon. The lesser and more obvious horrors of force are no longer his to choose; he is committed to lying from the first word he speaks in Hell. When Milton takes the occasion of Satan's deception of Uriel to denounce hypocrisy,

> the only evil that walks
> Invisible, except to God alone,
> By his permissive will, through Heav'n and Earth,
>   (III.683–685)

his words have a bite like those of Virgil on the beast that penetrates everywhere and pollutes the world.

But before Satan proves himself the master hypocrite he proves his mastery of deceptive rhetoric, and here he owes something to Dante's Ulysses. It is not by chance that careless readers have mistaken both the Ulysses of *Inferno* 26 and the Satan of Books I and II for heroic figures, prepared to venture into the unknown, determined to lead their followers to a better life—true Renaissance explorers eager to enlarge the confines of a limited world. It would seem that almost as large

a proportion of readers as of the speaker's own "fratri" have
been deluded by the persuasiveness of Ulysses into enthusiasm
for the disastrous voyage. The pattern of his deceitful oratory
is remarkably like Satan's, which is evident even in the initial
harangue to his "intrans't" followers. Each opens his appeal
with flattery:

> "O brothers!" I said, "who through a hundred
> thousand dangers have reached the West . . .
> >   (*Inf*. 26.112–113)

> Princes, Potentates,
> Warriors, the Flow'r of Heav'n, once yours, now lost. . . .
> >   (*P.L*. I.315–316)

Both use irony in depicting the threat of annihilation if action is
delayed, Satan with an elaborate emphasis on the pain that
goes with the threat:

> deny not, to this the brief vigil
> of your senses that remains, . . .
> >   (*Inf*. 26.114–115)

> If such astonishment as this can seize
> Eternal spirits; or have ye chos'n this place
> After the toil of Battle to repose
> Your wearied virtue, for the ease you find
> To slumber here, as in the Vales of Heav'n?
> Or in this abject posture have ye sworn
> To adore the Conqueror? who now beholds
> Cherub and Seraph rolling in the Flood
> With scatter'd Arms and Ensigns, till anon
> His swift pursuers from Heav'n Gates discern
> Th' advantage, and descending tread us down
> Thus drooping, or with linked Thunderbolts
> Transfix us to the bottom of this Gulf.
> >   (*P.L*. I.317–329)

Both end by offering a hopeful alternative in a ringing phrase
that precludes the very possibility of any third course:

> . . . experience of the unpeopled world behind the Sun.
> Consider your origin: ye were not formed to live like
> brutes, but to follow virtue and knowledge."
> (*Inf.* 26.116–120)

> Awake, arise, or be forever fallen.
> (*P.L.* I.330)

They are impressive, Ulysses and Satan, and they are also
successful:

> With this brief speech I made my companions so eager
> for the voyage, that I could hardly then have checked
> them.   (*Inf.* 26.121–123)

> They heard, and were abasht, and up they sprung
> Upon the wing.   (*P.L.* I.331–332)

Their great success is to lead those who follow to irrevocable
disaster.

Tennyson, perhaps unwittingly, confirms the resemblance in
the last line of his "Ulysses"—a portrait elaborated from
Dante's—with its metrical and thematic echoes of Milton's
Satan:

> To strive, to seek, to find, and not to yield.

But we need not explore Tennyson's reading of *Inferno* 26 to
surmise that Milton, seeing in Ulysses the very type of the
false counselor, accordingly endowed his archetypal deceiver
above all else with a spellbinding gift of oratory. Beelzebub is
characteristically the first, in both Book V and Book I, to

acknowledge its power:

> Leader of those Armies bright, . . .
> If once they hear *that voice*, thir liveliest pledge
> Of hope in fears and dangers, heard so oft
> In worst extremes, and on the perilous edge
> Of battle when it rag'd, in all assaults
> Thir surest signal, they will soon resume
> New courage and revive. . . .   (I.272–279)

Satan may owe many of his traits to Milton's reading of *Inferno* with its distinction between the evils of force and fraud, and, among those of fraud, its presentation of the deceptive orator in the magnificent-seeming Ulysses.[3]

[3] Kellett briefly notes a parallel between Satan and Ulysses as well as Farinata (p. 143).

The Valley of Serpents

Those who have insisted on the utter disparity between Milton's Hell and Dante's Inferno have generally discounted or disparaged as excrescences in *Paradise Lost* the allegory of Sin and Death, the building of the causeway from Hell to Earth, and the transformation of Satan and his crew into serpents. Indeed, if Milton had been concerned to allow dignity to evil, as those who contrast his concept with Dante's so often assert, he would have been repelled by the vulgar blasphemies and grotesque monsters of *Inferno*, and have avoided anything like them in his own poem. But apparently Milton too intended that Hell should be presented as ultimately, even if not initially, repellent. He was evidently impressed by the concept in Dante's lines on the "imperador del doloroso regno":

> If he was once as beautiful as he is ugly now,
>   and lifted up his brows against his Maker,
>   well may all affliction come from him.
>   (*Inf.*34.34–36)

Since the corruption of the best is the worst, the former beauty and present ugliness measure the distance between the initial perfection of the created being and the monstrous products of the evil will.

Dante and Milton

In both Dante and Milton it is the evil will that brings about evil. Dante uses the explanatory phrase in *Purgatorio* 5, where Buonconte says of the devil that had claimed his body, "He united that evil will, which seeks ill only, with intellect" (112–113). In *Inferno* itself the damned are "the wretched people, who have lost the good of the intellect" (3.17–18). Both phrases accord with Milton's view: the evil will uses intellect to evoke evil, and thus loses the very good of intellect. Milton treats the question both dramatically and allegorically. Satan's speeches of persuasion to Beelzebub and his assembled followers, at the outset of the war in Heaven, show the evil will making use of intelligence; by the time Satan reports on his conquest of Eden the evil he has willed has cost him his intelligence; and at points between we can note the progressive distortion of his thinking by his resolve to make evil his good.

The allegory of Sin and Death gives opportunity for a fuller account of the process by which the perverse will has summoned evil into being. The Dantean quality of the allegory may be gauged by the resemblance of certain of Milton's phrases for its chief personages to those used by Dante for the grotesque guardians of Hell. Satan's blazing eyes (I.193–194) may owe more to Virgil's than to Dante's Charon (*Aen.* VI.299–300; *Inf.* 3.109), but it is Dante's who tries to oppose the divine will (88–99) and speaks words that apply to both Dante's Hell and Milton's (85–87). Sin, as we have noted, confounding the human and reptilian (II.650–653), resembles Geryon (*Inf.* 17.10–12).

Beyond this, Sin gnawed at from within by her Hell-brood (II.795–800) is reminiscent of the Minotaur of *Inferno*: "quando vide noi sè stesso morse,/ sì come quei, cui l' ira dentro fiacca" (12.14–15). Death grins horribly (II.846), like Minos (5.4); he has a ravenous maw (II.846–848; X.597–599), like the three heads of Cerberus (6.27; cf. *Aen.* VI.421); he is monstrously indistinct of shape (II.666–673) like the fused bodies of Cianfa and the serpent Agnello (25.70ff.), and exercises a petrifying power (X.294) like Medusa's (9.52). Together Sin and Death are to become the scavengers of all the evil in the world (X.630–637), even as Inferno is its cistern (33.133). The images are all deliberately far more repellent than those in Virgil, of Tisiphone guarding the gates of Hell, or Tityos gnawed by the vulture (*Aen.* VI.555–556,595–600).[1]

The episode involving them is no less grotesque. Sin, conceived as an idea in the Satanic mind—his "Wisdom" as it were—became a reality when, mating with her, he began the war in Heaven. By a sympathetic motion she fell with his falling armies, already pregnant with Death, at whose birth, after she arrived in Hell and took her place as its wardress, her "nether shape thus grew/ Transform'd." (The characteristic pun suggests at once the transformation of her nether parts into reptilian shape and her assumption of the shape appropriate to the nether world.) Had Satan not fallen in love with his misconceived brain-child—that is, decided to make war in Heaven—all the unnaturalness of evil, symbolized by the incestuous union, would never have been.[2] Once the initial anti-natural choice was willed, all else that followed, perversion on perversion, was already implicit as consequence in that choice.

[1] The comments of Daniello on Dante's use of Geryon are pertinent here: "Certo è grandissimo lo 'ngegno, & ordine, che tiene questo Poeta ammirabile: il quale havendo posto nel secondo cerchio Minos sopra i lussuriosi; nel terzo Cerbero sopra i golosi; Plutone nel quarto a guardia de gli avari, & prodighi; nella palude Flegias; nella città di Dite le Furie; a guardia de' violenti il Minotauro; qui nell' ottavo cerchio, ove si puniscono dieci spetie di fraudolenti pone Gerione, che la fraude, & malitia significa" (p. 117).

And Mazzoni observes (p. 905) that Dante, by intentionally making his Furies as horrible as possible, surpassed other poets in describing Hell.

[2] Cf. Mazzoni: "Il peccato di Lucifero fu di lussuria, poichè egli amò sè stesso troppo disordinatamente" (p. 733). Mazzoni cites Scotus' view that the sin of Lucifer began in "lussuria" and ended in "superbia" (p. 734).

With the emergence of Death, crowned King of Hell at his birth, the anti-nature of the whole realm of evil is emphasized. Sin undergoes her monstrous metamorphosis; Death at once incestuously rapes her and begets the whole Hell-brood of further evils; they multiply, "hourly conceiv'd/ And hourly born," constantly returning to Sin's womb to gnaw at her entrails. None of this was part of the created cosmos. Only the initial perversity of willed evil could have brought it into being. Sin's birth-day might have been her death-day, had Satan not mated with her. At first sight she filled him, as she did everyone who beheld her, with horror; but then, as she puts it, "familiar grown,/ I pleas'd" (*P.L.* II.761–762), very much as the Siren of Dante's second dream in *Purgatorio* (19.7ff.) became alluring to his continued gaze. But the Siren and the dream vanished when Virgil uncovered her loathsomeness. Satan, on the contrary, found his Siren-daughter increasingly attractive.

The allegory of Sin and Death in Book II is thus not less grotesque, less grimly comic, less melodramatic than many a scene of *Inferno*. The building of the causeway through Chaos again involves a Dantean allegory. Sin burrowing her way like a mole recalls Geryon's arrival and descent in *Inferno* 17.19–27,100–105; Death smiting the shored-up soil with "his Mace petrific" and binding it with his look in "Gorgonian rigor" recalls the danger to the beholder of the presence of Medusa at the outworks of the City of Dis, and the freezing of sinners into the permanent distortions of the lowest circle. The bridge itself, "High Archt, . . ./ Of length prodigious . . . / . . . a passage broad,/ Smooth, easy, inoffensive down to Hell" (X.301–305), recalls the arches in varying states of disrepair in the later Hell that Dante traverses with Virgil. When Sin assures Satan,

O Parent, these are thy magnific deeds,
Thy Trophies . . .
Thou art thir Author and prime Architect,
(X.354–356)

the very phrase, as we have noted, recalls Dante. Its meaning
is even more Dantean: as in *Inferno* all the motions of evil in
the world proceed from the six wings of Satan, ceaseless in their
batlike flapping (34.46–52), so for Milton all the ills which
Sin and Death will now loose on the world spring from "the
Author of all ill" (II.381). The grotesque exchanges between
the daughter-wife and the father-husband hardly bear out the
common critical view of the dignity of Milton's infernal beings.

Our last view of Sin and Death is again Dantean. As the
Hell-hounds drawn forth by God they will be put to a fittingly
grotesque use:

. . . to lick up the draff and filth
Which man's polluting Sin with taint hath shed
On what was pure, till cramm'd and gorg'd, nigh burst
With suckt and glutted offal, at one sling
Of thy victorious Arm, well-pleasing Son,
Both Sin, and Death, and yawning Grave at last
Through Chaos hurl'd, obstruct the mouth of Hell
For ever, and seal up his ravenous Jaws.   (X.630–637)

The sudden shift from their self-estimate to God's view of them
has an effect like the reversed view of Satan in *Inferno* 34:
suddenly inverted, the terrifying becomes absurd. Before that
ultimate absurdity, however, the hellish kingdom founded in
Paradise Lost I–II may come to be more like Dante's City-state of
Dis. It already has a walled city (X.415–426). Its first grand
building, the Plutonian Hall of Pandemonium (I.710–730),
unmistakably baroque in design, is perhaps intended to recall

St. Peter's in Rome, much as Dante associates the red buildings in *Inferno* 8 with the mosques of Islam. To assign to Hell the architecture of an inimical religion is among the many Dantean touches in Milton's nether world.

Pandemonium, of course, has a façade of dignity that the City of Dis lacks. But everywhere behind the façade is evidence of the foulness that lurks, only waiting to become manifest. Those careless readers who suggest that the stench of Dante's Inferno is the kind of thing Milton avoided, have evidently ignored the "ever-burning Sulphur unconsum'd" of I.69 (as well as I.237, I.671, and II.69). Belial declares that they will all adjust to the "noxious vapor" of the realm (II.216), and Mammon in his crassness not only does not miss the "Ambrosial Odors" (245) of Heaven but fully expects all aspects of Hell to become agreeable, "our temper chang'd/ Into their temper" (II.276–277). Just before his seduction of Eve, Satan is compared to

> . . . one . . . long in populous City pent,
> Where Houses thick and Sewers annoy the Air . . .
> (IX.445–446)

The simile gains force because Hell is already such a city, though less populous than the turn of events in Book IX will presumably make it.

Satan's first recourse from the natural pleasure at finding himself in the countryside has been to descend into the body of the serpent, a body which, in a startling scene, he resumes in Hell. Along with the Dantean allegory of Sin and Death in Book II and the bridge from Hell in Book X, the transformation of Satan and his followers into serpents has been judged inappropriate to *Paradise Lost*. But apparently Milton thought decorum called for such a scene if the meaning of evil was finally to be clear. The evident analogue is the transformation of the thieves in *Inferno* 24–25, and Dante's passage may confirm the propriety and significance of Milton's as well as the insight with which he read the large meanings of *Inferno*.[3]

In *Paradise Lost* X, Satan, returning from what he thinks a wholly successful expedition, gives his triumphant report to the council of chief devils in Pandemonium, and just when he expects—and they are about to give—their applause, he hears himself hissed, sees his audience transformed into serpents, and finds himself similarly transformed. Then as they go to join the lesser devils waiting outside the hall, these too, after their first astonishment, are changed. Compulsively they swarm through a valley thronged with serpents of every kind, where sham trees have sprung up; compulsively they climb and eat, though the fruit turns to dust and ashes in their mouths.

Satan had chosen to descend into a serpent, had created a sham serpent to deceive the mother of mankind, had pretended to have eaten of a sham tree with supposedly magical fruit, which must, he knew, turn to dust and ashes in Eve's mouth. Now he is compelled to be the serpent he then chose to be, and to eat the fruit he then only feigned to have eaten. And since his followers, greater and lesser, were content that he should engage in the exploit and were ready to applaud and share its fruits, they must now share in the transformation and the eating. All that he did as their representative they are now bound to re-enact with him. As Arnold Stein has pointed out, it is significant that Satan's transformation follows that of his lieutenants, proving him the leader led. The details in the triple sequence of metamorphoses are thus not merely ornamental; they have been placed there because of their significance.

The passage from Ovid, generally taken as a source of Milton's and explicitly cited by Dante (*Metamorphoses* IV.576–603; *Inf.* 25.97), has no comparable meaning. Cadmus prayed

[3] Todd briefly observes the relation in his notes on X.525–526, but does not pursue it.

to be transformed into a serpent; his wife prayed for the same transformation, their prayers were granted, and "as of yore, they neither fear mankind nor wound them, mild creatures, remembering what once they were." The passage in Lucan, also cited by Dante (*Pharsalia* IX.700–733; *Inf.* 25.94) and regarded as one of Milton's sources, is little more than a list. But Satan and his followers are not the mere reptilian varieties of Lucan or the mild and harmless creatures of Ovid.

Only Dante could have suggested to Milton the idea of having the scene represent the penalty exacted by divine justice—that the criminal must go on being and doing involuntarily what he formerly was and did by choice. Dante's Hell is entirely peopled with those condemned endlessly to re-enact what they had chosen to be and to do on earth. In *Inferno* 24–25 the equation of crime with penalty is subtly worked out in the three kinds of transformation suffered by the three kinds of thieves. The serpent image with its suggestions of fraud, slipperiness, and malevolence clearly befits the nature of thieves, just as the elaborate thief image of *Paradise Lost* IV.188–192 befits Satan:

> . . . as a Thief bent to unhoard the cash
> Of some rich Burgher, whose substantial doors,
> Cross-barr'd and bolted fast, fear no assault,
> In at the window climbs, or o'er the tiles:
> So clomb this first grand Thief into God's Fold.

Satan began his exploit like a thief; it is appropriate that he should end the boastful account of his success by being transformed, like one of Dante's thieves, into a serpent, since the transformation of Dante's thieves is intended to suggest the likeness of their crime to that of the old serpent himself.

Of the three scenes Dante witnesses in the valley, the first occurs when one of the thieves is suddenly bitten in the throat

by a snake, whereupon he at once burns to a heap of ashes, and
then as suddenly resumes his human shape. The figure is Vanni
Fucci, thus punished for his sacrilege in robbing the sacristy
at Pistoia and for the merciless accusation that caused another
to be punished for his crime. After maliciously prophesying
defeat for Dante's party in the civil broils of Florence, Vanni
proceeds to blaspheme in word and gesture. He is stopped by
two serpents, one coiling itself about his throat, the other tying
his hands behind him. Presumably his burning and resurrection
represent a periodic visitation on those who now run about the
valley with their hands bound behind them by serpents, for off
he runs: "He fled, speaking not another word" (25.16).

Then as suddenly three new thieves appear, and with them
a six-footed reptile which attacks one of the thieves, linking
body with body until the two are so fused that their former
shapes are lost (25.46–78). And now another reptile comes
darting along, bites another of the thieves, and begins the third
metamorphosis. As serpent and thief eye each other, a cloud
of smoke issues from each; within the smoke they gradually
exchange forms from head to foot until "the one rose upright,
and prostrate the other fell" (121). Then the visages too
change, reptilian into human, human into reptilian, until finally

> The soul that had become a brute, fled hissing
> along the valley, and after it the other talking
> and sputtering. (136–138)

The first transformation is evidently the rarest kind in the
valley, the second probably less rare, the third commonest, for
all the serpents are presumably transformed thieves. Super-
ficially they share with Milton's scene little more than their
common sources in Ovid and Lucan. It is in the way the three
transformations support the meaning that Dante's valley of
serpents resembles Milton's. Thus Milton reverses the sequence

of the metamorphosis in Ovid as freely as Dante varies it. Since Satan's proceedings began with his head, first his visage turns reptilian, then his torso, then his legs, until he falls prone, and trying to address his already transformed grand councilors finds himself returning "hiss for hiss . . . with forked tongue/ To forked tongue" (X.518–519). The whole of Hell resounds with "din/ Of hissing" and swarms with "complicated monsters." In a typical Miltonic pun, "complicated" suggests both the coilings and the contorted complicity of the fallen angels. As in Dante, the visual image signifies the idea.

When Satan and his lieutenants go forth, the multitude waiting to see "In Triumph issuing forth thir glorious Chief," but beholding instead "a crowd/ Of ugly Serpents," scarcely have time for horror, so rapidly do they become like those they behold:

> down thir arms,
> Down fell both Spear and Shield, down they as fast,
> And the dire hiss renew'd, and the dire form
> Catcht by Contagion, like in punishment,
> As in thir crime.   (X.541–545)

Again the image signifies the idea. As the lieutenants, wishing to applaud, could only hiss—since praise from the wicked is the worst condemnation—so these, having backed Satan's decision to resort to fraud, lose even the appearance of the army that fought in Heaven, and assume the very shape of what they have encouraged their leader to become.

The changes are not distinguished by Milton as they are by Dante: his main point is that all the devils participated in one and the same crime with Satan in his theft of man's happiness. They therefore undergo one and the same transformation: those who might have stopped him if they had not shared his purposes are in fact changed even before he is, and those who merely went along with the rest now too go along. The metamorphosis is given in detail only for Satan, who remains "still greatest" and still midmost when "Dragon grown, larger than whom the Sun/ Ingender'd in the Pythian Vale." (Again the detail counts: a greater Apollo will one day slay this Python too.) Dante is not here concerned with size, and he distinguishes more than sequence, but he too gives importance to the metamorphosis "catcht by contagion."

Chiefly, however, he discriminates three processes of becoming a thief. Vanni is bitten by a sudden impulse that consumes him for the moment. When he comes to himself again, far from repenting of the impulse, he can take comfort only in maliciously awaiting the destruction of others. The characterless Agnello is fastened upon by the accomplished thief Cianfa and becomes one with him. The interchange of serpent and human forms in the third transformation suggests two separate processes: the susceptible becoming spellbound by the evil in the hardened thief, and the hardened thief seeking to regain touch with humanity by turning it into his own likeness.

Most of this was irrelevant to Milton's purpose, though some of Dante's particular insights resemble his own concept. Thus, like Vanni, Satan is cut off in the midst of a blasphemy by the appearance of serpents. He has been boasting his success in an oddly literal-minded fashion:

> [Man] by fraud I have seduc'd
> From his Creator, and the more to increase
> Your wonder, with an Apple . . . ,
> . . . worth your laughter . . .
> True is, mee also he hath judg'd, or rather
> Mee not, but the brute Serpent . . .
> . . . that which to mee belongs,
> Is enmity, which he will put between
> Mee and Mankind. . . .
> His Seed, when is not set, shall bruise my head:
> A World who would not purchase with a bruise?
> (485–500)

Appropriately, the literal mind sees its former pretense turn into literal fact—Dante's very way of meting out justice. Again, like the commingling of the serpent Cianfa and Agnello, or like the exchange of thief and serpent's shapes in the climactic transformation, Milton's scene emphasizes the spreading of crime; sight and hearing, as in *Inferno* bite and hypnotic stare, serve to transmit the contagion. And the most hideous aspect of the entire episode in Dante, the ceaseless recurrence of the infection, is the one Milton drives home: the metamorphosis of Satan and his crew is their final appearance in *Paradise Lost*, with its annual recurrence prophesied.

Then, in a characteristic shift of meaning, Milton relaxes the tension. The prophesied annual recurrence is, after all, only what "some say," while others say the devils-turned-serpents flooded the earth. And the poet turns from the scene to show Satan's partly reptilian progeny, Sin and Death, arriving to lay Eden waste, and make it an outpost of Hell, fit for that serpent brood. In *Inferno* Dante makes a like transition; in the first lines of Canto 26 he hails his native city: let Florence rejoice that she has thus colonized the valley of thieves! Thus he too links Hell with an infected world.

From Dante, Milton almost certainly drew the technique of juxtaposition and elaboration of images to convey an implied meaning. Neither poet merely depicts thievish devils or devilish thieves being turned into serpents, or sends them hissing through a valley, though even these details link the two scenes. Dante refers his reader to Ovid and Lucan, two of the poets, as it happens, who had welcomed him with Virgil into the castle of the enlightened heathen (4.90); but he himself makes of their merest suggestions one of the most striking episodes in *Inferno*. Little wonder, then, that its possibilities for his own devils struck Milton. Like Dante, he wished finally to emphasize the grotesque and the compulsive in Hell.

The Ultimate Fixity

On the terrace of Mount Purgatory that cures pride, Dante sees among the examples carved in bas-relief "him who was created nobler far than any other creature, on one side descending like lightning from heaven" (*Purg.* 12.25–27). In *Paradiso* he hears three comments on Lucifer's fall. Folco refers to him "who first turned his [shoulders] on his Maker, and from whose envy hath such wailing sprung" (9.128–129). Later, the Eagle of Justice speaks of "that first proud Being, who was the summit of all creation," but "because he would not wait for light," fell "unripe" (19.46–48). And finally Beatrice explains:

> The beginning of the fall was the accursed pride
> of him whom thou didst see constrained by all
> the weights of the universe.   (29.55–57)

The phrase in *Purgatorio* 12, "folgoreggiando scendere," along with the verb "ruina" in *Inferno* 33, for the soul that falls before the body's death into Ptolomaea (124–135), resembles the striking image of Raphael's account: "Hell saw/ Heav'n ruining from Heav'n" (VI.867–868), as well as the phrase that the Anarch of Chaos uses of the rebel angels' fall "through the frighted deep/ With ruin upon ruin" (II.994–995). The turning the shoulders to God in *Paradiso* 9 is an image more like that of Satan's march to the north with his followers, or Abdiel's march away from the rebels who had shrugged off God:

> . . . with retorted scorn his back he turn'd
> On those proud Tow'rs to swift destruction doom'd.
>
> (V.906–907)

The Eagle's phrase, as we have seen, may have suggested to Milton Satan's perverse relation to light.

Does the image of Lucifer "costretto" in the pit have any counterpart in *Paradise Lost?* Obviously not in the externally unconstrained general-orator-dictator of Books I through IX. Thus Thomas Nelson Page's comments on Milton's debt to Dante are too vague to be helpful. When he asks,

Can one familiar with Dante read Milton's magnificent picture of Lucifer and not feel the influence of Dante's picture—not feel that he has but redrawn the latter's mighty figure, with his vast wings like sails? (p. 148)

it must at once be answered, Yes, one can, and a great many have. The three-headed monster of the frozen pit has not, to my knowledge, struck anyone but Page as resembling Milton's Prince of Hell, except in his gigantic size and "Sail-broad Vans" (*P.L.* II.927; *Inf.* 34.46–48).

Yet it would be strange if Milton had not been impressed by Dante's Lucifer. Early in his description of Satan he uses the Leviathan image (I.201–208) much as Dante uses it near the end of *Inferno* (31.52–54) in a context of terrifying danger; and evidently he was impressed by the horn that sounds in the same canto (12–13), as well as by the towering size of the giants (31–33), the gross figure of Nimrod (46–48), the pine-measure (58–60), and the savage babble of his talk (67–81). Comparable passages occur in *Paradise Lost* on Satan (I.531–543,591,292–294) and on Nimrod, whom Milton associates with him, Nimrod having been the first tyrant on earth as Satan was the first tyrant of all (XII.36–42,55–62). He surely agreed with the comment in *Inferno* 32.7–9 that

> . . . to describe the bottom of all the Universe is
> not an enterprise for being taken up in sport,
> nor for a tongue that cries mamma and papa.

Dante's encounter in Canto 32 (76ff.) with Bocca degli Abbati may, as we noted, have given Milton the phrase on "Strength, or Chance, or Fate" (I.133); the Ugolino episode (33.13–78) doubtless impressed him as it has most readers; the explanation of Friar Alberigo (33.109–135), as we have just seen, suggests his use of the verb "ruin"; he too felt that rudeness to evil is true courtesy (33.150). It is unlikely that the final canto of *Inferno* offered Milton nothing to his purpose. We can in fact trace something of its impress on his handling of evil in *Paradise Lost*—more clearly the more we take it as Dante's summation of the meaning of Hell.

The relation of crime and penalty in *Inferno* had impressed Milton by the time he entered the note in his *Commonplace Book* on suicide (fol. 16). His own treatment of the metamorphosis of Satan and his crew into serpents suggests his grasp of Dante's meaning: the wrongly directed will obtains what it has desired, until it can desire nothing else; and at length, frozen into mechanical habit, it cannot be said to will at all. Francesca continues to be whirled along with Paolo, though she laments to the visitor from earth, "There is no greater pain than to recall a happy time in wretchedness" (5.121–123). Satan, arrived on earth, also experiences "the bitter memory/ Of what he was, what is, and what must be/ Worse" (IV.24–26). And later he too pines his loss when, rebuked by Zephon, he sees "Virtue in her shape how lovely"; but what he pines is "chiefly to find here observ'd/ His lustre

visibly impair'd" (IV.848–850). In their self-pity, neither
Francesca nor Satan pines for the rejected good; each continues to cling to the prize for which they still reject it. The
self-pity of Ugolino as he goes on gnawing at the skull of
Archbishop Ruggieri is also symptomatic. The self-pitier fails
to perceive any relation between his own crime and what he
pities himself for. So with Satan, gloating in advance over the
damage he intends to Adam and Eve, and yet declaring himself

> . . . no purpos'd foe
> To you whom I could pity thus forlorn
> Though I unpitied.   (IV.373–375)

Milton shares Dante's awareness that pity is wasted on one
who keeps choosing the crime that is its own penalty.

The relation is clearest in the presentation of Mammon, type
of avarice,

> . . . the least erected Spirit that fell
> From Heav'n, for ev'n in Heav'n his looks and thoughts
> Were always downward bent, admiring more
> The riches of Heav'n's pavement, trodd'n Gold,
> Than aught divine or holy else enjoy'd
> In vision beatific.   (I.679–684)

In Heaven, presumably, he had not been the slave of that impulse; but given the opportunity to make war on Heaven, the
impulse helped to determine his choice. Now in Hell it rules
him so completely that, provided Hell contains "Gems and
Gold," he demands to know "what can Heav'n show more?"
(II.271–273). Perhaps that fixed downward gaze of Mammon's
has some relation to the inverted posture of Dante's simonists
(*Inf.* 19) or to the avaricious in Purgatory (*Purg.* 19.70–75)
lying prone and sighing in self-castigation, "Adhaesit pavi-
mento anima mea." Milton may also have had in mind verse 25
of Psalm 119 (Vulg. 118) when he gave Mammon that charac-

teristic gaze at pavements, but his own concept is close to Dante's elaboration. Indeed, Milton's presentation of avarice shares notable features with Dante's. Canto 7 is one he cites in his *Commonplace Book* (fol. 12), remarking Virgil's comment on the avaricious priests, popes, and cardinals:

> These were Priests, that have not hairy covering
> on their heads, and Popes and Cardinals, in
> whom avarice does its utmost. (*Inf.* 7.46–48)

But he attended to more than the anticlericalism of the passage.

Significantly, it is Mammon's argument that almost wins unanimous approval at the Council in Hell, just before Beelzebub intervenes (II.290–298). Milton, like Dante, regards the desire for gain as the commonest taint of humanity. In the circle of the avaricious Dante saw "many more than elsewhere" (*Inf.* 7.25). And it is here that he first hints the transformation which the life effects in the appearance, a transformation that reaches its climax in his Lucifer:

> If he was once as beautiful as he is ugly now,
> and lifted up his brows against his Maker,
> well may all affliction come from him.
>   (34.34–36)

Of the avaricious he says simply that their mode of life has made them unrecognizable. But namelessness is an unusual penalty in both Dante and Milton. In *Purgatorio* 14.29–30 the valley of Arno deserves to have its name perish, just as in *Inferno* 3 "he who made the great refusal" deserves not to be named, or as Raphael in his account of the war in Heaven refuses to name any but a few of Satan's followers:

> Cancell'd from Heav'n and sacred memory,
> Nameless in dark oblivion let them dwell.
> For strength from Truth divided and from Just,

Illaudable, naught merits but dispraise
And ignominy, yet to glory aspires
Vain-glorious, and through infamy seeks fame:
Therefore Eternal silence be thir doom.
(*P.L.* VI.379–385)

And the unrecognizableness of the avaricious and prodigal in
Inferno has its bearing on the scene in Eden when Zephon
and Ithuriel fail to recognize Satan, and Zephon has to explain:

Think not, revolted Spirit, thy shape the same,
Or undiminisht brightness, to be known
As when thou stood'st in Heav'n upright and pure;
That Glory then, when thou no more wast good,
Departed from thee, and thou resembl'st now
Thy sin and place of doom obscure and foul.
(IV.835–840)

Like the citizens of Dante's Hell, Satan has been choosing his
face.

The distortion Dante invents as appropriate to the crime is
perhaps most notable in the backward-turned heads of the
diviners in *Inferno* 20. Seeing in them "our image so contorted,"
the visitor cannot refrain from tears: "Certainly I wept" (22–
25), though Virgil chides him (27–30). So too, at the sight
of the lazar-house in the pageant of man's future, "Adam could
not, but wept" (XI.495), crying out:

Can thus
Th' Image of God in man created once
So goodly and erect, though faulty since,
To such unsightly sufferings be debas't?
(XI.507–510)

And Michael has, like Virgil, to insist (515–525) on the
justice involved in the sufferings, which themselves resemble
Dante's simile of the hospitals in *Inferno* 29.46–51. But scene

122

leads to scene, as so often when we begin to trace the Dantean impulse in *Paradise Lost*.

The Lucifer of Canto 34 is the summation of many meanings in *Inferno*. If Milton's Satan reaches no such total deformity within *Paradise Lost*, he has come a long way from his former beauty even before Zephon remarks on his changed countenance. The "ire, envy and despair" that mar "his borrow'd visage" and thus betray him to Uriel (IV.115–128) are now his habitual expression, except as hypocrisy briefly masks them (II.815–816,968–970; III.681–685). The three passions, each with its distinctive pallor, correspond to the three variously colored heads of Dante's Lucifer. Daniello remarks that the vermilion-colored face signifies Ira, the livid one, between white and yellow, Invidia, and the black Accidia, the colors being chosen for the corresponding humors—choler, phlegm, and melancholy (p. 224). And Buommattei, though he does not himself agree, observes that some interpreters take the colors of the three heads to mean, the red Ira, the yellow Avarizia or Invidia, and the black Accidia (II.IV.132, p. 341). Renaissance commentators differed from others both earlier and later on the meaning of the three heads. And Ira, Invidia, and Accidia are clearly equivalent to the anger, envy, and despair by which Milton repeatedly characterizes Satan. (The reader who wishes to pursue the matter in *Paradise Lost* may turn to I.56,126,604; II.707–708,719–720; III.552–554; IV.73–74, 156,502–503,857,871,969; V.662–665; VI.340–341,792–794, 900; VII.139; IX.55–56,97–98,171–178). Whenever he appears, Satan is angry, envious, or desperate, though one of his tricks is consistently to attribute anger and envy to God (I.260; II.35–37; IV.103,516–517; V.61; IX.177,703–709,729; X.466).

He reveals his ultimate kinship to Dante's Lucifer in still other ways. "Fardest from him is best," he cries, hailing the remoteness of his new realm from God's surveillance (I.247); and that is where we find him, "As far remov'd from God and light of Heav'n" (I.73) as he can be. He is not, like the Lucifer of *Inferno* 34, fixed in his chosen abyss; his fixity is of the mind. Milton adapts Dante's geographic symbols only now and then, and without committing his poem to them. No one in *Paradise Lost* hails Satan as Pluto does when he clucks "Pape Satan, pape Satan" in *Inferno* (7.1); an irony so blatantly Protestant would only have distracted Milton's readers. But it is not by chance that in Milton's Hell no one names the Son as in Dante's no one names God, or that both Hell and the City of Dis are locked from within and guarded by dreadful shapes (*Inf.* 8.115ff.; 9.34ff.; *P.L.* II.871ff.).

Canto 34 proves Dante's Hell, like Milton's, a dreadful parody of Heaven. The opening line hails the banners of the infernal king as Fortunatus' famous hymn hails the cross: "Vexilla regis prodeunt—inferni." The three-headed monster frozen into the pit, with his six wings yet incessantly in motion, parodies the triune God who is the unmoved mover. But Dante's Hell has all along been suggesting an inversion of divine order. The damned show themselves fixed in their various rungs, whereas the blessed spirits will voluntarily descend from the Empyrean to manifest themselves in the various spheres of Heaven. Hell illustrates to its visitor a scheme that descends in narrowing circles from incontinence to violence to fraud, as Paradise illustrates for him an unfolding that rises in ever-widening circles through the more and more inclusive virtues.

The midmost point of the abyss holds the "imperador" of Hell; the ultimate point around which all Paradiso revolves proves to be its circumference as well. Milton's Satan is an even more obvious parodist of God, with his hierarchies and summonses to councils, his special Mount in the north of

Heaven and his Oriental despot's throne in Hell; he is the "Idol of Majesty Divine," as Raphael names him, in contrast to the true Image, the Son.[1] His very return to Hell in Book X is an emulation of God's mode of revealing himself (X.444–454; III.375–382), as his chariot on the battlefield is an imitation of the living chariot which the Son is later to mount (VI.99–102, 750–762). If God has his only begotten Son, his perfect image, in whom he is well pleased, Satan has a beloved daughter, Sin, who is his perfect image. If God can transfer power to his Son, Satan can assign his conquest, earth, to Sin and their joint offspring, Death. If God can create a universe, Satan can destroy it—or so at least he boasts. The pastimes of his followers, chosen to while away the tedium of Hell, similarly parody the purposeful activities of Heaven (II.523–573; III. 367–371; IV.549–554,779–798,977–979; V.266–270,563–566, 585–595,618–627,637–638,650–657).

The total inversion of the natural order which Dante figures in Lucifer as he is finally seen, head downward like the simonists in their holes, Milton presents in Satan's determination to be and do and will the opposite of what Providence seeks (I.162–165), simply as the opposite. He determines "Evil be thou my Good" (IV.110) until it comes to pass, and he laments, "All good to me becomes/ Bane . . . ;/ . . . only in destroying I find ease/ To my relentless thoughts" (IX.122–123,129–130). This is the sense in which God "Left him at large to his own dark designs,/ That with reiterated crimes he might/ Heap on himself damnation" (I.213–215). Dante shows Satan transfixed by the weight of all the damnation he has already heaped on himself and others.

The consequences of his willed inversion of the natural order, Satan had, of course, not foreseen. One of those consequences,

[1] Cf. J. M. Steadman, "Image and Idol," *JEGP* 59 (1960), 640–654; and Irene Samuel, "The Dialogue in Heaven," *PMLA* 72 (1957), p. 606, n. 9.

for both Dante and Milton, was a cataclysm corresponding to the introduction of evil into the moral order. When Satan fell "dal cielo/ folgoreggiando," (*Purg.* 12.26–27), all the land rushed from the hemisphere through which he passed, leaving the cavity that was to become his new realm and forming, at the earth's opposite extreme, Mount Purgatory (34.121–126). In *Paradise Lost* the same kind of convulsion tore Hell from the lower reaches of Chaos (II.1002–1003) to prepare a realm fit for the rebels. They too fell "headlong flaming from th' Ethereal Sky/ With hideous ruin and combustion" (I.45–46), "thunder-struck" (VI.858), while "Disburd'n'd Heav'n rejoic'd" (VI.878). On a less cosmic scale the fall of Adam and Eve introduces similar changes in their physical world.

But Dante's Hell, like his Paradise, is close to the end of time, its ranks nearly full, whereas Milton's is just beginning. With its "imperador" encased in ice from chest to knee, Dante's Hell has much the same aspect it will wear at the Last Judgment. The Oriental despot of Milton's Hell has still to increase his realm, but its end is sure: not he but Death will be its final ruler. When at Doomsday "Hell, her numbers full,/ Thenceforth shall be for ever shut" (III.332–333), what will be shut in is the universe of which Death was born king. We have seen his petrifying power in the building of the causeway to the newly fallen Earth; we can imagine the petrified realm under his ultimate sway as not unlike Dante's frozen abyss. Such fixity, the ultimate opposite to the spontaneity of life, is an exact symbol for Dante's view, and Milton's, of the end of evil. As the compulsively repeated choice becomes mechanical, purposeless, and ceaseless, it becomes the whole character, and the whole character thus becomes one fixed posture. The sepulchers that for the newcomer to the City of Dis are the first sight within its walls carry the same suggestion as the crown Death wears in *Paradise Lost*.

A premonition of that destiny of evil may be read in *Paradise Lost* (IX.465–466) when Satan, awed by Eve's beauty, stands for the moment

> Stupidly good, of enmity disarm'd,
> Of guile, of hate, of envy, of revenge—

disarmed, that is, of all that makes him Satan. Daniello makes the point in his comments on *Inferno* 34.22–25 that when Dante nearing Dis becomes "gelato" and "fioco," so that he is neither dead nor alive, the words signify "stupido" and "muto" (p. 223). Daniello's glosses here suggest the stupidity and momentary silence of Milton's Satan. In any event, the moment is telling. Without guile, hate, envy, revenge, Satan no longer has a self, his self being no longer his but the prisoner of these fixed purposes. As he goes on lying he becomes the lie; as he goes on choosing revenge, hate, guile, they cease even to be his motives, and he becomes their instrument. The mechanical fixity we see in Dante's Lucifer is only implied as the end of Milton's Satan. Within *Paradise Lost*, where the central concern is not with the destiny of evil, he is left in the reptilian shape that fits the parent of Sin, his ultimate future and that of his followers still not clear.

Yet the correspondences between the handling of the figures of evil by Dante and by Milton emphasize their common concern: to explore the traits that lead to misery. Milton's Hell is more obviously political than Dante's—a working tyranny with a marked class structure, the tyrant using every characteristic device to impose his will, gratifying his supporters' meanest wishes, and thus reducing them to a uniformity advantageous to himself. That is the main difference between Milton's nether world and Dante's; and that difference, deriving from Milton's Platonic thesis that the state is the individual soul writ large, may partly be accounted for by the simple difference in the time at which we see each of the two Hells. The likenesses are remarkable. We first meet Satan and his followers on a burning lake, a symbol not unlike Dante's for violence against God and nature; we later find them at home in the fair-seeming city that may yet come to resemble the City of Dis; our last sight of them is of no heroic figures but of a valley teeming with serpents like Dante's bolgia of the thieves. Inferno's populace too do not at first reveal its ugliness, though they lament its woe; in *Paradise Lost* too the woe is revealed as unmistakably chosen, and the deformity within soon gives its stamp to the once fair outward form. Like Dante, Milton unveils his Hell as a means of "esperienza," and he does not leave it until he has moved from what at first seemed merely all too human through deliberate fraud to the obsessively demonic.

Mazzoni makes the valuable point that just as the visitor to Hell crosses the river that represents the irascible faculty by means of Phlegyas, and the precipice formed by the river that represents the vices of the practical intelligence by means of Geryon, so he descends into the well of the frozen river that represents the vices of injustice by means of the giant Antaeus. He takes it that Dante wished to emphasize the difference in degree of a vice worse even than those above, a vice that turns men into demons and so may be called "indiavolamento" (p. 893). Our word "bedevilment" will not give Mazzoni's meaning here—no men are turned to demons in *Paradise Lost*— but the comment is suggestive of what happens to Satan's victims in Milton's account. His followers are literally turned from angels to devils; Eve and Adam are bedeviled into a like treachery against their Creator. And the chill that grips Eve in her dream, as it does Adam on first hearing of her crime, strangely echoes Dante's "gelato" as he feels the icy wind from the wings of Lucifer. But they, and Dante, can still escape.

Satan cannot. And Milton too ends by suggesting the fixity to which the perverted will finally dooms itself. Like Dante's wretched folk "who have lost the good of the intellect," and like the three-headed monster endlessly gnawing his three victims in the frozen pit, Milton's devils appear ultimately to have no identity but the endless repetition of some one role or gesture. Even in Book II Moloch is in process of turning himself into a habitually clenched fist, Belial into an indolent sprawl, Mammon into a calculating eye, and Beelzebub into a second voice for Satan. It is only Satan whose final doom Milton suggests; but all his henchmen, like all the damned of *Inferno*, are clearly launched on their headlong way into a cul-de-sac. The world is to be healed at Doomsday, and these would hardly know what to do in the presence of beauty and goodness but stand immobilized, like the Satan of that highly Miltonic oxymoron, "stupidly good."

V

Heaven and Eden

THE heavenly and earthly paradises in both the *Commedia* and *Paradise Lost* are so interconnected that they must be considered together. Commentators have noted frequent echoes in Milton's Eden of *Purgatorio* 28, where Dante enters the lost garden, and in Milton's Heaven of the images of radiance that dominate *Paradiso*. Such echoes, however, take on their full significance only in terms of what both poets had set out to do. The letter to Can Grande della Scala names one of Dante's purposes: "To remove those living in this life from a state of misery and to guide them to a state of happiness." Another main purpose was to fulfill the promise at the end of the *Vita Nuova* to write concerning Beatrice "what hath not before been written of any woman." That the two purposes prove one in Dante's handling needs emphasis: Beatrice, for Dante and thus for his reader, furnishes the guidance to the state of happiness and is herself part of it. The function of Milton's Heaven, presented in the context of an unfolding human action, is nowhere thus identified. But Milton's explicit invocation of Holy Light at the opening of Book III, in order that he "may see and tell/ Of things invisible to mortal sight," is like Dante's prayer at the opening of *Paradiso:*

> O divine Virtue, . . . so far lend thyself to me,
> that I make manifest the shadow of the blessed
> realm imprinted on my brain.
>
> (*Par.* 1.22–24)

133

Like Dante, Milton seeks to report the invisible world in order to guide men to "a state of happiness." Both *Paradise Lost* and the *Commedia* have recourse to the superhuman in order to define an ideal life for humanity. The vision communicated by both is of man's lot seen in the light of a realm where the permanent and immutable can reveal itself, where all that is can be right. Both present a Heaven and an Earthly Paradise in order to tell us what our life could be. Man has generally conceived of the perfect life under two rubrics: an ideal community or Utopia, set in the future, or laid up in Heaven as a pattern, or remote across the seas, or on some other planet; and an ideal rural privacy, lost in the remote past, sheltered as in a garden, irrecoverable in its simplicity and innocence. The Heaven of Dante and Milton is their Utopia, the Earthly Paradise their Golden Age. Like most visions of Utopia or the Golden Age, they have as their purpose not only to satisfy a yearning for perfection but to tell in what it would consist. Heaven, as the ultimate and eternal community, can most fully present the pattern of the ideal life.

Dante expounds the pattern in *Paradiso* largely through the successive spheres in which the blessed manifest themselves, though also in the angelic hierarchies and in the final vision where the poet for a moment experiences union with God himself. Milton too uses man, angel, and God to present the ideal life, but in his poem angelic and divine beings perforce have a larger role. Indeed, Milton's angels take the place of Dante's redeemed humanity, as they manifest in their traits and activities the perfections possible in created beings.

In *Paradise Lost* Milton's God, unlike Dante's, is himself shown speaking and acting. The difference has troubled many readers who compare the two: Dante, they assert, has taken the right way in presenting God indirectly, as a mystery behind the experience of the narrator, whereas Milton, in daring to report God's words and ways, offers a figure more appropriate to Homer's Mount Olympus—or a Sunday school. But here again the ground of comparison is at fault. In the *Commedia*, where the beholder and the narrator are linked in the "I" of the poem, it would have been puerile to concoct speeches and deeds for God. How could Dante declare, This is God as I saw him and these were his very words? But in *Paradise Lost*—unless one argues that it ought not to have been written at all—God must himself speak and act and not only manifest himself through other agents. From the earliest telling of the fall God has been a chief agent. To omit him from a narrative of man's first disobedience would be an impossible innovation. The proper ground for comparing *Paradise Lost* and the *Commedia* is not, then, the extent to which God is directly presented but what the presentation reveals about him.

The *Commedia*, if we attend to what is said of God by all authoritative speakers as well as by the poet, reveals far more of the divine than is commonly assumed, and what it reveals is far closer to the substance of *Paradise Lost*. The revelation in the one poem comes more largely through statement, in the other through demonstration, but in each the God revealed is transcendent in his infinity and omnipotence, unknowable in his omniscience, perfectly benevolent in his transmission of life, light, and joy to all beings, the creator and sustainer of every part and aspect of the universe, immanent in his creation, the center and circumference of all things. If the *Commedia* insists upon the transcendence and unknowability of God and of Heaven as well, the insistence is appropriate in the report of a mortal's vision of the immortal realm. But it is worth noting that in Dante's Heaven the redeemed are as much at home in the presence of God as the angels are in Milton's. Dante in his role as narrator may insist at each stage that what he experienced in Paradise cannot be fully told; Milton, representing the angelic life, whether directly or through Raphael's narrative, is careful to stress the insufficiency of his representation to the actuality.

But the incommensurability and the disparity are conveyed by Dante and Milton in remarkably similar terms. Dante begins *Paradiso* with an account of the transcendent light of Heaven and of his incapacity to report more than "the shadow of the blessed realm." Milton, before beginning his account of Heaven, invokes light as the central fact of the realm, and, as we have noted, prays for illumination in dealing with his transcendent theme (*P.L.* III.1-6, 51-55). And when Milton's Raphael prepares to tell Adam of the war in Heaven, he uses a premonitory phrase that recalls Dante. Raphael asks:

> . . . how shall I relate
> To human sense th' invisible exploits
> Of warring Spirits?
>
> (*P.L.* V.564-566)

and gives the answer himself:

> . . . what surmounts the reach
> Of human sense, I shall delineate so,
> By lik'ning spiritual to corporal forms,
> As may express them best, though what if Earth
> Be but the shadow of Heav'n?
>
> (*P.L.* V.571-575)

His terms remind us too of Beatrice explaining to Dante his first vision of the communion of saints:

> "The river and the topaz-gems that enter
> and go forth, and the smiling of the grasses
> are the shadowy prefaces of their reality.
> Not that such things are harsh as in themselves;
> but on thy side is the defect, in that thy sight
> not yet exalteth it so high."
>
> (*Par.* 30.76-81)

Raphael goes on to suggest that, since Earth is the shadow of Heaven, "things therein" may be "Each to other like, more than on Earth is thought" (*P.L.* V.575–576). Yet Dante too, for all his repeated insistence on the unlikeness of earth and heaven, not only does report the realm that "surmounts the reach of human sense," but reports it in terms available to human understanding.

Both poets warn that Heaven is beyond space: Milton denies that it has geometric shape—"th' Empyreal Heav'n, extended wide/ In circuit, undetermin'd square or round" (*P.L.* II.1047–1048), and Dante denies that it is subject to the laws of geometry:

> Near and far addeth not nor subtracteth there,
> for where God governeth without medium
> the law of nature hath no relevance.
> (*Par.* 30.121–123)

Both significantly attribute to it an art "inimitable on Earth" (*P.L.* III.505–509; *Par.* 18.109–111). Both insist that words cannot rightly convey its realities. Thus Milton has Raphael preface his story of the creation:

> . . . to recount Almighty works
> What words or tongue of Seraph can suffice?
> (*P.L.* VII.112–113)

and again

> Immediate are the Acts of God, more swift
> Than time or motion, but to human ears
> Cannot without process of speech be told.
> (*P.L.* VII.176–178)

Similarly Dante prefaces his mounting above earth:

> To pass beyond humanity may not be told in
> words . . .   (*Par.* 1.70–71)

137

And again Milton suggests Dante when he has Raphael advise Adam to "be lowly wise" (*P.L.* VIII.173), since

> God to remove his ways from human sense,
> Plac'd Heav'n from Earth so far, that earthly sight,
> If it presume, might err in things too high,
> And no advantage gain.   (*P.L.* VIII.119–122)

Dante reports that he questioned Peter of Damian "umilmente" after he had been adjured:

> And to the mortal world, when thou returnest, take
>   this report, that it presume not more to move its
>   feet toward so great a goal.
>
> (*Par.* 21.97–99)

But for all the humility proper to Adam and Dante in asking about Heaven's ways, or to Milton and Dante in representing them, both poets do venture to relate what they imagine of the unknowable in order to present a paradigm, in available human terms. William Haller observes (p. 225) that Dante regularly proceeds from politics to theology, Milton from theology to politics. Although Haller suggests a contrast, the likeness is more impressive: the Heaven and Eden of both poets offer models to man as citizen, and not only "of that Rome whereof Christ is a Roman" (*Purg.* 32.102), but of the earthly state that should be patterned on the heavenly city.

Commentators on the two Heavens have largely ignored such purposes. For those critics who have simply misread Milton's God, or Dante's, we may borrow the witticism of Douglas Bush on William Empson's "notable gift for reducing order to chaos." But many readers cannot disentangle the Heaven of either Dante or Milton from the confusions that becloud lesser minds the instant such words as Heaven, God, angels, Eden—or for that matter Utopian, perfect, ideal—are uttered.

Shelley, for all his admiration of both poets, declared that both used "distorted notions of invisible things," though granting that they were perhaps aware of the disparity between their own and common views. Lamartine evidently thought the same, but he put more emphasis on the error of making such unfortunate materials the subject of poetry. For him, Dante was "a monk of a barbarous age," who dreamed and then awoke to relate "strange, bizarre, trivial, atrocious, sometimes sublime things, never before related" (p. 4). At least, Lamartine continues, Dante's originality is to his credit, whereas Milton borrows his supernatural subject and Christian theogony, and "recites the Bible" with an intermixture of "fables, adventures, long discourses" (p. 20). Dante and Milton alike, therefore, are true poets only when they are pagan, when they refashion the Christian Heaven into a new Mount Olympus (p. 27)—not when they attempt to teach theology. Lamartine's distaste for what he saw as the misguided purpose of the two poets at best provided him with an epigram: "Quand on chante ses dieux, on est bien près de les profaner" (p. 3). But it kept him from a real understanding of either poet, let alone any relation between the two. In some measure, William Haller shows a like failure of sympathy when he calls Dante's Heaven "an academy of the blest speculating upon the mystery which is God," and Milton's "a parliament listening to speeches from the throne and engrossed in the conduct of affairs" (p. 225). Such belittling of major concerns of two major poets gives readers little insight.

Less dogmatic is the skepticism of Shaw when he assigns to the reality-denying Devil of the dream-sequence in *Man and Superman* the diatribe against "two of the greatest fools that ever lived, an Italian and an Englishman." The Italian,

when he was not lying about me, was maundering about some woman he saw once in the street. The Englishman described me as being expelled from heaven by cannons and gunpowder; and to this day every Briton believes that the whole of his silly story is in the Bible.

Apparently Shaw's Devil is so much the enemy of reality that he cannot even get the events of Milton's war in Heaven right. But as the Shavian Don Juan answers, "All this is old." Voltaire and Lamartine had made much wittier remarks on Milton's war in Heaven and on Dante's absurdities.

Walter Savage Landor too thought Milton erred when "like Dante, [he] . . . mixed the Greak mythology with the Oriental" (p. 441), wrote a line "too much in the manner of Dante" (p. 444), followed "the schoolmen and the crazy philosophers," and put "most of the worst verses and much of the foulest language . . . into the mouth of the Almighty" (p. 467). Though Landor protests that he has studied Dante attentively and with delight, he is appalled at the exaltation in his time of the *Commedia*, where

the characters are without any bond of union, any field of action, any definite aim. There is no central light above the Bolge; and we are chilled in Paradise even at the side of Beatrice. (p. 475)

We may wonder why Landor expected light in what Dante intended as the blackest pit, or fireside warmth in highest Heaven.

But still worse than the frank antipathy to the whole effort of either poet is the apologist's determination to show that Milton did the poetical right thing only when he departed from Dante or only when he didn't. The balance was weighted in Dante's favor by Keble in the *Quarterly Review* for 1825, as well as by Carlyle, James Russell Lowell, and Ruskin, and in Milton's favor by an anonymous critic in the *Quarterly Review* for 1827, as well as by Stebbing and John Addington Symonds. We need not pursue the argument through the scholarly journals of the present century, since it only leads into Bolge as lightless as those Landor complained of. The nineteenth century at least varied its argument: Milton's God and Heaven are either less or more spiritual than Dante's; either Dante or Milton surpassed the other in combining poetry with doctrine; one or the other had a better idea of what to do with Heaven, or did it better. (See, for example, Coleridge, *Notes and Lectures*, 1818; *North American Review*, 1819; and Henry Hallam, *Introduction to the Literature of Europe*, IV, 236–239.)

Even comparisons that suggest a relation between Milton's Heaven and Dante's often hit on a wrong relation or suggest only some minor resemblance. Thus Richardson, in all equanimity, decided that Milton took from Dante much of the notion for his angels, on the ground that he uses the words "splendors" and "ardors" for them just as Dante used "splendori" and "ardori." Austin finds them alike in their "fanaticism and bitter partisanship" (p. 167); Kellett agrees that both were lonely and humorless men (pp. 129–130); for Kuhns, the major resemblance is apparently in the golden stairs of *Paradiso* 21.28–30 and *Paradise Lost* III.510. Sister Margaret Teresa collects numerous parallels between *Paradiso* and *Paradise Lost*, but stops short of trusting her own insight, and hazards only the generalization that "we know [Milton] better if we know Dante and his use of Dante" (p. 177). Her work is, however, the most solidly based of the many comparisons of the two poems.

Milton's use of *Paradiso* cannot be limited to explicit references and analogies of phrase any more than his use of *Inferno*, though as with *Inferno* they prove helpful pointers. Of *Paradiso* he cites only Canto 20, on the Gift of Constantine, in *Of Reformation*, and Canto 8.140–148 in his *Commonplace Book* (fol. 111), where he praises Dante's opinion on the talent bestowed by nature but pushed into the wrong career by the world.

But echoes of *Paradiso* and the last cantos of *Purgatorio* are everywhere in *Paradise Lost*. For the pleasant garden alone (in Book IV), Todd and Kuhns collected from *Purgatorio* 28 an impressive number of parallels, conveniently printed together in Toynbee (I, 127–128). They include the location atop a steep mountain, the divine forest, the fragrant ground, the pure air and perfumed breezes, the branches tremulous in the breeze, their leaves murmuring, the birds singing joyously, the fountain feeding the descending stream, Eden as the true Golden Age fabled by pagan writers, the reminiscence of Proserpina, the conjunction of eternal spring and its flowers with fruit of every kind in enameled colors, and the constant equable climate, all arranged by divine beneficence for man's greatest possible comfort and joy. Assuredly Milton reread Dante's along with other accounts of paradisal gardens before creating his own. And more important than the likeness of descriptive detail is the intended use of the garden as the place in which man might grow fit for Heaven (*Purg.* 28.77–78; 33.145; *P.L.* V.497–500; VII.155–161).

Comparable likenesses associate the activities of the two Heavens. Unanimous singing, dancing, beholding, and rejoicing characterize them both (e.g. *Par.* 12.22–27; *P.L.* III.416–417; V.618–627). In both, Jacob's ladder supplies an image to link lower and upper reaches of Heaven (*Par.* 21.28ff., 22.70–72; *P.L.* III.510–512). For the ultimate realm of the beatific vision like phrases are used (*Par.* 27.7–9, 29.76ff.; *P.L.* III.60–62, 260–265,338); and the intuitive power of Heavenly beings is similarly made explicit (*Par.* 30.100–102; *P.L.* V.486–490). Their brightness at one point in each of the poems exceeds the sun on which they are beheld (*Par.* 10.40–42; *P.L.* III.622–628). The attributes of God again are accorded like phrasing— not only the infinity, omniscience, omnipotence, omnipresence, and perfect benevolence of the Creator, but also his uniqueness in being alone able fully to enjoy and understand his creation (*Par.* 30.19–21; *P.L.* IV.201–203), which was fashioned according to his Platonic Idea (*Par.* 13.52–54; *P.L.* VII.557).

In this last, *Timaeus* may be independently at work on both poets; and indeed we have constantly to remember that even when Milton's phrasing is closest to Dante's their common heritage may have suggested diction or image to each separately. But the parallels are frequent—so frequent, indeed, that for the longer lists from *Inferno* the explanation may simply be that the compilers of such parallels grow as weary of copying out passage after passage from *Paradise Lost* and *Paradiso* as readers do of scanning them.

If the markings in the copy of *L'Amoroso Convivio* bound with the della Casa volume Milton owned are also his, they show that he was interested, among other topics, in Dante's teaching on the fall of the angels and the making of man to replace them, on the Trinity, on the lady Philosophy, on friendship, and on inward sight. These are all dealt with in *Paradiso* and in the last five cantos of *Purgatorio* more fully than elsewhere in the *Commedia*. Back in 1905 Kenneth C. M. Sills remarked that the reference to Dante by Edward Phillips in his *Theatrum Poetarum* of 1675 would imply that *Paradiso* was for him the most important part of the *Commedia*. And while Sills may be wrong in believing this was Milton's own opinion, surely a student of Milton's relation to Dante must at least entertain the possibility that a nephew and pupil would first have heard of Dante as a major poet from his famous mentor. Phillips says of "Dantes Aligerus, a most Renowned Florentine, and the first of Italian Poets of any Fame or Note for Vernacular Verse," that what "most proclaims his Fame to the World is his Triple Poem entitled *Paradice, Purgatory,* and *Hell*." (The Latin version of 1679 is entitled *Compendiosa Enumeratio Poetarum qui a tempore Dantis Aligerii usque ad hanc aetatem claruerunt.*) Perhaps Phillips attached primary importance to *Paradiso* out of some preference of his own. But probably John Milton's views are also at work here.

Coleridge may have been right in declaring Dante less successful than Milton in fusing doctrine with poetry; but for that fusion Milton took him as a model. Or Carlyle may have been right in declaring Milton less concerned than Dante to explore the "deep things" in man's soul; but it was precisely that exploration in *Paradiso* that impressed Milton. He did not agree with Dante on every point, but it was probably Dante who suggested to him what must be dealt with if Heaven and Eden are to be paradigms of the ideal.

If nothing else, a comparison of their doctrinal agreement may end the repeated declaration that Milton lacked a Beatrice (Austin, p. 159; Whiting, pp. 476–477; Sayers, p. 151). No one, apparently, has thought to answer that Dante's Earthly Paradise lacks an Eve. Obviously an Eve would have no more place there than a Beatrice in *Paradise Lost*. Perhaps the easy assumptions about Milton's misogyny prepare readers to see dreadful implications in his choosing for the central action of *Paradise Lost* the story of a woman who tempted her husband to his destruction. But Dante accepted the story as fully as Milton. The speaking tree of the Purgatorial terrace where gluttony is cured refers to its parent tree "which was eaten of by Eve" (*Purg.* 24.116), as though Adam had not shared in the eating; and the Dante who finds himself in the Earthly Paradise experiences such delight that

> . . . righteous zeal made me reprove
> Eve's daring,
> who, there where heaven and earth obeyed, a
> woman alone and but then formed, did not
> bear to remain under any veil,
> under which, if she had been devout, I should

have tasted those ineffable joys ere this,
and for a longer time.   (*Purg.* 29.23–30)

No one accuses Dante of antifeminism for accepting the
Biblical tale, or reads his private life into his public utterance
merely because, while scattering members of the Donati family
through the *Commedia*, he never names Gemma or so much as
intimates that he had a wife and children.

A proper conclusion is that the love for Beatrice is relevant
to Dante's poem, the error of Adam's wife to Milton's. It is
not, perhaps, the only conclusion. But those misreaders who
harp on Milton's antifeminism need to be reminded that Voltaire, Chateaubriand, and Lamartine all thought the representation of the love of Adam and Eve among the poetic
glories of *Paradise Lost*, and none of those three Frenchmen, so
remarkably unlike in temperament, has ever been accused of
antifeminism.

Perhaps too the comparison of doctrine may suggest that to
exalt Dante's sense of mystery, or Milton's ability to transcend
the narrow and familiar, is to miss the point: just as Dante
dares to represent himself as having beheld and penetrated the
Heaven of Heavens, Milton dares to represent Heaven as
declaring itself more like familiar Earth than "on Earth is
thought." Indeed, to attend to what the *Commedia* and *Paradise
Lost* say on Heaven and Eden proves an antidote to the irrele-
vances that have been reiterated about Dante and Milton separately or by way of comparison. To perceive what they present
is to learn their recommendations to us. That may indeed be
why readers falter before the presentation.

The Chain of Being

If God himself is hardly seen in *Paradiso* except in the blinding vision at the end, a good deal can still be learned about him in the ascent through the heavenly spheres. He shows himself in his creation, not only as its shaper (*Par.* 10.10–12) but also as its source (*Par.* 13.52–63). What he reveals is above all the infinite plenitude of his being, which delights to overflow into other beings and then to behold them (*Par.* 19.40–51,88–90). The magnanimity of the creator is thus the first attribute revealed by his creation. But in its infinite complexity the creation itself is unknowable except to its maker (*Par.* 21.83–99), though something of its plan may be grasped from its superlative order (*Par.* 10.1–6). The book of creation speaks the mind that made and sustains cosmos.

No doubt such axioms of theology and metaphysics are not the peculiar property of the *Commedia*, and Milton hardly needed to study it in order to make them his. But Dante may sometimes have contributed to Milton's phrasing. Thus we may hear in

> . . . because I am who fill
> Infinitude, nor vacuous the space,
> Though I uncircumscrib'd myself retire,
> (*P.L.* VII.168–170)

a Miltonic version of Dante's

> e regna sempre in tre e due e uno,
> non circonscritto, e tutto circonscrive.
>
> *(Par.* 14.29–30)

Again, Abdiel on God's care of the angels' dignity—

> Yet by experience taught we know how good,
> And of our good, and of our dignity
> How provident he is   *(P.L.* V.826–828)

—may recall Carlo Martello:

> and not only is provision made for the diverse-natured
> creatures, by the mind that is perfection in itself, but
> for their weal too, co-related with them.
>
> *(Par.* 8.100–102)

And when Raphael refers to

> Things not reveal'd, which th' invisible King,
> Only Omniscient, hath supprest in Night,
> To none communicable in Earth or Heaven,
>
> *(P.L.* VII.122–124)

his way of stating that neither he nor his hearer can plumb the
divine intention recalls Thomas Aquinas addressing Dante on

> The providence which governeth the world,—with
> counsel wherein every creature's gaze must stay,
> defeated, ere it reach the bottom.
>
> *(Par.* 11.28–30)

More important, the *Commedia* may have suggested a way
of presenting the attributes of the creator who is known
through his creation that Milton found useful in writing *Paradise Lost.* Both poets faced the immense self-imposed task of
dealing with nothing less than the universe, and of dealing with
it authoritatively—and not because either Dante or Milton con-

sidered himself, or even wished to be, a cosmologist. But each poet, having set himself to deal in moral terms with the whole range of human life, must give it an adequate setting, both physically and metaphysically. Why and how was man made at all? what is his place in the universe in which he finds himself? what is his relation to, his destiny in, that universe? Such questions bear inevitably on how man gains and keeps, or loses but can regain, his happiness. Facing that question as the central issue of their poems, Dante and Milton were both obliged to deal with the cosmos. When Milton came to the problem in writing *Paradise Lost* he had the precedent—among others—of Dante.

Paradiso resolves the dilemma of providing authoritative answers to cosmic questions by assigning the questions to the mortal Dante and the answers to the immortal inhabitants of Paradise. Even where the mortal Dante records his own experiences of the celestial realm, he hedges his report, as we have seen, insisting in every possible way that he cannot adequately record the experience because even at the time it surpassed his comprehension (21.140–142), or because his memory now fails him (1.10–12), or because his wit is inadequate to provide symbols for what he beheld (14.103–105). We have observed how Milton adopted the device to guard against seeming to say in his own person what mere man cannot say. What remains that must be said is attributed to figures who can speak with authority. The angelic instructor Raphael in *Paradise Lost* fills a role like that of Beatrice and other heavenly beings in their illumination of Dante through the circles of *Paradiso*, dealing in comparable ways with comparable questions. In both poems, the chief question concerns the universal scheme.

Like Beatrice early in *Paradiso*, using the puzzlement of Dante when he finds himself ascending above the earth as occasion to sketch the cosmic plan, Raphael early in his visit takes Adam's puzzlement, over an angel's ability to eat human food, as occasion to deal with the same subject. The tuition of the lesser creature by the superior thus in both poems begins with the chain of being. The parallels are so many that both passages must be quoted at length.

> "All things whatsoever observe a mutual order; and this is the form that maketh the universe like unto God.
>
> Herein the exalted creatures trace the impress of the Eternal Worth, which is the goal whereto was made the ordinance now spoken of.
>
> In the order of which I speak all things incline, by diverse lots, more near and less unto their principle;
>
> wherefore they move to diverse ports o'er the great sea of being, and each one with instinct given it to bear it on.
>
> This beareth the fire toward the moon; this is the mover in the hearts of things that die; this doth draw the earth together and unite it.
>
> Nor only the creatures that lack intelligence doth this bow shoot, but those that have both intellect and love.
>
> The Providence that doth assort all this, doth with its light make ever still the heaven wherein whirleth that one that hath the greatest speed;
>
> and thither now, as to the appointed site, the power of that bowstring beareth us which directeth to a joyful mark whatso it doth discharge.
>
> True is it, that as the form often accordeth not with the intention of the art, because the material is dull to answer;
>
> so from this course sometimes departeth the creature

that hath power, thus thrust, to swerve toward some
other part,
(even as fire may be seen to dart down from the cloud)
if its first rush be wrenched aside to earth by false-
seeming pleasure.
Thou shouldst no more wonder, if I deem aright, at
thine uprising, than at a river dropping down from
a lofty mountain to the base.
Marvel were it in thee if, bereft of all impediment,
thou hadst settled down below; even as were stillness
on the earth in a living flame."

(Par. 1.103–141)

Raphael's account phrase by phrase recalls Beatrice's, though
with significant changes:

O Adam, one Almighty is, from whom
All things proceed, and up to him return,
If not deprav'd from good, created all
Such to perfection, one first matter all,
Indu'd with various forms, various degrees
Of substance, and in things that live, of life;
But more refin'd, more spiritous, and pure,
As nearer to him plac't or nearer tending
Each in thir several active Spheres assign'd,
Till body up to spirit work, in bounds
Proportion'd to each kind.

(P.L. V.469–479)

Before examining the divergence of the two accounts, we
may note that Raphael introduces the cosmic explanation as
his first step in a colloquy designed to prevent the fall of man.
In *Paradiso* 7 Beatrice reverts to the theme in order to explain
the fall. And since it is here that the points with which Milton
takes issue are elaborated, we may excerpt the phrases most
clearly related to Raphael's speech. Here the divine goodness

imprints its seal directly and without intermediary upon the human creature, which is thus immune, as are the angels, to change from without.

> It is more close conformed to it, therefore more pleasing
> to it; for the sacred glow that rayeth over everything,
> in what is most like itself is the most living. . . .
> Sin only is the thing that doth disfranchise it, and
> maketh it unlike to the highest good, so that its
> light the less doth brighten it.
>
> (Par. 7.73–75,79–81)

Unlike angels and humanity,

> . . . the elements . . . and all the things com-
> pounded of them, have by created virtue been
> informed.
> Created was the matter which they hold, created was
> the informing virtue in these stars which sweep
> around them.
> The life of every brute and of the plants is drawn
> from compounds having potency, by the ray and
> movement of the sacred lights.
> But your life is breathed without mean by the supreme
> beneficence who maketh it enamoured of itself,
> so that thereafter it doth ever long for it.
>
> (133–144)

It will be obvious at once that in Raphael's speech Milton has introduced some notable variations. *All* things, in his account, proceed directly from God, and *all* seek to return to him. All are perfect in their kind, and all can be depraved, deprived of, and thus turned from the highest good, by losing their own goodness. All are made of matter, and all are stamped with their forms by the maker himself. In the light of Beatrice's account, Raphael's takes on a special emphasis.

In Beatrice's version, defect may enter the cosmic scheme in two ways: through the impediments inherent in matter (*Par.* 1.129) or through the sentient creature's willful swerving from his proper goal (*Par.* 7.79). In Raphael's version, defect cannot be attributed to matter, the substratum of all created beings at every level. There can be no inherent flaw in the stuff of which all parts of the universe, each perfect at its own level, are made. Nor can the various forms, again each perfect in its own kind, be badly impressed on resistant matter. Only by being "deprav'd from good," vitiated in its whole nature as formed matter, can any part of the creation lose its initial perfection. That is to say, there is only one way, according to Milton, that defect enters the universe: by a distortion of form into deformity. Hence the immediate response throughout nature to the distortions introduced by the fall of Eve and Adam (*P.L.* X.651–707,1063–1068). If there is defect in the world we know, according to Milton, its source is not matter but the human will, which has distorted and deformed what was created entirely good. Thus, in Milton's scheme far more than in Dante's, man makes his world.

Not, of course, that every level of being has the same perfection. Milton's Raphael posits in the universe a growth from level to level which allows perfection in each without doing away with the range of higher and lower. We grasp the concept best by recognizing that a dog is not a defective man, but can in fact be perfect in itself, and yet is necessarily something lower in the scale than a man, perfect or imperfect. One reason for this major difference in the chain of being as elaborated by Beatrice and by Raphael is perhaps the different function of time in the cosmic schemes of *Paradiso* and *Paradise Lost*. When Beatrice later, in *Paradiso* 29, explains the realms of matter and form more fully, she gives a new emphasis to the simultaneity of all creation. Here too the explanation starts with the generous goodness of the Creator:

> Not to have gain of any good unto himself, which
> may not be, but that his splendour might, as it
> glowed, declare, *I am*.
> In his eternity beyond time, beyond all other compre-
> hension, as was his pleasure, the eternal love revealed
> him in new loves.
>
> (Par. 29.13–18)

That is, of course, Milton's view as well, presented in Adam's
very first speech in the poem:

> . . . needs must the Power
> That made us, and for us this ample World
> Be infinitely good, and of his good
> As liberal and free as infinite.
>
> (P.L. IV.412–415)

But Beatrice's next assertion, that there was no *when* before
the creation, the whole of which occurred simultaneously,
Milton could not accept.

> Nor did he lie, as slumbering, before; for nor before
> nor after was the process of God's outflowing over
> these waters.
> Form and matter, united and in purity, issued into
> being which had no flaw, as from a three-stringed
> bow three arrows; . . .
> so the threefold effect of its Lord rayed out all at
> once into its being, without distinction of be-
> ginning.
> Co-created was order and co-woven with the sub-
> stances; and those were the summit in the universe
> wherein Pure Act was produced.
> But Potentiality held the lowest place; in the midst,
> Power twisted such a withy with act as shall ne'er
> be unbound.
>
> (Par. 29.19–36)

True, Milton does have Raphael say in his account of the creation,

> Immediate are the Acts of God, more swift
> Than time or motion, but to human ears
> Cannot without process of speech be told.
>
> (*P.L.* VII.176–178)

True, too, that the simultaneous creation of matter, form, and formed matter had no more flaw at this stage according to Beatrice's account than according to Raphael's. But Dante makes plain that the lower levels of formed matter are subject to defect from the start (*Par.* 13.61–78). And even here Beatrice is impelled to argue at some length against Jerome's view that the angels were in being eons before the rest of the universe was created (29.37–45). The very fall of the rebel angels is hardly allowed time in which to occur: it happened in less time than it takes to count to twenty (49–54), and their fall is what disturbed the substratum of the elements (50–51). A vitiation introduced so all but immediately is hardly distinguishable from a defect in the stuff itself.

In Raphael's account of the war in Heaven, the very first assertion is that time is part of the eternal scheme, and that there has been process in the creation all along:

> As yet this World was not, and Chaos wild
> Reign'd . . . when on a day
> (For Time, though in Eternity, appli'd
> To motion, measures all things durable
> By present, past, and future) on such day
> As Heav'n's great Year brings forth . . .
>
> (*P.L.* V.577–583)

Whereas Dante cherishes above all else the stability in which the universe begins and ends, Milton cherishes our familiar sense of sequence in time, of an evolving universe. Not only was the stellar universe created after the fall of the angels, so that it cannot have been vitiated by their rebellion; that fall itself occurred long after the cosmos had been created in its perfection. Not, of course, that Milton opposed to creation *ex nihilo* a God who had to work with matter already in being; for him too, matter had to be created by God, who created all things (*Doct. Christ.* I.7.12). But since for Milton there is no level of created being that does not have matter for its substratum, his chain of being is more of a continuum than Dante's three realms of pure matter, formed matter, and pure form. In the parts of a continuum that develops and changes in time, the differences are not to be explained as deficiency.

The emphasis on continuity constitutes in fact the second main theme of Raphael's account:

> So from the root
> Springs lighter the green stalk, from thence the leaves
> More aery, last the bright consummate flow'r
> Spirits odorous breathes: flowr's and thir fruit
> Man's nourishment, by gradual scale sublim'd
> To vital spirits aspire, to animal,
> To intellectual, give both life and sense,
> Fancy and understanding, whence the Soul
> Reason receives, and reason is her being,
> Discursive, or Intuitive; discourse
> Is oftest yours, the latter most is ours,
> Differing but in degree, of kind the same.
>
> (*P.L.* V.479–490)

That is why, Raphael goes on to say, he can partake of the same food as man. So he has said before, in a prelude to this speech on the universal continuum:

> . . . food alike those pure
> Intelligential substances require

155

As doth your Rational; and both contain
Within them every lower faculty
Of sense, whereby they hear, see, smell, touch, taste,
Tasting concoct, digest, assimilate,
And corporeal to incorporeal turn.
For know, whatever was created, needs
To be sustain'd and fed; of Elements
The grosser feeds the purer . . .

(P.L. V.407–416)

The doctrine is then illustrated from the elements and from the celestial bodies of sun and moon, as well as, in the later speech, from plant and animal life. As the illustrations and reaffirmations mount, Milton has Raphael emphasize a concept that is the very antithesis of Dante's: the lower realms of being not only aspire to, but feed and are absorbed into the higher realms. The figure Raphael uses for the chain of being is precisely the one in which Adam sums up his teaching: he has set "the scale of Nature . . . / From centre to circumference" *(P.L.* V.509–510). The steps are not those of a ladder but rather of a series of concentric circles, each outer circle including all those within, the outermost the most inclusive.

The phrase itself echoes the magnificent line which begins Canto 14 of *Paradiso:* "Dal centro al cerchio, e sì dal cerchio al centro"; it recalls too the arresting image in *Paradiso* 28.16–39, of the angelic hierarchies in their nine circles whirling about the fixed point of light. But if Milton uses here both the same words and the same images as Dante, he does so with a major difference. In the Dantean chain of being the impulse is entirely from higher to lower realm, as the higher draws the lower into motion and guides it. For Milton there is a reciprocal impulse between higher realm and lower, each drawing its own perfection of kind directly from the source of all kinds, and all sustaining each other in interdependence.

Nor doth the Moon no nourishment exhale
From her moist Continent to higher Orbs.
The Sun that light imparts to all, receives
From all his alimental recompense
In humid exhalations, and at Even
Sups with the Ocean. (*P.L.* V.421–426)

Such dependence both ways is, of course, the very opposite of the emphatic doctrine of *Paradiso:*

These organs of the universe go, as thou seest
now, from grade to grade; for from above do
they receive, and downward do they work.
(*Par.* 2.121–123)

Milton may indeed have had *Paradiso* in mind, for he has Raphael explain the dark spots on the moon in terms of his cosmic theory as Beatrice had explained them in terms of hers. Raphael accounts for them as "vapors" which the moon has not yet digested "into her substance" (*P.L.* V.419–420), Beatrice as owing to the fusion of form and resistant matter. Just how important the cleavage between Milton and Dante on this issue of dependence is, we shall see in discussing the life of bliss as each details it. Here we may note simply that it entails the difference between a highest realm of created being that utterly transcends matter, however benignly it looks down upon and guides it, and a highest realm of created being that transforms matter into spirit.

Dante's emphasis here may be less Christian than Virgilian. At any rate, it corresponds to implications in the passage of *Aeneid* VI from which the *Commedia* takes its impetus:

First of all, heaven and earth and the liquid fields, the shining orb of the moon and the Titanian star, doth a spirit sustain inly, and a soul shed abroad in them sways all their members and mingles in the mighty frame. Thence is the generation of man and beast, the life of winged things, and the monstrous forms that ocean breeds under his glittering floor. Those seeds have fiery force and divine birth, so far as they are not clogged by sinful bodies and dulled by earthy frames and limbs ready to die.   (725–732, tr. Mackail)

Virgil apparently follows Plato in the whole passage; and Dante, though he knew only *Timaeus* at first hand, may here be more Platonic in his cosmology than the Platonist Milton. They divide on the issue; and since Dante's has been, in literature at least, the more familiar doctrine from antiquity down to the nineteenth century, Milton's warrants attention for its novelty.

That there are higher and lower levels of being, Milton and Dante agree; so much the very concept of a chain of being involves. And on the worth of the various levels they also agree; so much is implicit in the very terms higher and lower. The worth of the higher level is, for both poets, that it is more inclusive. But for Milton the greater inclusiveness also means a greater power to transform matter into its own substance. A flower has no less matter than a stone; but that matter is more informed with life. So too as between a flower and an animal, an animal and a man, a man and a celestial being: the difference is in vitality. To the difference in being and vitality ("substance" and "life," in Milton's terms), as we advance through the "several active Spheres" from the limited least to the inclusive outermost, corresponds a difference in definiteness, in spiritedness, and in distinctness; Raphael's terms are "more refined, more spiritous and pure." Indeed, Raphael's exposition of the chain of being suggests that the major scientific innovation of the nineteenth century, the doctrine of evolution, would not have disturbed Milton's essential thought any more than the major Renaissance innovation, the Copernican theory, had. The implications of Milton's cosmic scheme come prophetically close to the thought of Teilhard de Chardin.

The levels of being nearer to their source, "or nearer tend-ing," transmute their material substratum more completely into what is distinctly themselves and nothing but themselves. We might suppose it easier for a stone to be itself and nothing but a stone than for a man to be entirely human and nothing but himself. But Milton, with the scholastics, says just the opposite: a stone is necessarily more like every other stone than a man like any other man. And as soon as we have grasped the concept, it illuminates Milton's whole scheme. Between the ordinary man and the extraordinary the difference is very much of the sort that Raphael notes between man and angel, a difference "in degree, of kind the same." Whereas the ordinary man is more like other ordinary men, less distinctly himself— more dependent on the plodding steps of discursive thought, less spirited in transforming all that he takes from the outer world into his own nature—the extraordinary man, more dis-tinct, more intuitive, more active, absorbs and transmutes and makes part of himself all that by which he, like the rest of men in his dependence, is sustained. The pseudo-spirituality of pretending to need no sustenance from the outer world is thus for Milton the depth of folly.

And here, strikingly enough, the divergence of Milton's thought brings him back to an important agreement with Dante. If Dante does not, like Milton, admit a dependence of higher realm on lower, Milton does, like Dante, regard the vitality and freedom of all things as consistent with acknowledged dependence, and indeed as consisting in the acknowledgment. He has less interest than Dante in apportioning vitality to the various beings within the several grades. Dante's blessed are more and less free as they feel "più e men l'eterno spiro" (*Par.* 4.34–36), "più vivace" the more they conform to that source of freedom (*Par.* 7.70–75). Always in *Paradiso* we are aware of grades and ranks among the redeemed as among the angelic hierarchies, whereas in *Paradise Lost* we are aware only of large classes. But that difference apart, both Dante and Milton assert with equal force that the universe created by the overflowing divine abundance, being an order, a cosmos, involves interrelation and dependence.

As order it reveals at all levels the glory of its Maker. What Raphael says of the starry heavens, he implies of all aspects of the universe: "Heav'n/ Is as the Book of God before thee set,/ Wherein to read his wond'rous Works" (*P.L.* VIII.66–68). The same book, naturally enough, bespeaks the same author to Dante (*Par.* 1.1–3; 10.1–6). For the cosmos answers to the idea of its artist, both in Thomas's phrase in *Paradiso*

> Ciò che non more e ciò che può morire
> non è se non splendor di quella idea
> che partorisce, amando, il nostro sire,
>
> (13.52–54)

and in Raphael's in *Paradise Lost:*

> . . . this new created World
> . . . how it show'd
> . . . how good, how fair,
> Answering his great Idea. (VII.554–557)

If for Dante's Thomas the idea may be marred by the matter on which it is imprinted (*Par.* 13.67–69,73–78)—that is, if the defects of the universe are yet again attributable to matter—such defects are of minor consequence compared with those introduced into the universe by a will alienated from its source. Here Dante and Milton are at one. Inversely the highest virtues of created beings stem from their receptiveness. According to Beatrice,

> The beginning of the fall was the accursed pride of him
> whom thou didst see constrained by all the weights of
> the universe.

> Those whom thou seest here were modest to acknowledge
>   themselves derived from that same Excellence which
>   made them swift to so great understanding;
> wherefore their vision was exalted with grace illuminating
>   and with their merit, so that they have their will full
>   and established.
> And I would not have thee doubt, but be assured that 'tis
>   a merit to receive the grace by laying the affection
>   open to it.   (29.55–66)

The passage might stand as summary of the debate between
Satan and Abdiel (*P.L.* V.803–895), or of the interchange
between Satan and Gabriel in Eden (*P.L.* IV.877–1015). When
the sign of the balances appears in the sky to show that Satan
will lose if he insists on hand-to-hand combat, Gabriel points it
out and reads its meaning for them both:

> Satan, I know thy strength, and thou know'st mine,
> Neither our own but giv'n; what folly then
> To boast what Arms can do, since thine no more
> Than Heav'n permits, nor mine . . .
>   (*P.L.* IV. 1006–1009)

Gabriel can acknowledge the gift, Satan cannot—and it is the
measure of the gulf between them.

Raphael too in his exposition of the chain of being shows
himself "modesto" in acknowledging his relation to the universe
and its maker, and thereby shows himself also "meritorio."
But his emphasis on the likeness of man and angel—product
of his merit and his modesty at once—implies almost the whole
of what is distinctive in Milton's theory. The modesty is not
only toward God, nor even toward fellow angel, but also
governs his attitude toward lesser creatures—man, animal and
plant life, and even the very elements from which the higher
forms of life unfold, to which they owe their sustenance, and
with which they share their source of being.

The implication is clear. We have noted that for Milton far more than for Dante our world is what we make it, since the stuff from which it is made is without inherent defect. And all of us make our world on much more nearly the same terms, since the levels and grades among us are matters of degree rather than of kind. We are dependent on what is below and around as well as on what is above us. But for Milton, as for Dante, we make our world best if we start by acknowledging our dependent relation to the totality of things. That is why the instruction of Dante by Beatrice, and of Adam by Raphael, begins with an account of the chain of being. Our human life, to which both celestial instructors wish to attribute all possible dignity, may be a little lower or a little higher in the eyes of the one than of the other—a little more dependent on or independent of the stuff of the universe, the stuff itself may be inherently excellent or recalcitrant, the fabric of the universe more or less homogeneous, the parts disjunct but coeval or a continuum that unfolds in time. But on the habit of mind which alone can lead to the life of perfect creatures in perfect joy, the agreement of the two poets is complete.

The Life in Bliss

Like the redeemed of *Paradiso*, Milton's angels enjoy the life of Heaven, and their joy is the measure of its rightness as well as their own. The beatific vision in both realms is literally the sight that makes for happiness. So far as the angelic hierarchies of *Paradiso* have that and other joys in common with the redeemed, they resemble the angels of Paradise Lost; but Dante in fact says little about them before Canto 28. The redeemed have the large role in *Paradiso* and the larger relation to *Paradise Lost*. In *Inferno* and *Purgatorio*, angels appear to great effect— swift, radiant, of exceptional beauty and power, fulfilling high offices. The heavenly messenger who opens the gate of the infernal city with the touch of his wand and his sharp words to the "outcasts of Heaven" (*Inf.* 9.85–103) resembles Ithuriel unmasking the toad with the mere touch of his spear, and demanding "which of those rebel Spirits adjudg'd to Hell" has dared invade the bower of Eden (*P.L.* IV.810–826). Again the two angels who quickly put to flight the symbolic serpent in *Purgatorio* 8 resemble Ithuriel and Zephon coping with the revealed Satan. The glorious apparition who steers the newly dead to the shore of Purgatory, "plying the air" like a "bird divine" (*Purg.* 2.13–51) anticipates the figure of Raphael speeding phoenixlike from Heaven to Eden (*P.L.* V.266–272).

The guardian of Purgatory proper speaks, acts, and explains as prompted by his office (*Purg.* 9.82–132), and the angels of the cleansing circles heal Dante's brow of its seven *P*'s and bid him ascend (*Purg.* 12.79–99; 15.22–36; 17.43–47; 19.43–48; 22.1–6; 24.133–54; 27.6–13,55–63), all very much as Milton's angels proceed in their services to man.

But these are offices outside Paradise. Inside it, human spirits perform such functions. When the angelic hierarchies appear, from Canto 28 on, they are the explained, not the explainers. As Meozzi noted (p. 127), they are figures or designs rather than persons, relatively undifferentiated in presentation. According to Dante, they are, of course, as according to Thomas Aquinas in the tradition of angelology going back to Dionysius, the most highly differentiated of created beings, each in the nine orders a distinct species in himself. But within Paradise they have no occasion to reveal their distinctions. What is said about them by Beatrice has more relevance to Milton's heavenly beings; she names "Gabriel and Michael, and him too who made Tobit sound again" (4.47–48) in the course of explaining the anthropomorphic representation of God in Scripture, and of angels by the church. Milton similarly, in *Christian Doctrine* I.2, justifies the language of anthropomorphism as an accommodation to human understanding; and he uses it in *Paradise Lost*, where the same three angels, Gabriel, Michael, and Raphael, play important roles. In *Paradiso* the returned traveler, who has been empowered, however briefly, to see ultimate realities, cannot use the same anthropomorphism; nor would fuller representation of the angelic life have served Dante's purpose in describing the life of the heavenly city.

Macaulay's comment that "Dante's angels are good men with wings" applies far better to Dante's wingless redeemed, or to Milton's angels, and indeed sheds light on their meaning—provided we understand "good men" as Dante and Milton did, and recognize the angelic wings as not merely ornamental. The goodness is necessarily human, though far above common human goodness. Milton could even assert that "the affections which in a good man are good, and rank with virtues, in God are holy" (*Christ. Doct.* I.2). What he and Dante saw no reason not to attribute to God, always recognizing the incommensurability of all terms for the Infinite, they did not hesitate to attribute, Milton to the angels, Dante to the redeemed. The six wings of the seraphs—in which both poets follow Isaiah 6:2—add a beauty and power beyond the human, and are signs of an enlarged consciousness and capacity. A reader who disapproves of wings can easily disregard them since they are seldom mentioned in either poem except where swiftness is involved. The heightening of human goodness is another matter.

The goodness of the redeemed in *Paradiso* and of the angels in *Paradise Lost* shows itself in dance and song, and in radiance. Both poets use light as the virtual equivalent of joy, particularly in the analogy of God to the sun. In Dante's phrase, God is "il sol degli angeli" (*Par.* 10.53); in *Paradise Lost*, we first behold the angels about his throne receiving "from his sight . . ./ Beatitude past utterance," while "on his right" sits the "radiant image of his Glory . . . ,/ His only Son" (*P.L.* III.61–64). In *Paradiso* as Dante ascends the spheres to the Empyrean, he enters realm after realm of ever more intense light, until he must bathe his eyes in the River of Light itself to behold the "candida rosa" of the heavenly court; and even then he will lose his sight in the blinding radiance of his final vision of God. In *Paradise Lost* the first words that introduce Heaven similarly concern light, and God's radiance is celebrated by the very angels as blinding (*P.L.* III.375–382).

The angels themselves glow with the brilliance they draw from that fountain, as Dante's redeemed, otherwise invisible, glow in *Paradiso*. When Raphael arrives in Eden, Adam describes the "glorious Shape/ . . . this way moving" in a phrase that recalls Dante:

> . . . seems another Morn
> Ris'n on mid-noon.
>   (*P.L.* V.310–311)

So for Dante first rising above earth in *Paradiso* 1:

> And, of a sudden, meseemed that day was added
> unto day, as though he who hath the power,
> had adorned heaven with a second sun.
>   (*Par.* 1.61–63)

But fallen Adam, having lost the power to sustain such radiance, sees Michael approach in "Darkness ere Day's mid-course" (*P.L.* XI.204). When Milton undertook to describe the angelic figure Uriel in the sun, glorious even in the "place . . . beyond expression bright" (*P.L.* III.591), he was perhaps accepting the challenge of Dante's words in *Paradiso* 10:

> How shining in itself must that needs be which
>   in the sun, whereinto I had entered, itself re-
>   vealeth not by hue, but light!
> Though I should summon genius, art, tradition,
>   ne'er could I so express it as to make it
>   imaged; but it may be believed—and let
>   men long to see it.   (*Par.* 10.40–45)

At any rate, he obviously shares with Dante such images of radiance for the blessed.

He shares with Dante, too, the imagery of song and dance to evoke the intense vitality of the heavenly life. Both are concerned to emphasize recognizable human delights. But Dante, concerned also to emphasize their transfiguration, does not attempt to reproduce the songs except here and there in a familiar word or phrase from the liturgy (*Par.* 3.121–122; 7.1–3; 8.29; 14.62; 23.128; 24.113–114; 26.69; 32.95), sometimes explaining that even at the time the song surpassed his understanding (*Par.* 14.118–126), sometimes that his memory cannot recapture it (*Par.* 20.10–12; 24.22–25), but more often that it cannot be known except as heard in Heaven (*Par.* 10.70–75,145–148; 12.1–9; 19.37–39), and once at least that the song was suspended out of compassion for his human limitations (*Par.* 21.58–63; 22.10–12). Milton ventures to compose songs for his angels, but carefully prepares the reader to accept the recognizable words as heavenly, adapting much of Dante's technique as well as of his substance (*P.L.* III.345ff.; VI.885–886; VII.256–260,274–275,449–450,565ff.,601ff.; X.643–648). The resemblances, in view of the unlike actions of the two heavenly realms, are striking. Dante, with all *Paradiso* in which to stress the theme, again and again has the heavenly songs explicitly accompanied by dance (*Par.* 10.76–81; 12.22–24; 13.28; 14.19–24, 18.76–79; 23.109; 24.22–25). Milton, with far less opportunity to repeat any detail of angelic activities, uses one magnificent passage, when Raphael introduces the occasion of Satan's rebellion:

> That day, as other solemn days, they spent
> In song and dance about the sacred Hill,
> Mystical dance, which yonder starry Sphere
> Of Planets and of fixt in all her Wheels
> Resembles nearest, mazes intricate,
> Eccentric, intervolv'd, yet regular
> Then most, when most irregular they seem:
> And in thir motions harmony Divine
> So smooths her charming tones, that God's own ear
> Listens delighted.   (*P.L.* V.618–627)

The comparison of the angelic dance to the movements of the stars recalls the elaborate figure in *Paradiso* 13.1–21.

Beyond the evidence of joy, both Dante and Milton use these heavenly song-dances to assert that harmony arises from diversity. Thus Justinian declares:

> Divers voices upon earth make sweet harmony,
> and so the different degrees in our life render
> sweet harmony amongst these wheels.
>
> (*Par.* 6.124–126)

Milton takes an early opportunity in Heaven to remark:

> No voice exempt, no voice but well could join
> Melodious part, such concord is in Heav'n.
>
> (*P.L.* III.370–371)

Doubtless the reader is to contrast this with Hell, where only one group sang (*P.L.* II.546–555); but the meaning is not only that all in Heaven took part, but that the parts they took were distinct, and so composed the concord.

The significance of the musical image, that diversity is necessary to perfect harmony, is a major theme in *Paradiso*. Set forth by Piccarda (*Par.* 3.70–90), repeated by Justinian, re-emphasized by Carlo Martello (*Par.* 8.97–102), and applied to the angelic hierarchies by Beatrice in the beautiful metaphor of the mirrors (*Par.* 29.136–145), the insistence on variety-in-unity as what Heaven delights in explains why various persons who inhabit the same Empyrean manifest themselves to Dante in the different spheres (*Par.* 4.34–39), why they can say in their various ways "la sua volontate è nostra pace" (*Par.* 3.85), and why Dante has Carlo Martello specifically apply the principle as a prescription for our world (*Par.* 8.115ff.). Carlo urges that it is better for man to be a citizen; a community requires that divers kinds of people fill divers offices; a fit education would encourage each talent in its proper exercise; and we err by ignoring individual bent and imposing alien tasks. The last is the substance of the passage from *Paradiso* noted in Milton's *Commonplace Book* (fol. 111):

Of the Education of Children. See of the Knowledge of Literature.
The nature of each person should be especially observed and not
bent in another direction; for God does not intend all people for
one thing, but for each one his own work; whence comes Dante's:
"And if the world down there put its mind on the foundation that
nature lays," &c. See Paradiso cant:8.   (trans. Mohl)

Evidently Milton was impressed by the explicit application to
earthly affairs of the idea so pervasive in *Paradiso*. When he
affirms a similar idea of his Heaven, he too has in mind its
applicability to man as citizen.

By the time he wrote *Paradise Lost* he took the doctrine
with a difference. Because he does not make such categorical
distinctions among the angels as Dante makes among the human
redeemed as well as among the angelic hierarchies, Milton
needs some other means of showing unity in diversity. Dante
insists that Heaven has no near or far (*Par.* 30.121–123; and
cf. 3.88–89); Milton has Raphael talk of regions in Heaven
(*P.L.* V.750–756; VI.1–2). Dante assigns specialized functions
to the orders of the blessed; Milton suggests, rather, in his
angels a versatility that permits them to hold offices assigned
"by Lot" (*P.L.* IV.561–563). Both are concerned, however,
to stress a kind of unanimity and a kind of variety as desiderata
of the supremely happy community. For Dante the variety con-
sists in ranks and functions, the unity in equidistance from God,
the omnipresent center. Milton prefers to use what makes at
once for pleasing diversity and for essential community in the
world we know.

He varies the Heavenly scene with "change delectable"
(V.629) of evening and morning, "Heav'n's great Year," sleep
after festivity, the garden city with its combination of buildings
and park, the rural space with its hills and valleys. Heaven is
recognizably of no less "various view" than Eden (IV.247), for
which it is indeed the model (IV.208). Similarly he varies the

Heavenly life by ascribing versatility to its citizens in the range of offices they can fill. They resemble the products of his own proposed educational system, fitted "to perform justly, skilfully, and magnanimously all the offices, both private and public, of peace and war." Hell is a place of specialization (*P.L.* II.521–576); but the citizens of Heaven all sing and dance, make war if need be, guard Eden or instruct it, engage in games, or celebrate a returning hero. Evidently they do have special skills: Uriel is sharp-sighted, Michael a warrior, Raphael accomplished in social discourse; but their special skills do not preclude their engaging in all the various activities: Raphael has taken part in the war in Heaven; Uriel directs a seemingly youthful angel; Michael instructs Adam in the future of mankind. To Satan, Gabriel and his angelic troop guarding Eden are mere "gay Legions," better at singing hymns than at fighting (IV.942–945)—or so he hopes—just as he boasted during the war that "train'd up in Feast and Song,/ . . . the Minstrelsy of Heav'n" would be easily defeated (VI.167–170). His insult is, of course, the highest tribute: the angels prefer civilized pleasures to civic broils, though they can descend to battle if they must. Milton will have his angels no more one-sided than his properly educated man, and no more given to the resort to force than God himself (VI.695–703,801–810), though no less prepared to wage the war that is thrust upon them (VI.262–280). They are indeed the models of what "a complete and generous education" should aim at, as are the citizens of Dante's ideal community.

In their habits too Milton's angels recall *Paradiso*. They move with swirling speed, and take in meanings with a speed still greater;[1] they speak modestly of their own excellence, praise

---

[1] On the intuitive power of the blessed, see especially *Par.* 9.61–63, 73–75,80–81; 11.19–21; 17.14–19; and on the same power in Milton's angels, see especially *P.L.* V.487–490.

each other, and delight in the addition to their community of those who can share in and thus increase their joys; they rejoice at the growth in comprehension of others, and show unfailing courtesy to intimate and newcomer alike. Their lives are a "high great festival" (*Par.* 12.22), but not because they see, hear, know no evil. In *Paradiso* there is repeated comment on the ills of thirteenth-century Europe; in *Paradise Lost* Raphael relates with sharpest insight the twistings of the Satanic mind. But evil cannot touch their own joy, perhaps because, able to admit their own mistakes freely, they have no need to concentrate on the mistakes of others. Their admission of error wastes no time on either self-exculpation or self-castigation: thus Piccarda (*Par.* 3.97–107) and Cunizza (*Par.* 9.25–36), referring to their past lives, or Uriel reporting his error (IV.561–590). They are concerned instead with inducting others into the heavenly life. Milton's tutorial angel Raphael, in his discourse with Adam, thus resembles Peter, James, and John examining Dante on faith, hope, and charity (*Par.* 24–26). Their "ardent courtesy," always notable, is best illustrated by the praise Thomas Aquinas and Bonaventure each give to the founder of the other's order, St. Francis and St. Dominic (*Par.* 11–12), and by the "joy and acclamations" that greet Abdiel on his return, "not lost" (VI.22–25). Magnanimity is the chief heavenly trait.

Dante gives it more emphasis, *Paradiso* constituting a full third of the *Commedia*, while heavenly scenes occupy less than a fifth of Milton's poem. But the virtues and the duties to one's neighbor detailed in *Christian Doctrine*, II.12–13, show Milton's essential agreement with Dante on the matter, and indeed shed more light on the angelic nature enacted in *Paradise Lost* than does the brief chapter on the special government of the angels. As it happens the argument there (I.9) against angelic omniscience also coincides with what Peter Damiani affirms in

Dante and Milton

Paradiso on the limitations of every created being's knowledge:

> But that soul in heaven which is most illuminated,
>   that Seraph who hath his eye most fixed on
>   God, had given no satisfaction to thy question;
> because so far within the abyss of the eternal
>   statute lieth the thing thou askest, that from
>   all created vision it is cut off.

(Par. 21.91–96)

A like humility makes Raphael again and again assert to Adam that angels do not know God's full purposes, but stand in much the same relation to him as perfect man, of whom they think as their "fellow servant" favored with God's "Equal Love" (*P.L.* VIII.224–228).[2]

Like Dante's redeemed, Milton's heavenly beings are thus profoundly concerned with the affairs of earth, though nothing can violate their bliss (X.25). The concern is natural enough since they are introduced in relation to the human story, as Dante's redeemed are introduced to welcome an earthly visitor to Paradise. Beyond the demands of the action, however, both groups have a common hope of sharing their community with earth's inhabitants. Because of that hope, they show a like indignation at threats to the welfare of man. Milton's angels are no more uniformly mild than Dante's redeemed. They display a range of feelings, among which—not unnoticeably—is an anger so overwhelming that we might hardly suppose it appropriate to the life of bliss. But Milton evidently agreed with Dante that wrath may be not only appropriate but neces-

---

[2] Cf. John Arthos, who contrasts Milton and Dante on this score: "Milton does not challenge divinity—he admires, adumbrates, and serves. . . . This is the achievement one puts beside the efforts of Dante . . . to rival the Creator, and to undertake the very work of creation" (p. 120). It will be evident that I find Dante as careful as Milton to insist that man—or angel—cannot possibly rival, or indeed fully comprehend, the Creator.

172

sary in Heaven. The variety of mood in both Heavens again reminds us of the position Milton takes in *Christian Doctrine* II.8, when he lists the affections as love, hate, joy, sorrow, hope, fear, and anger, and indicates the propriety of each: hatred, for example, should be proportionate to the hatefulness of the object. Neither Dante nor Milton ever suggests that what is damnable deserves less than condemnation, though both carefully make their heavenly beings distinguish between the error and the person who errs.

In both Heavens, impulse and law can be one and the same. Since the one law is love of the one inclusive good, unanimity characterizes both citizenries. Yet Dante and Milton are aware that Hell too has its unanimity, bred of envy and spite, as Heaven's is bred of fulfillment and generosity. "Devil with Devil damn'd/ Firm concord holds" (II.496–497), as well as saint with saint or angel with angel. To be of one mind is not always to be of sound mind. But in Heaven perfect justice rules with perfect harmony, wisdom, and love as these have nowhere ever ruled the earthly scene. In such a kingdom, the freest spirit is gladly the most law-abiding, the law of love, wisdom, justice being part of his own nature. Peter Damiani states the principle for Dante:

" . . . the deep love which holdeth us prompt servants
of the counsel which governeth the world, maketh
assignment here as thou observest."
"Yea, I perceive, O sacred lamp," said I, "how free
love in this court sufficeth to make follow the
eternal providence . . . "   (*Par.* 21.70–75)

Raphael is equally explicit for Adam and Eve:

. . . freely we serve,
Because wee freely love, as in our will
To love or not; in this we stand or fall.
            (*P.L.* V.538–540)

And again in his narrative he has Abdiel, repudiating Satan's defense of the rebellion, specifically declare:

> Reign thou in Hell thy Kingdom, let mee serve
> In Heav'n God ever blest . . . (VI.183–184)

Milton had not forgotten Satan's magniloquent "Better to reign in Hell than serve in Heav'n" (I.263) when he gave Abdiel that priority in phrase-making. "Non serviam" is a fit protest against injustice in power; against justice it has the meaning Abdiel assigns it:

> Unjustly thou deprav'st it with the name
> Of Servitude to serve whom God ordains,
> Or Nature; God and Nature bid the same,
> When he who rules is worthiest, and excels
> Them whom he governs. This is servitude,
> To serve th' unwise, or him who hath rebell'd
> Against his worthier, as thine now serve thee,
> Thyself not free, but to thyself enthrall'd.
> (VI.174–181)

Such issues, presumably, have long since been resolved in Dante's Paradise, and Inferno has long served unwisdom. Milton shows more of the choice of service in process, the whole of *Paradise Lost* defining the "disobedience" of the opening phrase of the poem. But so too the whole *Commedia* may be said to define "the straight way" that had been lost. Milton offers guidelines for the choosing: "God and Nature bid the same," "Right reason for thir Law" (VI.42), and pre-eminently, the Son's words on the Father,

> Whom to obey is happiness entire. (VI.741)   *

The happiness of the creature being the will of the creator, obedience to that will is itself the measure of happiness. The point cannot be too emphatically stated against readers of both

174

Dante and Milton who assume that the unhappiness of the creature is the Creator's will, so that they must repudiate either the Creator or what nature and reason self-evidently declare to be man's happiness. Casuists of all parties can make out cases for all manner of unnatural, irrational obediences and disobediences. But Dante is as little of their persuasion as Milton. When William J. Grace accuses Milton of failing to guard against the subjective errors that lead to anarchy—though allowing that he stays closer to orthodoxy in *Paradise Lost* than elsewhere (p. 187)—and praises Dante for accepting established offices (p. 186), he blurs both a recognizable emphasis in the *Commedia* and Milton's commitment to *right* reason. Mere self-assertion Milton assigned to Satan, and what Dante sanctioned was not a simple acceptance of established power. As William Madsen has said in another context (*The Idea of Nature in Milton's Poetry*, p. 274), in the Middle Ages there was "no *one* orthodox view." Of course Dante believed there could be both an ideal church and an ideal papacy, just as he believed in an ideal monarchy and in unity under an ideal emperor. For the realities of degenerate state and church in his time he had words as harsh as any Milton ever used in a political pamphlet. In Dante's Paradise and in Milton's Heaven, the joy of the citizenry shows the rightness of the city. But the very nature of its life, founded in devotion to justice and wisdom, prescribes a mood far from bland acceptance when they behold injustice and folly.

Wrath in Heaven

Man cannot be reconciled to injustice. He can turn his eyes from it or pretend to have accepted it. He can train himself to forgive the unjust if their injustice ceases. But with the injustice itself, especially cherished injustice, forgiveness would have no meaning. Hence both Dante and Milton attribute anger to Heaven, Dante the more surprisingly in scene after scene of *Paradiso*. The most shocking of these comes in *Paradiso* 27, a canto that evidently impressed Milton from his early reading since it involves a matter on which he felt deep sympathy with Dante, the evil inflicted on the world by a corrupt clergy. The scene is meant to shock. Set in the highest glory of the redeemed, put as the words of St. Peter himself, introduced abruptly after one of the most joyous passages in the poem, the denunciation takes on a terrifying force. The canto opens with a sound of such sweetness and a look of such brightness that it seems a smile of the universe. Milton perhaps recalls the phrase in his lines for the newly created Earth ready to house Man: "Earth in her rich attire/ Consummate lovely smil'd" (VII.501–502). Dante, remembering the experience of sight and sound, exclaims:

> O gioia! o ineffabile allegrezza!
> o vita intera d'amore e di pace!
> (27.7–8)

The lines suggest the same "Beatitude past utterance" (*P.L.* III.62) that Milton attributes to Heaven. Suddenly, following this climax of joy and peace, a unanimous silence falls over the hushed choir of the blessed, and a light approaches, whose words will shortly reveal it to be St. Peter. When he speaks, it is first to call attention to the phenomenon that Dante is about to witness:

> If I transform my hue, marvel
> thou not; for, as I speak, thou shalt see all
> of these transform it too.   (27.19–21)

And indeed as he continues, both he and the assembly of the redeemed turn fiery red with anger (28–30), while even the face of Beatrice darkens (31–36). St. Peter's words are an anguished castigation of his present successor in the papacy, culminating in a command to the poet, when he returns to earth, to speak out and not hide what Peter himself has not hidden. The force of the denunciation comes in part from the contrast with its setting, in part from the startling metaphors, in part from the extraordinarily effective repetitions. With three hammer-strokes,

> Quegli ch' usurpa in terra il loco mio,
> il loco mio, il loco mio,

St. Peter demolishes every pretension of the incumbent pope, declares the usurped place vacant in the eyes of God, thunders that his burial ground has been turned into a "cloaca/ del sangue e della puzza," and proceeds through an elaborate series of parallel constructions ("Non fu . . . Non fu . . . nè che . . . nè ch' ") to contrast his and the present use of the papal office:

> "The spouse of Christ was not reared upon my
> blood, and that of Linus and of Cletus, that
> she might then be used for gain of gold; . . .

177

It was not our purpose that on the right hand
of our successors one part of the Christian
folk should sit, and one part on the other;
nor that the keys given in grant to me should
become the ensign on a standard waging war
on the baptised;
nor that I should become the head upon the
seal to sold and lying privileges, whereat I
often blush and shoot forth flames.

(27.40–42,46–54)

The antithesis of his martyred blood both with the gold sought
by misused power and with the blood that flows mixed with
filth through a papacy transformed into a sewer, the figures
of his keys converted into a battle-sign against the baptized,
and his own image the seal of the traffic in unlawful privileges—
how Milton read the passionate denunciation we know from
Lycidas, with its echo of St. Peter's lines:

In garb of pastors ravening wolves are seen from
here above in all the pastures.   (55–56)

Presumably Dante's lines gave Milton the idea of using St.
Peter himself to call the corrupt Roman church "the grim
wolf with privy paw" and threaten the vengeance soon to
overtake a similarly corrupt Church of England.

Paradise Lost has few occasions for such outbursts of just
anger as mark the journey of Dante, not only in Hell and Purgatory but in Heaven itself. In comparison with the *Commedia*
its tone is unpolemical. The anger of *Paradiso* is, to be sure,
unlike the habit of anger that is punished in *Inferno* and eradi-
cated in *Purgatory*. But *Paradise Lost*, though it attributes wrath
to Heaven, seldom shows it. Thus God, in the words of the
Son, rather holds his foes in derision; the Son himself speaks
in calm judgment as he drives against the Satanic forces or

pronounces sentence on Adam, Eve, and the serpent; even Abdiel shows more astonished revulsion than anger at Satan's blasphemies. Ithuriel and Zephon do, it is true, match Satan's scorn with scorn of their own, but without anger; and Michael on the field of battle maintains a Homeric dispassion. That Satan constantly attributes rage to God of course means nothing. Significantly, in fact, Milton makes wrath, along with despair and envy, the mark of Satan himself; even the displays of ill temper by Adam and Eve are clearly the effects of their fall into his snare.

All the more impressive, then, are the resemblances to *Paradiso* 27 that do occur in *Paradise Lost*. A natural occasion for just anger comes in Michael's account to Adam of the degeneration of the church. He echoes Dante's St. Peter:

> Wolves shall succeed for teachers, grievous Wolves,
> Who all the sacred mysteries of Heav'n
> To thir own vile advantages shall turn
> Of lucre and ambition, . . .
> Places and titles, and with these . . . join
> Secular power, though feigning still to act
> By spiritual . . . ;
>   . . . and from that pretense,
> Spiritual Laws by carnal power shall force
> On every conscience. . . .
>   . . . so shall the World go on,
> To good malignant, to bad men benign,
> Under her own weight groaning.
>
> (XII.508–539)

Michael too then promises an end to such evil, though only at Doomsday. But while he notes many of the same abuses as Dante's saint, his tone is less denunciatory than explanatory. His speech constitutes in Milton's poem no such high moment as St. Peter's tirade in *Paradiso* 27. Its most effective line, "To good malignant, to bad men benign," it owes to another of Dante's denunciations, in *Inferno* 19.105, where the phrase "calcando i buoni e sollevando i pravi" condemns the avarice of Nicholas III and his breed. But Michael detailing the sad future to Adam, while trying to send him from Eden comforted and hopeful, cannot, as Dante among the simonists or St. Peter regarding the usurper of his office can, give way to anger, however justified. As always in *Paradise Lost*, the principle of decorum holds.

Decorum allows Milton only one occasion for the flush of rage in celestial faces. That he uses it suggests that he felt as free as Dante to attribute indignation to Heaven. Indeed, had *Paradise Lost* dealt as largely as the *Commedia* with the world of the poet's own time, decorum might have permitted him more such outbursts. The sight of evil in places of power was certainly no more tolerable to him than it was to Dante. But the one occasion in his poem does not directly concern his own time. Satan, having exercised his powers of insult and then called the reply to him insulting, prepares to take on Gabriel and all his troop at once; and Gabriel, duly angry in his turn, accepts the challenge. Although the angelic guard restrain their own wrath, and permit Gabriel by himself to meet Satan's threat of force, they change color like Peter and the other saints in Dante's Paradise:

> . . . th'Angelic Squadron bright
> Turn'd fiery red, sharp'ning in mooned horns
> Thir Phalanx.   (IV.977–979)

Two elements distinguish this from other presumptive occasions for anger in *Paradise Lost*: the threat of force from Satan and the self-imposed nonintervention of the angels. Neither Uriel when he finds he has been tricked by Satan, nor Gabriel when he learns of the trick, wastes emotion on rage. Neither even takes immediate action: Uriel can wait until sunset to report the incident, Gabriel until night to seek out the intruder without disturbing Eden. Both show the habitual confidence of Milton's angels in the triumph of right when the time for action comes. So too Ithuriel and Zephon when they lead Satan before Gabriel, Abdiel among the rebels, Michael and the other loyal angels on the battlefield, and Gabriel at the end of this scene when he observes the scales in heaven and lets Satan go.

But here the angelic guard deliberately hold back while their chief by himself confronts Satan, though he has called them cowards and incompetents and threatened to quell the lot of them singlehanded. The combination of wrath with a seeming false position—since they do outnumber him and cannot in their dignity make use of the advantage—is what brings the flush to their faces. Thus Milton in the one episode in his poem where the good are in the grip of frustrated anger uses the same image as Dante. It may be mere coincidence that the simile of a horned shape and a constellation appears in *Paradiso* 27 at just this point: "when the horn of the heavenly Goat is touched by the sun" (68–69). Or it may be that Gabriel's troop sharpening their phalanx "in mooned horns" was Milton's more or less conscious recollection of the wrath of the blessed in *Paradiso* 27. The collocation of resemblances suggests, at any rate, how much the passage impressed Milton. St. Peter's final words to Dante surely must have done so:

> . . . open thy mouth
> and hide thou not the thing which I hide not.
> (65–66)

In the opening section of *The Reason of Church-Government*, II, Milton imagines a similar voice bidding him speak out on a similar theme, and he had not done with speaking out when he wrote *Paradise Lost*.

The commonplaces on Dante as an angry poet or Milton as an embittered man conveniently ignore what they were angry about. Neither was willing to turn his gaze from the injustice he saw; neither was given to pretenses of forgiveness. Milton on an early page of his *Commonplace Book* raises the question why God permits evil, and answers that it can constitute the "ratio" of virtue as virtue is tested, brought to light, or exercised by evil (fol. 4). He did not hold that virtue needs evil—the doctrine sometimes misread into *Areopagitica*—and he did not condone the evils of willed injustice. Satan is the fit target of just anger in *Paradise Lost* as in himself and his policies he sums up every evil detailed in the human panorama of Books XI and XII. The wrath in *Paradiso* is directed where Milton directed the heavenly wrath in *Paradise Lost*—not against lapses in pious observance, but against injustice. And the Milton who wrote in *Tetrachordon*, "The end of every ordinance [in the Bible] . . . is the good of man; yea, his temporal good not excluded," would not have thought merely vindictive the diatribes of Cacciaguida, St. Peter, and Beatrice on the injustices of the world to which their hearer was to return. Nor would he have thought it wrong to represent the citizens of Paradise as bidding Dante to speak out against evil. Milton had survived his private disasters when he composed *Paradise Lost;* he had chosen a subject that put the immediate at a distance. But for Dante Beatrice was irrevocably gone and Florence would never again be his home; and his subject included his immediate world.

Had Milton written the proem to Book VII to display his own feelings he might have done more than imply a kinship between "the barbarous dissonance/ Of Bacchus and his Revellers" and the restored monarchy. Like Dante he thought of himself as an exile. The *Commedia* gave opportunity for the poignant words in Cacciaguida's prophecy:

> Thou shalt abandon everything beloved most
>   dearly; this is the arrow which the bow of
>   exile shall first shoot.
> Thou shalt make trial of how salt doth taste
>   another's bread, and how hard the path to
>   descend and mount upon another's stair.
>
> (Par. 17.55–60)

Paradise Lost offered Milton no fit place to speak what he wrote to Peter Heimbach: "What you call policy, but I would rather have you call loyalty to one's country,—this particular lass, after inveigling me with her fair name, has almost expatriated me. . . . One's country is wherever it is well with one" (tr. Masson). The sense of exile, transmuted into Eve's lament, and Adam's, at learning of their dismissal from Eden (XI.263ff.), is heard from Milton directly in *Paradise Lost* only once, when he presents himself as

> . . . fall'n on evil days,
> On evil days though fall'n, and evil tongues;
> In darkness, and with dangers compast round,
> And solitude. (VII.25–28)

And even then his situation is introduced so that he may assert himself

> . . . yet not alone, while thou
> Visit'st my slumbers Nightly, or when Morn
> Purples the East: still govern thou my Song,
> Urania . . . (28–31)

Aware of the poetic emphasis in the *Commedia* that derives from the narrative as in some sense the journey of an everyman, Milton would have been aware as well of the poetic use that Dante as narrator made of his private joys and woes. And he would have had enough ground of his own for sympathizing with the sufferer from injustice not to think the denunciatory passages of *Paradiso* excessive.

Yet while he reproduced something like Dante's episode of sanctioned wrath in the encounter of the angelic guard with Satan, it would seem that Milton on the whole preferred to have his Heaven look to the time when "wrath shall be no more" (*P.L.* III.264; XI.251–258,334–354). Difference in the distance of the two poems from the world of their time accounts, as we have said, for much of this difference in emphasis. And if in *Paradiso*, with Heaven's numbers so nearly complete (30.130–132), we could wish to hear more assurance of the approaching state, in which vengeance will no longer need to be thought of, Milton himself gives no sign of making that judgment. The wrath of Dante's redeemed may disturb the reader; it does not disturb their own joy in Dante's Heaven, and apparently did not disturb Milton. He could assign it at the right moment to his angels; and making joy the dominant note in his own Heaven, he could yet draw many of the signs of that joy from the life of bliss that is detailed in Dante's *Paradiso* more explicitly than in any other poem.

The Earthly Paradise

From Dante's Earthly Paradise Milton drew far more than phrases and descriptive details; but even the correspondences Todd and Kuhns noted between *Purgatorio* 28 and *Paradise Lost* IV are impressive. Whenever Milton recurs to the Eden theme, the Dantean echoes recur. Thus Eve among the flowers in Book IX (425–432,455–460) recalls Matilda in a like setting and engaged in a like activity (*Purg.* 28.37ff.). But fair ladies tending gardens do not of themselves make an Eden, nor does a rural scene however idyllic. What Milton's Earthly Paradise chiefly shares with Dante's is the concept of a place from which man might rise naturally to Heaven. The Dantean idea could be summed up in the words of Milton's *Reason of Church-Government* where he considers "which way will lead man best to this hill top of sanctity and goodness above which there is no higher ascent but to the love of God" (Yale I, p. 842). In its paradigmatic function, however, Milton's Eden has even more in common with Dante's *Paradiso*.

For Dante the Earthly Paradise is the "place chosen for *nest* of the human race" (*Purg.* 28.77–78), and in that sense the "place made as proper" to it, so designed by the creator:

> The highest Good . . .
>> made man good and for goodness, and gave
>> this place to him as an earnest of eternal peace.
>>> (28.91–93)

Dante and Milton

For Milton too Eden is the home designed for man, even more closely linked with Heaven since it is

> A Heaven on Earth; for blissful Paradise
> Of God the Garden was, by him in the East
> Of Eden planted.   (*P.L.* IV.208–210)

From this Eden too man was intended to rise to Heaven (*P.L.* VII.155–161; V.493–500). As homes for fledgling humanity, both Edens offer every delight to the senses. Indeed, Puritans may misread them as too sensuous. But they offer delight not to the senses alone: Adam and Eve have intellectual and artistic employments, and exercise all their faculties with delight, working at the pleasant art of landscape gardening, entertaining an angelic visitor, hearing the music of the "spiritual creatures" who walk the earth, and conversing with each other. If the emphasis in Eden falls on sensuous pleasures, Milton's Heaven delights the senses as fully, though with less emphasis because other faculties have wider scope. In their lives as in their natures, angel and man in *Paradise Lost* differ "but in degree, of kind the same." The joys of Eden are more largely of the senses than those of Heaven proportionally, not absolutely.

The life that was to have been led in Dante's Earthly Paradise is less clearly defined, but what remains in the setting implies a like emphasis on pleasure for sight, smell, and hearing, accompanied by imaginative, intellectual, and social activity. The brevity of Adam's stay according to Dante—a mere six hours—makes it possible to say little more than that the lost garden *would* have been a happy nest for man (*Par.* 26.139–142). In the scheme of the *Commedia* it has a different use. As the goal achieved by the pilgrim after his purgatorial ascent, it is the scene for his parting from Virgil, his reunion with Beatrice, and his witnessing in the form of a pageant the whole wretched history of the relations between church and empire—after which he is fully prepared to rise to the stars. Little of this could be relevant to Milton's Eden, the chief scene of *Paradise Lost*, or to the action there. The time for dwelling in Eden is extended; and the focus shifts from the garden irrevocably lost to the kind of life that could be led there, as a pattern for the kind of life man might lead even now. Milton designs his earthly Paradise to arouse not simply a nostalgia, but a yearning such as Dante wishes to arouse only for his Paradiso. The difference is instructive. The "Paradise within" that Adam is to regain and that Christ will re-establish, corresponds to the life of this lost garden; the Paradiso to which man may ascend from the lost garden is a wholly other world.

Eden as well as Heaven thus has an exemplary value in *Paradise Lost* such as only Heaven has in the *Commedia;* hence Milton's stress on the likeness of angel and prelapsarian man. Like man, the angels have bodies and senses, only more perfect than man's:

> Spirits . . . live throughout
> Vital in every part . . .
> All Heart they live, all Head, all Eye, all Ear,
> All Intellect, all Sense, and as they please,
> They Limb themselves, and color, shape or size
> Assume, as likes them best, condense or rare.
> (VI.344–345, 350–353)

In the perfection though not in the mutability, they resemble the saints of *Paradiso* as they will be after the Last Judgment, when they have assumed their celestial bodies (*Par.* 14.43–60), rather than the incorporeal, purely intelligential substances of Dante's angelic hierarchies. That eventual embodiment of the redeemed, according to *Paradiso* 7.145–148, is to restore to them such "human flesh" as "the first parents" had. Dante's

Heaven thus again corresponds in some sort not only to
Milton's Heaven, but to his Heaven on Earth.

Significant features also link Eden with the summit of Dante's
purgatorial mount. Virgil in his farewell speech to his pupil
bids him:

> now take thy pleasure for guide. . . .
> Free, upright, and whole is thy will, and 'twere a fault
> not to act according to its prompting.
>
> (Purg. 27.131,140–141)

The assurance, as it turns out, is somewhat premature; it cannot
hold until Dante has crossed and drunk of both Lethe and
Eunoe. But the meaning is clear: freedom is the first condition
for true paradise; and given a healthy taste, pleasure is the
right guide. The two features are notable in the life of Milton's
Eden. Save for the one easy prohibition, as Eve puts it to the
serpent,

> . . . we live
> Law to ourselves, our Reason is our Law.
>
> (P.L. IX.653–654)

The assertion is so emphatic that we need not urge it as a
notable aspect of the Edenic life: the upright reason and will
of perfect man is his law, he needs no other. Concomitantly,
the healthy pleasure of perfect man can be his guide. Dante's
words for the Edenic state, "honest laughter and sweet play"
("onesto riso e dolce gioco," *Purg.* 28.96), echo in Adam's
defense to Eve of their interrupting their gardening with

> . . . this sweet intercourse
> Of looks and smiles, for smiles from Reason flow,
> To brute deni'd, and are of Love the food,
> Love not the lowest end of human life.
> For not to irksome toil, but to delight
> He made us, and delight to Reason join'd.
>
> (IX.238–243)

(The smile that feeds love is itself a main theme in Dante's praise of Beatrice.) It is only after the fall, when Eden has been lost, that pleasure and good, like other seemings and realities, are dissociated. Then Michael must admonish Adam:

> Judge not what is best
> By pleasure, though to Nature seeming meet.
> *(P.L.* XI.603–604)

When the taste has been vitiated, delight is no longer a safe guide to real good as it was in Eden, where pleasure itself was an index of perfection.

More important to the scheme of the *Commedia*, the regained garden becomes the setting for Dante's reunion with Beatrice. Clearly all the literature of romance, as well as the story in Genesis 1–3, has determined that the most idyllic garden is ideal only if in it one is united with the beloved. But the meaning of that union for Dante, unlike any that Genesis or the romances had foreseen, is not to be known in the Earthly Paradise. Chided, accepted, instructed, he must be led through all the realms of Paradiso before Beatrice is properly his; and then he will be far more hers. We have obviously reached a point of divergence between Dante and Milton. The love of Adam and Eve, the dominant feature of Milton's Eden, has little in common with Dante's worship of Beatrice or even with Beatrice's benevolence toward Dante.

Although it was as the "famous renowner of Beatrice" that Dante first delighted Milton, by the time he wrote *Paradise Lost* his view of that celebrated devotion had apparently changed, and with it his view of what constitutes for man a perfect love, life, and paradise. The three are inseparable. Beatrice, as the personification of Beauty, arrives in the Earthly Paradise only to lead Dante from it. Eve, as the domestic companion Adam asks for, is bestowed on him to make his Eden complete. For all her beauty, Eve gathers to herself rather the "onesto riso e dolce gioco" of Dante's concept than the character of the lady who arrives in the processional chariot of *Purgatorio*. As Hatzfeld noted,[1] the very appearance of Beatrice rather than Christ at the climactic moment (30.19–33) is intended to astonish by defeating expectation: "Benedictus qui venis" hails the lordly lady who will proclaim, "Guardami ben: ben son, ben son Beatrice." She could have no place in Milton's Eden. When Adam needs instruction, angels come. As little could an Eve help Dante at that point in his journey, when he must learn the meaning of his lost love, and by returning to it gain his ascent to the stars.

Eve is Adam's wife, and Milton's concern in first presenting them is to define the ideal marriage as well as the ideal man and woman. Eve's subordination is to Adam, and it does not signify a general subordination of women to men any more than Beatrice's relation to Dante signifies a general subordination of men to women. Other women in the *Commedia* are not thus exalted; and Eve's sons, we must suppose, were not to be her superiors. Some of the misattributions of woman-worship to Dante and woman-subjection to Milton come from misconstruing a particular bond into a universal relation between the sexes. Milton is as far from thinking every man fit to be every Eve's "head and guide" as Dante is from thinking every woman fit to adorn the chariot in which Beatrice arrives. Eve represents womankind in so far as most women would prefer a relation like hers with Adam—as undoubtedly most husbands also would prefer an Eve. A Beatrice on the domestic scene might be overwhelming. But clearly Beatrice does not belong on the domestic scene. She is the guide to Heaven, Eve the helpmeet on earth.

"Joy and love" is the leitmotiv of Milton's Eden, and a main theme of his poem is "without love no happiness." "Luce ed

[1] "The Art of Dante's *Purgatorio*," *SP* 49 (1952), 25–47.

amore" is the repeated phrase of *Paradiso*, and "without light no happiness" might summarize its teaching. This difference, deeply rooted in each poem, implies other differences. We may conveniently localize them in *Paradiso* 28, from which Milton borrows a number of phrases, each time with a marked change. Deliberate or not, the changes measure his divergence from Dante.

The divergences begin almost at once with the line "quella che imparadisa la mia mente" (28.3) echoed in Satan's phrase for Adam and Eve "Imparadis't in one another's arms/ The happier Eden" (IV.506–507). In spite of Satan's leering jealousy, Milton himself would have approved the phrase and what it implies. By itself the shift might mean nothing; but at once *Paradiso* 28 introduces a point of light which will prove to be the center of the universe, the triune God to whom Dante's vision arrives at the grand climax of his poem in Canto 33:

> a point I saw which rayed forth light so keen,
>   needs must the vision that it flameth on be
>   closed because of its strong poignancy;
> and whatever star from here appeareth smallest,
>   were seen a moon neighboured with it, as star
>   with star is neighboured.   (28.16–21)

The passage surely suggested to Milton Satan's first view of the stellar universe:

> This pendant world, in bigness as a Star
> Of smallest Magnitude close by the Moon.
>   (II.1052–1053)

The point of light which will expand and change as it is approached until it assumes another appearance altogether, the collocation of smallest star and moon to suggest the infinitesimal point of light—such a correspondence cannot have arisen by chance. But Milton has transferred Dante's figure for God to the newly created universe, even shifting Beatrice's words, "Da quel punto/ dipende il cielo, e tutta la natura" (41–42), so that the emphasis falls on "this pendant world" suspended "in a golden chain" from Heaven, rather than on God, from whom all Heaven and nature depend.

Now clearly for Milton as well as for Dante, God is the light from which all else proceeds, and for him too, love imparadises the lover's mind. The reason for his shift of the two phrases to the stellar universe and to Adam and Eve embracing emerges in his revision of another passage in the same canto.

At lines 55–56 Dante, wondering that the smallest circle around the point of light should consist of the seraphic rulers of the largest celestial sphere, asks Beatrice why "l' esemplo/ e l'esemplare non vanno d' un modo," and Beatrice not only accepts the assumption but indeed asserts that the earthly copy and the heavenly pattern are opposites. Milton was concerned to assert the contrary. As we have noted, Raphael, preparing to tell Adam of the war in Heaven, hesitates at first, uncertain how to relate "To human sense th' invisible exploits/ Of warring Spirits" (V.565–566), and then deals with his own uncertainty:

> . . . what surmounts the reach
> Of human sense, I shall delineate so,
> By lik'ning spiritual to corporal forms,
> As may express them best, though what if Earth
> Be but the shadow of Heav'n, and things therein
> Each to other like, more than on Earth is thought?
> (571–576)

Of course this is prelapsarian man and earth of which he speaks; yet regardless of all the changes that are to occur after the fall, in human sense and the earthly scene, Milton intended Raphael's words to hold for the present too—if only because he meant that his readers too should understand what follows. The doctrine is of utmost importance: the earthly copy is not the inverse, but the very image of the heavenly pattern. In his view, to assert what Dante asserts is to disparage earth in a mistaken effort to exalt Heaven.

The humanist vein in Milton's thought is patent. Here, in his reading of *Paradiso* 28, he presumably discerned in Dante an opposite tendency. Yet the phrase on "l' esemplo e l' esemplare" has no such general application in the *Commedia* as Milton's contrary statement does in *Paradise Lost;* it applies specifically to the relation between the angelic hierarchies and their spheres.[2] Here too, however, Milton differed from Dante.

Beatrice explains that the circle closest to the point of light must rule the largest sphere since

> "Greater excellence hath purpose to work greater weal;
> and greater weal is comprehended in the greater body
> if that the parts be equally consummate. . . .
> thou wilt see a wondrous agreement of greater unto
> more and smaller unto less in every heaven with its
> Intelligence."
>
> (67–69,76–78)

Raphael, in Book VIII, asserts just the opposite to Adam:

> . . . consider first, that Great
> Or Bright infers not Excellence: the Earth,
> Though, in comparison of Heav'n, so small,
> Nor glistering, may of solid good contain
> More plenty than the Sun that barren shines.
>
> (VIII.90–94)

If size and goodness did correspond, the earth would be in danger

[2] But cf. Beatrice in *Par.* 4.67–68: "For our justice to appear unjust in mortal eyes is argument of faith." Milton would not have approved any such even momentary dissociation of heavenly and earthly justice.

of being little prized. Again the thesis has no general application for Dante; it concerns only the spheres and the angelic hierarchies. But again Milton diverged from Dante. According to the system of Dionysius the pseudo-Areopagite which Beatrice is expounding, the nine orders of angels who rule the spheres through which Dante has ascended—realms greater in proportion to their greater goodness—are more greatly good in proportion to their proximity to God.

Milton chose to disregard the Dionysian hierarchies, deliberately avoiding questions of rank among the angels. Only Hell boasts a caste system, with its division into nobility and commoners (I.789–797). When God addresses Heaven,

> Hear all ye Angels, Progeny of Light,
> Thrones, Dominations, Princedoms, Virtues, Powers,
> (V.600–601)

the names indicate no hierarchical arrangement, as is clear from Abdiel's echo of the lines (V.837–841). But when Satan adopts the same words in his rebellion-inspiring speech, he attaches a new meaning of caste and privilege to them:

> Thrones, Dominations, Princedoms, Virtues, Powers,
> If these magnific Titles yet remain
> Not merely titular. (V.772–774)

For the republican Milton, in God's view angels are all the "Progeny of Light," their differences minor; in Satan's view, the titles count. There are distinctions among the heavenly beings, of course, and Satan is clever enough to avail himself of them when he assumes the disguise of a cherub so as to get information from Uriel. Still, properly, according to any system, a cherub is of the second highest order, not one of the lower angels. Yet Milton deliberately gives to the term its associations with youth rather than with angelic status, and no less deliberately has Satan, ever conscious of rank, address Uriel as "Brightest Seraph" while Uriel simply calls the supposed cherub by the generic name "Fair Angel" (III.667, 694). The whole scene, though it involves the courtesies appropriate between lowlier and "superior Spirits," is played in terms of youth and age rather than of caste.

So too Gabriel is named "Chief of th' Angelic Guards" of Eden, but those under his command are called simply "Th' unarmed Youth of Heav'n" (IV.550,552). It would be impossible to tell from the conversation between Gabriel and Uriel which one, if either, is the superior spirit (IV.561–588). But Satan insists with Ithuriel and Zephon on their inferior status (IV.827–831), and perhaps with the intention of adding insult to insult calls Gabriel "Proud limitary Cherub" (971). Milton himself is content to name Gabriel "the warrior Angel"; of so little consequence, to his way of thinking, is rank to any but the Satanic mind. Raphael does indeed explain to Adam that the angels arrived at the heavenly council:

> Under thir Hierarchs in orders bright
> Ten thousand thousand Ensigns high advanc'd,
> Standards and Gonfalons [which] . . .
> . . . for distinction serve
> Of Hierarchies, of Orders, and Degrees;
> Or in thir glittering Tissues bear imblaz'd
> Holy Memorials, acts of Zeal and Love
> Recorded eminent.   (V.587–594)

And he describes them standing "in Orbs/ Of circuit inexpressible . . . / Orb within Orb" (594–596). The passage takes from *Paradiso* 28 the orbs and the orders, but not the correlation of rank and worth. Denial could hardly be more explicit. Out of a like commitment to republican principles, Milton transfers to Hell the idea of a secret court that Dante uses for Heaven. The "aula più segreta, co' suoi Conti" of

Paradiso 25.42 is God's; in *Paradise Lost* I.790ff., the language of Court and Lords sitting in "secret conclave" is used of the council of Hell. The point is perhaps minor. Milton, as well as Dante, thought God's ultimate purposes unknowable; and Dante had as little regard as Milton for secrecy in human affairs. Under no illusion about the correspondence of rank with worth, of size with goodness, in this world, he carefully distinguished their relation in the heavenly model and in the earthly copy.

But all this leads to a doctrine important in the *Commedia*, from which Milton differed no less sharply. Beatrice explains:

> And thou shouldst know that all have their delight in
>   measure as their sight sinketh more deep into the
>   truth wherein every intellect is stilled.
> Hence may be seen how the being blessed is founded
>   on the act that seeth, not that which loveth, which
>   after followeth;
> and the measure of sight is the merit which grace be-
>   getteth and the righteous will; and thus from rank
>   to rank the progress goeth.

(28.106–114)

Although the word "amore" dominates *Paradiso*, vision is primary; it is the source of love, and the great aim of the journey. So in *Paradiso* 14.40–42, the ardor is consequent upon the vision; in *Paradiso* 5.7–9, the seeing of the light kindles love; in 26.28–30, it is again the understanding of good that "accende amore"; climactically, in 30.40–42 the very sequence of phrase defines the doctrine of the whole *Commedia* on vision and love:

> luce intellettual piena d' amore,
>   amor di vero ben pien di letizia,
>   letizia che trascende ogni dolzore.

First light or vision, then love, then happiness, so that the three are virtually interchangeable. Faith may be the evidence of things unseen, but love is the effect of the seeing. (Cf. *Par.* 1.120; 5.9; 10.83–84; 13.79; 14.37–42; 27.112; 28.54; 30.14ff.; 31.27.)

This is unlike Milton's first premise on knowledge and love, explicitly recorded in Book I, Chapter 1 of his *Christian Doctrine:* "Obedience and love are always the best guide to knowledge, and often lead the way. . . ." Love is so primary that it is itself the spring of happiness, as Raphael tells Adam:

> Let it suffice thee that thou know'st
> Us happy, and without Love no happiness.
> (VIII.620–621)

The statement clarifies the theme of "love and joy" which dominates *Paradise Lost* as "luce ed amore" dominates *Paradiso*. With much of Dante's doctrine of love Milton agreed, both largely taking their views, directly or indirectly, from Plato. But here Milton reconsiders. If vision, light, understanding must come first, and love and joy be the consequence, then joy must wait. But if obedience and love are the guides even to vision and understanding, man can have joy here and now. Milton will not put off the *summum bonum*, or make its prerequisite a grasp of things impossible to man.

Now Dante in fact gives understanding primacy only in the highest realm. Near the middle of *Paradiso*, in the Cacciaguida episode, the visitor alludes to the great difference between mortal and redeemed man in this respect:

> "Love and intelligence [*l'affetto e il senno*],
> soon as the prime equality appeared to you,
> became of equal poise to each of you . . .
> But unto mortals, will and instrument [*voglia ed argomento*], for reasons manifest to you, unequally are feathered in their wings."
> (15.73–75,79–81)

He assumes that here the "heart" is the better guide (82–84), and his assumption is presumably correct: the relations of love and understanding are necessarily unlike for earthly and heavenly beings—that is, before and after the beatific vision. Milton abjures any such dichotomy, taking what is familiar on earth as the true image of the highest possibilities of created life and man's sole path to the Creator. Man and nature have indeed been tainted since the fall, but also—and even in advance—redeemed. In essence, with only the taint and nothing of what is human and natural removed, they are still, for Milton, as they were at their creation, far more like the "spiritual forms" of Heaven than is commonly supposed. The "esemplo" is not the inverse of the "esemplare," but its shadow. And Paradise is to be reconstituted on earth, even if on an earth that has become "waste Wilderness," no longer a garden

> Chos'n by the sovran Planter, when he fram'd
> All things to man's delightful use.
>
> (IV.691–692)

It is telling that in Eve's nightmare the flight above the earth which in Dante's dream in *Purgatorio* stands for the purifying ascent toward Heaven becomes (V.86–89) the symbol of unloving disobedience, and that for fallen Adam and Eve the joy of Dante's actual ascent in *Paradiso* becomes a delusion:

> As with new Wine intoxicated both
> They swim in mirth, and fancy that they feel
> Divinity within them breeding wings
> Wherewith to scorn the Earth.
>
> (IX.1008–1011)

It is also telling that Adam's reference to the earth as "a spot, a grain" (VIII.17), which brings sharp reproof from Raphael (VIII.90–94), is the very view to which Beatrice directs Dante in *Paradiso* 22.151–154 and 27.79–87. "To scorn the Earth," to belittle the human condition, is for Milton to take a grave misstep. Not by seeing earth as "a spot, a grain," or presuming a Heaven wholly unlike it, nor by postponing human joy until he attains superhuman comprehension, can man fulfill the promise of his humanity. For Milton, we do better not to ask a home in Heaven until we have learned to keep house on earth. For Dante, postlapsarian earth can never again be man's true home.

When Dante back in Canto 27 looks down from the circle of the fixed stars to behold "il sito/ di questa aiuola" (85–86), this little earth, and back again to Beatrice, he makes two observations that are remarkably like those for which Raphael rebukes Adam in Book VIII. The first, which is further elaborated in *Paradiso* 28, concerns the triviality of earth compared with the stellar universe; the second (like Adam's confession of disturbance in his love for Eve) concerns Dante's delight in the beauty of his lady:

> . . . whatsoever food nature or art e'er made, to
> catch the eyes and so possess the mind, be it
> in human flesh, be it in pictures,
> if all united, would seem naught towards the
> divine delight which glowed upon me when I
> turned me to her smiling face.   (27.91–96)

The whole speech of Adam to Raphael in Book VIII, contrasting "in all things else delight indeed" with the "commotion strange" produced by "the charm of Beauty's powerful glance" (521–559), reads like a reduction of Dante's lines:

> . . . so absolute she seems
> And in herself complete, so well to know
> Her own, that what she wills to do or say,
> Seems wisest, virtuousest, discreetest, best;
> All higher knowledge in her presence falls
> Degraded, Wisdom in discourse with her
> Loses discount'nanc't, and like folly shows.
>   (547–553)

And it will not do to say that Adam is speaking of his wife, Dante of his divinely appointed guide through Heaven, since Milton has Raphael, even in the course of his rebuke, make human love the stairway to "heav'nly Love" (589–592). It is a difference in doctrine that makes Milton think praise of any person as the one thing that matters an error at any stage. At any stage—for Milton certainly read *Paradiso* through to the end, and learned that Dante withdraws his gaze from Beatrice to fix it on the source of her—and of all—beauty. Yet in some sense Milton deliberately revalues two chief values of the *Commedia:* earth matters more, and the best-loved person less, to man's full growth. For him as for Dante, the developed power of loving rightly is the source and end of human joy; but for him, right love has a different meaning.

For Milton love entails responsibility, a care for the well-being of the beloved; that is why Raphael rebukes Adam for turning Eve into an idol. For Dante love is a beholding. *Vision* is the key-word of the *Commedia*. What originates as an act of seeing rises by degrees into intellectual insight. Where sight ends and insight begins it is impossible to say: in some measure the first always signifies the second. Thus, for example, still in Canto 28 of *Paradiso*, the reference to Beatrice's "beauteous eyes whence love had made the noose to capture me" (11–12) accords with the use of "veder" a little later for the seraphs and cherubs:

> So swift they follow their withies that they may liken
> them unto the point as most they may; and they
> succeed in measure as they are sublime in vision.
>
> (100–102)

The sight of Beatrice's eyes drew Dante on into insight, as the angels' sight of God is their insight into his nature. The greater nearness to God, which Milton deliberately blurs in Raphael's phrase "nearer to him plac't or *nearer tending*" (*P.L.* V.476), for Dante always signifies a greater power of vision, and hence of love. But for Milton, the greater resemblance of Adam to God involves the greater responsibility of his protective relation to Eve, as that of Raphael and Gabriel involves their protective relation to Adam and Eve, or that of Uriel his protective relation to the seeming cherub. Clearly Dante too is concerned to show the more illuminated in helpful relation to the less: all the celestial court, not Beatrice alone, undertake to instruct the visitor so that he too may mount to the beatific vision. But the helpful relation is not of first moment for Dante. Milton's revisions of Dante on these matters are thus presumably intended. When his words resemble Dante's, they are not mere echoings but a careful rethinking of Dante's thought, assimilating or discarding what accorded or jarred with his own. His purpose in *Paradise Lost* is doctrinal, and his awareness of Dante as a doctrinal poet consistently guides his use of the *Commedia*.

The doctrine of Dante, as of the Platonist Milton, starts from something like the Platonic stairway of love in the *Symposium*. Adam paraphrases Raphael's teaching:

> Love thou say'st
> Leads up to Heav'n, is both the way and guide.
> (VIII.612–613)

Dante uses the same image of the stair when he has Thomas Aquinas say:

> the ray of grace,—whereat true love is kindled,
> and then doth grow, by loving,
> multifold—doth so glow in thee as to conduct thee
> up upon that stairway, which, save to reascend,
> no one descendeth.   (*Par.* 10.83–87)

Love draws Dante up the stair, increasing as his vision grows more perfect; but his sight, and hence his love, of Beatrice is truest when he sees her back in her place in the great rose of Heaven, returning her gaze to the "eterna fontana" of all vision, as he then prepares to turn his own (*Par.* 31.73–93). *Paradiso* 10.59–63 briefly prefigures what will happen after the final vision. As Momigliano[3] puts it in his note on the passage, "The pilgrim's ardent abandonment in God eclipses Beatrice; Beatrice's smile of joy on seeing Dante rapt in God draws Dante without detaching him from the thought of God." The consciousness of her smile momentarily divides him from himself and God, and such dividedness will end only with his final vision.

For Milton, as for Dante, God is the supreme object of all love. So John proclaims in the examination scene: "Of thy loves keep for God the sovereign one" (*Par.* 26.48; cf. 10.59–61); and Raphael urges Adam, near the end of their discourse, "Love, but first of all/ Him whom to love is to obey" (*P.L.* VIII.633–634). But the meaning of the sovereign love is not the same for the two: in Dante it finally absorbs every lesser love; in Milton it constantly supports and sustains them. A comparable distinction marks the vision of God in the *Commedia* and *Paradise Lost:* for Milton God is the light given rather for us to see by than to fix our gaze upon, as Dante finally for one moment, and the redeemed in Paradise eternally, fix their gaze, seeing all else within that light. For Dante, because difference in degree constitutes a difference in kind as well, the life not only of his angels but of his human redeemed is finally a life to be prepared for but not to be lived on earth. But Raphael's whole exposition is designed to assure Adam that man and angel are more alike than different. Perfect man in Eden eats and drinks, marries, works at landscape

[3] See the note on *Par.* 10.59–63 in *La Divina Commedia*, ed. Attilio Momigliano (Florence, 1946).

gardening, rests in the cool of an arbor from the midday sun, sleeps and wakes—in short, does as imperfect man does, with the great difference that he knows neither evil nor pain nor death. And not only perfect man engages in such ordinary human doings, but angels as well. Milton indeed uses his angels, along with Adam and Eve in their perfection, to assert with all possible emphasis that there is nothing amiss in the human condition. Thus Raphael corrects Adam's mistaken notion that human food is unfit for angels. One great theme of *Paradise Lost* is that nothing human is too lowly to form part of the highest existence conceivable by man. In *Paradiso*, as in other parts of the *Commedia*, simple human activities appear often, but generally in simile and metaphor, as figures of something else, not themselves part of the life of Paradise. In Milton's Eden, man with all his familiar attributes and activities, only fully humanized, can not only live but even converse with God. As for the supposed need to transcend earth and the human condition expounded in the *Commedia*, Milton would evidently have declared, as Raphael does to Adam:

> Oft-times nothing profits more
> Than self-esteem, grounded on just and right . . .
> (*P.L.* VIII.571–572)

Earth in *Paradise Lost* is not the mere proving ground, but the very shadow of Heaven here and now.

Which of the two poetic paradigms puts the greater burden on man? It may be that to assure fallen man that he can regain Eden here if he will only learn to guide his life in generosity, humility, and due self-esteem, in admiration of the admirable and scorn of the contemptible—it may be that this is to ask too much of imperfect man. It may be that to tell him that he can train himself now for the communion of saints, but that he cannot expect its joys in this world, is to postpone too much the fulfillments by which humanity grows. Either counsel is a counsel of perfection, such as Utopias generally prescribe; and either means a burden as well as a promise. Chateaubriand casually remarked that in presenting Heaven Milton errs out of timidity, Dante out of fatigue (p. 294); but in fact both the *Commedia* and *Paradise Lost* present their Heaven and their Eden in order to call us to a courage and an effort before which the faint-hearted quail. Clearly both poems must offer not only a goal, but also a way.

VI

The Purgatorial Way

APART from Kuhns (1898), who listed a number of parallel phrases, and Herford (1924), who observed a relation between Virgil's climactic speech to Dante (*Purg.* 27.140ff.) and Michael's to Adam (*P.L.* XII.575ff.), James Holly Hanford has been alone in remarking Milton's interest in *Purgatorio*. In "The Chronology of Milton's Private Studies" he commented on the entry in the *Commonplace Book*, fol. 197:

The Dante entry in the *Paradise Lost* hand is from the *Purgatorio*, whereas those made in the Horton period were from the *Inferno* and the *Paradiso*. The two last named books alone are referred to in *Reason of Church Government* (1641), although the authority of Dante on the separation of Church and State is more clearly stated in the passage here copied out from the *Purgatorio*. Can it be that a discriminating Puritanism made Milton pass over the second part of Dante's epic in his first reading? In reality the human atmosphere of Purgatory is far more congenial with Milton's thought than that of either Hell or Paradise, and it is interesting to find him rereading the second book of the *Commedia*, perhaps in the very period when he was undertaking the actual composition of *Paradise Lost* (1658). His appreciation had already been recorded in the exquisite close of the sonnet to Harry Lawes.   (PMLA 36 [1921], 304–305)

Clearly we have not found *Inferno* and *Paradiso* uncongenial to Milton, but *Purgatorio* does have a larger relation to *Paradise Lost* inasmuch as both concentrate on the earthly scene. It is the relevance of Dante's work that determines its impression on Milton's, not some restrictive impulse.

Any of the three parts of the *Commedia* can be taken as subsuming the others both in doctrine and through allusion; *Purgatorio* subsumes *Inferno* and *Paradiso* in yet another fashion, by using matter appropriate to both as illustrations of the wrong and the right ways at each level of the Mount. Further, it treats paradigmatically of human affairs as they could lead toward Inferno—except as the saving impulse returns them, if they have not gone too far astray, toward Paradiso. Milton employs a similar paradigm in the earthly scene of *Paradise Lost*.

Because Purgatory is located on the antipodal surface of the earth, according to Dante's invention, it has recognizable weather, times of day, sights of sun, shadow, stars, vegetation, and landscape—seashore, valley, mountain, stream, and plain. So too Milton's Eden, where every sight is familiar, with only such difference as "without thorn the rose" implies. More important, the people of the Mount and its environs are thoroughly human, differing from mortal mankind only in their assured escape from ultimate disaster—just as Adam and Eve are human even before the fall, in their immortality and perfection, as well as after they have been assured of their ultimate restoration.

Verbal echoes suggest that Milton recognized the relation between the Edenic valley of *Purgatorio* 7–8 and the Earthly Paradise of Cantos 28–33—the one preceding, the other following the seven steps of the purgation itself. One is a foretaste, unsatisfying because it keeps the negligent from moving on; the other is a fulfillment, and sends the healed spirit upward. Milton uses both in his Eden. The earlier scene provides an evening piece (8.1–6; *P.L.* IV.598ff.) with something like the relaxed atmosphere of Eden, a fit background for a dream. The resemblance between the pattern of the dream itself and Eve's in *Paradise Lost* suggests that Milton recognized the

Purgatorial Mount as relevant to the life of Eden. And this idyllic valley has its serpent:

> On that side where the little vale hath no rampart,
>   was a snake, perchance such as gave to Eve the
>   bitter food.
> Through the grass and the flowers came the evil reptile,
>   turning round now and again its head to its back,
>   licking like a beast that sleeks itself.
>   (*Purg.* 8.97–102)

Surely Milton recalled the passage when he wrote in Book IX:

> Such ambush hid among sweet Flow'rs and Shades.
>   . . . the Fiend,
> Mere Serpent in appearance, forth was come . . .
> In Bow'r and Field he sought, where any tuft
> Of Grove or Garden-Plot more pleasant lay . . .
>   . . . Oft he bow'd
> His turret Crest, and sleek enamell'd Neck,
> Fawning, and lick'd the ground whereon she trod.
>   (*P.L.* IX.408–526)

Other verbal parallels may be of less importance. We need not decide how much the Siren of Dante's second dream, first foul, then fair, then foul again (*Purg.* 19), contributed to the figure of Sin in *Paradise Lost*—who to Satan first appeared foul, then fair, then foul again, only to be later hailed as his "Fair Daughter" (II.741–745, 759–765; X.384). The proem celebrating the transition from Inferno to a realm of light (*Purg.* 1.1–9) contains matter, as we have seen, related to all four proems of *Paradise Lost*. The dawn imagery of Canto 1,

> Sweet hue of orient sapphire . . . was gathering
>   on the clear forehead of the sky, pure even to
>   the first circle. . . .
> The heavens seemed to rejoice in their flames,
>   (1.13–15,25)

may have no more than the natural enough word "orient" in

common with the dawn imagery of Book V,

> Now Morn her rosy steps in th' Eastern Clime
> Advancing, sow'd the Earth with Orient Pearl,
>
> (V.1–2)

and the natural enough suggestion of rejoicing in common with that of Book IX:

> Now whenas sacred Light began to dawn
> In Eden on the humid Flow'rs, that breath'd
> Thir morning incense, when all things that breathe,
> From th' Earth's great Altar send up silent praise
> To the Creator . . .   (IX.192–196)

In *Purgatorio* angels fill offices for man like those of Raphael and Michael in *Paradise Lost*. The six-winged Raphael (V.275–285) may recall *Purgatorio* 29.94, as well as the Book of Ezekiel. And fallen Adam's inability to see Michael's approach as he had seen Raphael's, "another Morn/Ris'n on mid-noon" (V.310–311), resembles Virgil's comment to Dante in *Purgatorio* 15, "Thou drawest darkness from true light" (66); Adam's tainted vision sees the glorious apparition as "Darkness ere Day's mid-course" (XI.204). Earlier, Adam's account of the two states of trance on his first day in life, one when he was led into Eden, the other when Eve was taken from his side, recalls a number of passages in *Purgatorio*. Adam explains:

> My earthly by his Heav'nly overpower'd, . . .
> As with an object that excels the sense,
> Dazzl'd and spent, sunk down, and sought repair
> Of sleep . . .
> Mine eyes he clos'd, but op'n left the Cell
> Of Fancy my internal sight, by which
> Abstract as in a trance methought I saw,
> Though sleeping where I lay, and saw the shape
> Still glorious before whom awake I stood.
>
> (*P.L.* VIII.453–464)

Dante similarly relates a trance:

> There meseemed to be suddenly caught up in a
> dream of ecstasy . . .   (15.85–86)

He describes among several waking experiences of overpower-
ing brightness one in which

> . . . a light . . . was there, so bright that
> it vanquished me, and look upon it I could not.
>   (27.59–60)

He associates a sudden brightness with a reference to Eve
(29.16–24), and details the effect of a dazzling angelic figure
(9.81). He also elaborates a trancelike vision made possible by
a light derived from heaven:

> O fantasy, that at times dost so snatch us out of our-
>   selves that we are conscious of naught, even though
>   a thousand trumpets sound about us,
> who moves thee, if the senses set naught before thee?
>   A light moves thee which takes its form in heaven,
>   of itself, or by a will that sendeth it down. . . .
> and here my mind was so restrained within itself,
>   that from outside came naught which was then
>   received by it.   (17.13–18,22–24)

Here too the fancy, directly impressed by divine illumination,
shows a truth that the physical eye would be unable to sustain.

Milton plays with the theme in yet another way when the
Son appears on the battlefield to end the war in Heaven: what
to the loyal angels is a glorious apparition, to Satan and his
rebels is in more than one sense an unendurable sight (*P.L.*
VI.791ff.; cf. V.664–665). But the use of light, vision, and
darkness is so frequent in both the *Commedia* and *Paradise Lost*
that we can seldom relate any one passage from Milton exclusively to any one from Dante.

Dante and Milton

The life of Eden also contains reminiscences of *Purgatorio*. Thus Adam's explanation to Eve:

> Millions of spiritual Creatures walk the Earth
> Unseen . . .:
>   . . . how often . . . have we heard
> Celestial voices,   (*P.L.* IV.677–682)

resembles the phrasing of *Purgatorio:*

> e verso noi volar furon sentiti,
>   non però visti, spiriti, parlando
> (and, flying towards us were heard, but not seen,
>   spirits, speaking).   (*Purg.* 13.25–26)

Again, when Adam uses faculty psychology to explain Eve's nightmare (*P.L.* V.100–113), the language may be reminiscent of *Purgatorio* 4.1–12 and 25.58–78, as well as of their common sources. Or Adam wiping Eve's tears (V.129ff.) may recall Virgil performing a like office for Dante (*Purg.* 1.127–129). But such parallels, together with many others that could be remarked, have little bearing on the chief correspondences between *Purgatorio* and *Paradise Lost*. Again it is as a doctrinal poet that Dante made his chief impression, and specifically in his doctrine on the curative way for humanity.

The one citation from *Purgatorio* in Milton's *Commonplace Book* is of Canto 16.106–112, 127–129. Apart from his reference to the Casella episode, it is the one citation of *Purgatorio* in all his extant writing. And while it cannot be taken as necessarily the passage that interested him most, that it did interest him is suggestive. The passage comes midway in *Purgatorio*, and in a context of central explanations. The thematic material of Canto 16, with its preliminaries in Canto 15 and development in Cantos 17–18, establishes the main doctrines of *Purgatorio*.

Canto 16 opens with lines that recall Milton's as well as Dante's Hell:

> Gloom of Hell and of a night bereft of every
> planet under a meagre sky, darkened by cloud
> as much as it can be,
> made not to my sight so thick a veil, nor of a
> pile so harsh to the feel, as that smoke which
> there covered us.   (1–6)

Dante and Virgil have entered the terrace of the wrathful, and the striking association of wrath with Hell's darkness may suggest why Milton so deliberately restricted anger to the character of Hell and Satan. In any event, the image of the blind man in the following lines could not have failed to impress the blind Milton:

> Even as a blind man goeth behind his guide in order
> not to stray, and not to butt against aught that
> may do him hurt, or perchance kill him.
>   (10–12)

In the darkness Dante hears voices singing in full concord (16–21). That he hears without seeing these "spirti" (22) again recalls Adam on the celestial voices (*P.L.* IV.678–682). Then one voice, which will later identify itself as Marco Lombardo, addresses him and answers his query why virtue has deserted the world. Marco denounces the habit of blaming stellar influences, asserting at some length the doctrine of free will, charging evil leadership with responsibility for the world's going astray, and thus providing a context for the lines Milton cited in his *Commonplace Book*. The speech is a crux of the *Commedia*.

The stars may have their influence on men's affairs, but that influence cannot be strong enough to move the world "di necessitate." For man is given free will, "libero arbitrio," by God himself, and "lume . . . a bene ed a malizia," light by which to know good and evil (67–75); he is given "libero voler," which can be nurtured, and with it mind, "mente," which the stars cannot direct (76–81). Herein he is subject only to God (79–80). The cause of the world's error, then, must be in men themselves: "In voi è la cagione, in voi si cheggia" (83). The soul, issuing from God's hands, naturally turns to what is pleasing, and needs the curb of law lest it go astray in its loves (85–93). That is why man must have a "ruler who might discern at least the tower of the true city" (95–96). Man must have law, he must have a shepherd; and bad leadership is to blame for the world's ills, not the nature that has been given to man, though that can be—as it has been—corrupted by bad leadership (97–105).

Thus Marco comes to speak the lines in which, as Milton noted, Dante shows that the fusion of church and state is ruinous to both:

> Rome, that made the good world, was wont to have two suns, which made plain to sight the one road and the other; that of the world, and that of God.
> One hath quenched the other; and the sword is joined to the crook; and the one together with the other must perforce go ill. (106–112)

In fact, Marco declares, there are only three old men left in all of Lombardy who pursue the good way, and they long for death. The great source of evil is Rome's temporal power, according to the further lines that Milton quoted:

> Say henceforth, that the Church of Rome, by confounding two powers in herself, falls into the mire, and fouls herself and her burden.
> (127–129)

Such an emphasis on free will, combined with a denunciation of bad leadership and the confusion of church and state in papal Rome, would naturally be agreeable to Milton, and he surely

did not miss the beauty of Marco's lines on "l' anima sempli-
cetta" issuing from the hand of God (85–90).

The prelude to this canto, in which Marco is evidently helped
to cure his wrath by turning it against a suitable object, shows
Dante leaving the second terrace of Purgatory. There the
"splendore" who erases the *P* of envy from his brow is so
bright that he has to shield his eyes from the "soperchio
visibile" (15.15). The phrase is among many such passages in
Purgatorio and *Paradiso* that resemble Milton's famous "dark
with excessive bright" (*P.L.* III.380); probably their cumu-
lative effect rather than any one passage suggested the phrase
to him. (The line on the sun, "per soperchio sua figura vela,"
in *Purgatorio* 17.53, is another example.) But the experience
here is given emphasis (15.7–27) by Virgil's explanation that
as Dante mounts higher it will be easier for him to enjoy such
sights (28–33). Virgil's words are among the many passages
that suggest the great difference already noted between the
appearances of Raphael and of Michael to Adam. Here the
angel assures Dante that the ascent iself will be easier as he
mounts (34–36).

The pilgrims have now left the envious behind, and Virgil
uses the interval to discuss the great difference between love
of true good and desire for worldly gain. The "infinito ed
ineffabil bene" responds to all love, without diminution; indeed, the more who love well, the more good there is for all
(67–75), as Beatrice will explain more fully when Dante has
completed his Purgatorial journey (76–81). The emphatic
contrast between the goods that diminish as they are divided,
and this good, which increases as more partake of it, bespeaks
the same doctrine as the one Satan admits in his terrible self-
accusation, the doctrine of "Heav'n's free Love dealt equally
to all" (*P.L.* IV.68). One who must have pre-eminence, as
Satan must, cannot enjoy sharing equally with all, or under-

stand that he has more the more he shares. Envy, the sin that grudges another's good, is therefore naturally a chief trait of his, along with the pride from which it stems and the anger it produces. As Virgil puts it,

> Forasmuch as your desires are centred where the
> portion is lessened by partnership, envy moves
> the bellows to your sighs.   (15.49–51)

At the entrance to the ledge where he is to meet Marco Lombardo, Dante beholds in a totally new manner the examples designed to counteract anger, as "in una visione/ estatica" (85–86). In Canto 17.13–24, he is similarly to behold the deadly effects of anger with his inner eye alone—a mode of vision, as we have noted, that corresponds to Adam's trances (VIII.289–294,460–464). Here it may be significant that from Mazzoni Milton would have come to regard Dante as the poet of dreams par excellence. Trances, dreams that correspond to reality, visions that come to the inner eye alone, the poetic vision itself—these were all of interest to Milton no less than to the poet of *Purgatorio*.

In Canto 15, one of the inner visions is of the killing of St. Stephen:

> Then saw I people, kindled with the fire of anger,
> slaying a youth with stones, and ever crying out
> loudly to each other: "Kill, kill!"
> and him saw I sinking towards the ground, because
> of death, which already was weighing him down,
> but of his eyes ever made he gates unto heaven.
>   (15.106–111)

The subject resembles Adam's first chastening vision in *Paradise Lost* XI, when Michael shows him the murder of Abel by Cain, who

Smote him into the Midriff with a stone
That beat out life; he fell, and deadly pale
Groan'd out his Soul with gushing blood effus'd.
(XI.445–447)

Later he has a similar vision of Enoch, whom

. . . old and young
Exploded, and had seiz'd with violent hands,
Had not a Cloud descending snatch'd him thence.
(XI.668–670)

Like Dante's vision of St. Stephen murdered, Adam's are of the just man beset by a mob, a theme that Milton favored in the Abdiel episode (V.803ff.), here with Enoch, again with Noah (XI.719ff.), and in the whole account of Christ's atonement (XII.404ff.). He uses it again implicitly throughout *Paradise Regained* and in *Samson Agonistes;* the resemblance of his own treatment of the theme to Dante's can hardly have escaped him. And Michael's recourse to the vision as a mode of instruction may owe something to Dante's experience on the terrace of anger.

As the second night on the mountain nears, Virgil while they pause in their climb explains the scheme of Purgatory: the seven terraces for the seven capital sins are designed to eradicate perverse, defective, and excessive love (17.91ff.). Virgil's discourse not only elaborates his earlier contrast between the goods that increase and those that diminish by sharing, but also uses Marco Lombardo's account of the developing soul's need for guidance. In Canto 18, this central portion of *Purgatorio* is concluded with an analysis of love and free will (13–75), which Beatrice is to complete in *Paradiso.*

If we are here at the heart of *Purgatorio*—and, in a sense, of the entire *Commedia*—we are also at the heart of Milton's interest in Dante. It was as a love-poet that Milton first took

217

note of him, and here is the most explicit treatment of Dante's doctrine of love. The whole purport of *Purgatorio* is the search for liberty, and here is Dante's most elaborate treatment of free will. In his political writings Milton cited Dante as an ally against the temporal power of the church; and here is the ground of Dante's condemnation of that misappropriation—a major theme which the pageant in the Earthly Paradise will amplify. Like Milton, or anyone trained in classical philosopy, Dante saw politics as doubly related to ethics: first, because it is the extension into the community of the principles that should guide the private life; second—and perhaps more important—because a community that does not foster such principles publicly in fact diminishes them privately. When politics fall short of ethics, they help to destroy them. The goal of the *Commedia* is the communion of saints; but every community has a responsibility for helping its citizens toward that goal. The point cannot be overemphasized in Dante, nor for that matter in Milton. *Paradise Lost* too is a political poem—not that, as romantic misreaders supposed. Satan's dictatorship could possibly represent Milton's ideal republic, but because the relation of ethics in the private and the communal life dominated Milton's thought as it dominated Dante's.

The relation between Heaven and Eden cannot be the same in *Paradise Lost* as in the *Commedia*. Milton can show the as yet unlost paradise as a "Heav'n on Earth," a garden that might have become the home of a community like its parent Utopia (*P.L.* XI.342–346). The earthly paradise atop Mount Purgatory has no future except as the place from which the redeemed rise to heavenly communion. Eden is the chief setting of Milton's poem, a brief way station in Dante's. The two have a common meaning only as they suggest what might have been the fostering home of human nature.

In like manner, the fall and the redemption, though of course central to the theology of both Dante and Milton, cannot have the same importance in the two poems. In the *Commedia* both the crime of Adam and the vicarious atonement of Christ are accomplished facts that have shaped the universe through which Dante makes his pilgrimage. In *Paradise Lost*, the fall is anticipated through two-thirds of the poem; and the atonement, though determined in advance, is still far in the future when at the end Adam and Eve go into exile. Thus Dante's presentation in *Paradiso* of a perfect humanity ought to suggest the habits not only of Milton's angels but also of his unfallen man and woman, and *Purgatorio* what comes after the fall. For just as *Purgatorio* and *Paradiso* concern two distinct states, the one needing correction, the other only illumination, Book IX of *Paradise Lost* divides fallen from unfallen man. Before, Adam and Eve need only to develop, afterward to be corrected, changed, reformed.

Beatrice, in the terrestrial paradise, confronts the still imperfectly mended Dante with the demand,

> How didst thou deign to draw nigh the mount?
> knewest thou not that here man is happy?
> *(Purg. 30.74–75)*

The implied concept resembles God's explanation of the expulsion from Eden:

> . . . longer in that Paradise to dwell,
> The Law I gave to Nature him forbids:
> . . . I at first with two fair gifts
> Created him endow'd, with Happiness
> And Immortality: that fondly lost,
> This other serv'd but to eternize woe;
> Till I provided Death; so Death becomes
> His final remedy . . .
> *(P.L. XI.48–49,57–62)*

The introduction of sin and death and misery, death's harbinger, has ended, beyond all recapture, the *Paradiso*-like growth in Eden from perfection to perfection. What remains, as on Dante's Purgatorial Mount, is to straighten what has become crooked (*Purg.* 23.125–126), to enlighten what has gone blind (*Purg.* 26.58), to set free what has been enslaved (*Purg.* 1.71; *Par.* 31.85–87). Michael's purposes in *Paradise Lost* XI–XII thus more nearly resemble the purposes of *Purgatorio*, Raphael's in *Paradise Lost* V–VIII more nearly those of *Paradiso*.

But the dividing line only partly clarifies the relation of Milton's poem to the last two-thirds of the *Commedia*. The neat division does not entirely hold. *Paradiso* bears on *Paradise Lost* IX–XII as well, and *Purgatorio* on Eden before the fall. The interrelation of all parts in each poem, the recurrence in each of themes begun in one section to be clarified by their elaboration elsewhere, means that if Milton was impressed by Dante's treatment of a given matter, the whole treatment left its traces on his whole treatment of like matter. Perhaps too Dante's phrase on the Earthly Paradise as a "nido" for humanity (*Purg.* 28.78) suggested to Milton an Eden designed for perfect man not only to live but to grow in. The possibility of growth, emphasized in Raphael's discourse with Adam (*P.L.* V.497–500; VII.155–161), is unmistakably a main feature of Eden. *Purgatorio* concerns itself with re-education; but in the terms available to readers of both *Paradise Lost* and the *Commedia*, education and re-education have much in common.

Love, free will, and politics—or the search for true good, the confirmation in right modes of living, and the proper role of power in promoting both—are the themes at the center of *Purgatorio*, from which Milton quoted the brief political passage in his *Commonplace Book*, fol. 197. These, and the way of education in them, are the main areas of his debt to Dante.

The Two Instructions

A sense of urgency dominates *Purgatorio* and the last two books of *Paradise Lost*. "Reflect that this day never dawns again," Virgil prods; and Dante comments, "Right well was I used to his monitions never to lose time" (*Purg.* 12.84–86). Among the slothful he naturally hears the counsel, "Haste! Haste! let no time be lost" (18.103). Among the gluttonous, Forese cries, "Time is precious in this realm" (24.91–92). Books XI and XII convey a similar sense that a difficult progress must be accomplished in little time. Michael pauses after the covenant of the rainbow like "one who in his journey bates at Noon,/ Though bent on speed" (XII.1–2). The sheer compression of human history into less than a thousand lines of verse suggests haste. Like Virgil in *Purgatorio*, Michael has a vast course of instruction to complete; like Dante, Adam has much to learn before a momentous change.

Paradiso and the instruction of Raphael are more leisurely. The effortless ascent of Dante from sphere to sphere, the easy conversation between Raphael and Adam with "no fear lest dinner cool," and a full afternoon for questions and answers, permit an expansiveness of tone that parallels the expanding universe which Dante enters and to which Adam is introduced. But re-education of any kind involves stress. That is the great difference between *Paradiso* and *Purgatorio*, between the instruction of Raphael and of Michael. Whereas Raphael can assume that if he does his part Adam will grasp his meaning, and can therefore discourse or narrate without pausing to see how much Adam has understood, affording opportunity for discussion and query afterward, Michael must not only provide a series of examples in vision and narrative before proceeding to exposition, but must pause after each to discover from Adam's comments what in his teaching still needs clarification. Michael's instruction thus more nearly resembles the pattern of *Purgatorio*, and the progress of his pupil that of Dante under Virgil's tuition. Adam gradually learns to draw the right inference from what he is told or shown, much as Dante's burden of error grows lighter with his purgatorial climb. And at the end of each educative process, the instructor can reward the pupil with deserved praise. Thus Virgil to Dante:

> Free, upright, and whole, is thy will, and 'twere
> a fault not to act according to its prompting;
> Wherefore I do crown and mitre thee over thyself.
> (*Purg.* 27.140–142)

And Michael to Adam:

> This having learnt, thou hast attain'd the sum
> Of wisdom.   (*P.L.* XII.575–576)

Michael, to be sure, must add a caution that would be inappropriate from Virgil:

> hope no higher, though all the Stars
> Thou knew'st by name, and all th' ethereal Powers,
> All secrets of the deep, all Nature's works,
> Or works of God in Heav'n, Air, Earth, or Sea,
> And all the riches of this World enjoy'dst,

And all the rule, one Empire; only add
Deeds to thy knowledge answerable, add Faith,
Add Virtue, Patience, Temperance, add Love,
By name to come call'd Charity, the soul
Of all the rest: then wilt thou not be loath
To leave this Paradise, but shalt possess
A paradise within thee, happier far.

(XII.576–587)

Dante, after all, is about to proceed where Virgil cannot enter, whereas Adam must be reminded to use all he has learned when he descends to a lower, troubled world.

The instruction of Michael thus resembles in some measure that of Dante's heavenly guides as well. He has to prepare Adam's sight to receive vision, as Dante has to bathe his eyes in the river of light (*Par.* 30.82–90) in order to behold the "candida rosa" of Heaven. Directing Adam "now ope thine eyes, and . . . behold" (*P.L.* XI.423), he translates Beatrice's bidding to Dante: "Apri gli occhi e riguarda" (*Par.* 23.46). His résumé of the future resembles Justinian's of the past (*Par.* 6.34–96). His teaching on the redemption naturally resembles what Dante appropriately hears in *Paradiso* (*P.L.* XII. 358ff.; *Par.* 7.19ff.). His pupil too, like Dante in *Paradiso*, is instructed in order that he may confront a difficult life ahead. But Adam at the end, of course, cannot match the climactic achievement of the tutored Dante in *Paradiso*, when, his vision attained, his will and desire move at one with God's. "The sum of wisdom," though larger than Virgil's teaching, necessarily falls far short of the ecstatic communion to which Beatrice's leads. Indeed, only the Son predicting the eventual redemption, when

> . . . with mee
> All my redeem'd may dwell in joy and bliss,
> Made one with me as I with thee am one,
>
> (XI.42–44)

names the ultimate goal for man that Dante experiences, however temporarily, in *Paradiso*. Milton evidently thought fallen
man could hardly hope for total re-education unless where
Dante found it, beyond this world. The instruction of Michael
has a humbler aim for chastened Adam.

Even unfallen Adam can assert no such final harmony with
the universe, or within himself, as Dante at the end of *Paradiso*.
He too needs guidance and assurance, and these Raphael gives
him. The substance of Raphael's instruction, designed to prevent the fall, involves the chain of being, the story of the war
in Heaven, the account of the creation of Adam's world, and—
as answers to queries spoken or implied—lessons in astronomy
and the right way of love. It is thus related to the substance of
what Dante learns, first in the earthly and then in the celestial
Paradise. The story of the war in Heaven has a value like that
of the schematic history of church and state in the pageant
introduced by Beatrice: here is the pattern of how evil begins,
works, and defeats itself. And Raphael's emphasis on the Son's
effective elevation, which both precipitates and concludes the
war in Heaven, may be likened to the quick survey by Justinian
of Rome, the chosen and effective power, in *Paradiso* (6.31–99):
both, though at different levels, illustrate divine providence
at work through a complex series of events. Raphael in explaining the creation of the universe has a purpose, not only like
Beatrice's in her exposition of the same subject, but also like
that of Cacciaguida telling of Dante's forebears and of the just
city Florence had been in his time (*Par.* 16.34–154). A sense of
purposeful continuity and lofty origins is to evoke a due self-
esteem.

But the purpose of Raphael's instruction is also to guide
Adam into a due humility, to enlighten him on the nature of
evil, to give him the self-understanding needed to prevent his
doing the one thing forbidden, and to confirm his pursuit of

good. It is thus closely related to Virgil's instruction in *Purga-torio*. Raphael's parting words sum up his teaching:

> Be strong, live happy, and love, but first of all
> Him whom to love is to obey, and keep
> His great command; take heed lest Passion sway
> Thy Judgment to do aught, which else free Will
> Would not admit; thine and of all thy Sons
> The weal or woe in thee is plac't; beware.
> I in thy persevering shall rejoice,
> And all the Blest: stand fast; to stand or fall
> Free in thine own Arbitrement it lies.
> Perfet within, no outward aid require;
> And all temptation to transgress repel.
> (VIII.633–643)

The preventive aim here corresponds to Virgil's curative aim in *Purgatorio*, as the emphasis on self-dependence suggests (*Purg.* 27.140–142). And minor resemblances support the correspondence. At intervals in *Purgatorio* Dante uses the word "sete" for his desire to know more (18.4–6; 21.1,39,74). Adam uses the same term to thank Raphael for having "allay'd [his] thirst . . . of knowledge" (*P.L.* VIII.7–8), and again to praise his discourse as sweeter "Than Fruits . . . pleasant-est to thirst/ And hunger both" (212–213). The effect of the instruction on Adam recalls Dante listening to Manfred, spellbound, completely absorbed in what he hears (*Purg.* 4.1–9). So Adam when Raphael has concluded his story of the creation:

> The Angel ended, and in Adam's Ear
> So Charming left his voice, that he a while
> Thought him still speaking, still stood fixt to hear.
> (*P.L.* VIII.1–3)

Query, answer; the thirst to know satisfied by an account that leaves the hearer as under a spell; a new query eliciting new

Dante and Milton

information, advice, warning: the pattern links Raphael's instruction with *Purgatorio*.

At intervals, to be sure, a like pattern occurs in *Paradiso*. Thus Dante hesitates to put his question to Benedict (*Par.* 22.25–36), as Adam hesitates to question Raphael. Or gratitude to his instructor leads him to speak a doubt raised by the instruction (*Par.* 4.118–135), as it does Adam (*P.L.* VII.59ff.). The instructor of each gives assurance that he does not blame the question and is ready to answer it (*Par.* 5.13ff.; *P.L.* VII.111–112; VIII.66), explaining that Heaven has in fact commissioned him to satisfy the questioner (*Par.* 10.88–90; 21.67–72; *P.L.* VII.112–120) although there are limits to what he can explain (*Par.* 21.91–99; *P.L.* VII.120–124; VIII.71–75). Each learner comments that the instruction produces no satiety but begets an eagerness for more (*Par.* 2.11–12; *P.L.* VIII.211–216).

A more important feature again links Raphael with Beatrice. The monitory tone with which the angel answers Adam's way of putting his doubt on astronomy, and reproves his way of describing his love for Eve, resembles Beatrice's tone with Dante, not only in the Earthly Paradise (*Purg.* 31.10–12,22–30,52–57), but in parts of *Paradiso* (1.88–102; 17.10–12). Michael will be gentler with fallen Adam, as Virgil was with Dante still struggling up the mountain. But the tutor who properly assumes right-mindedness in the learner can be more stern than one coping with the delinquent.

Michael does not treat Adam as a virtual equal, as Raphael had. Even more than Virgil with Dante, he is the declared guide. Raphael, more like Beatrice, is determined to raise his hearer into the same relation to the scheme of things as he himself enjoys. But Michael must make great allowances in his instruction, especially at first when he has to correct almost everything Adam says; and yet he must be firmly declarative. His

226

concern is to fulfill his assigned mission, not only to drive "from Paradise of God/ Without remorse . . . the sinful Pair," but to hide "all terror" and "Dismiss them not disconsolate," so that they may depart "though sorrowing, yet in peace" (XI. 104–117). It is a difficult enough task, and for some of Milton's readers Michael does not accomplish it satisfactorily. But in fact he attempts far more than his explicitly named duty. Sweeping through Biblical story, he uses it to outline central doctrines of Christian theology, humanistic ethics, and politics. Revealing the whole dismal future, the widening aftermath of the fall, he nonetheless gives increasing assurance that all will eventually come right. Revising at first every mistaken inference of his bewildered pupil, he yet manages to instill in him renewed confidence that he can cope with his damaged world. If further error on Adam's part can be prevented, Michael designs his teaching to prevent it.

But Raphael's teaching too is designed to be preventive. Before he leaves, everything possible has been done and said to strengthen Adam and confirm him in his happiness: he has been praised, chided, given maxims and examples, assured of the involvement of the universe in his future, told his probable destiny, warned exactly how he may err, and then left to his own responsibility—as any free creature must be. He has also been made responsible for Eve and their progeny (VI.908–909; VIII.637–638). The sending of Raphael as well as of Michael to Adam thus resembles the sending of Virgil to Dante. All are involved in a kind of rescue work commissioned by higher powers who name the purpose of the mission but leave the agent free to perform it in his own way (*P.L.* V.229–245; XI.99–117, *Inf.* 2.94–118).

In short, the two instructions in *Paradise Lost* cannot be neatly paired with the two instructions in the *Commedia*. Since Michael's is linked with that of Raphael, Virgil's with that of Beatrice, each of Milton's instructors in some measure resembles both of Dante's. In so far as Michael's purpose is to illuminate, it resembles that of Raphael and Beatrice. In so far as Raphael's is to prevent error, it resembles the curative purposes of Michael and Virgil.

The burden of cure rests chiefly on Michael in dealing with fallen man. He must prepare Adam for the new terms on which he is to live—subject to death, disease, debility, in a world where appearance no longer matches reality, where immediate joy no longer rewards virtue and evil does not immediately come to grief, a world with horrors of war, flood, tyranny, every possible wretchedness. What is harder still, he must prepare him for the new self with which he will confront his now shattered world. The specific doctrines of Michael's instruction concern us elsewhere; here we note its direction and method.

Before Adam is ready to learn from Michael, he must recognize with full contrition what he has done. Then he can, even while mending his ways, begin to face the irremediable consequences in the world as well as the remediable consequences in himself. Milton takes the same charitable view as Dante, that the destroyed self can be restored; but on the causal relation of deed and effect he too is stern. Hence the harshness of the panorama Michael sets before Adam. An emerging truth can comfort the one responsible for loosing such ills on the world: however immutable the consequences inherent in the crime, new deeds too will have their consequences; and as these meet, match, and finally overcome the effects of the crime, the world can be renewed. That is possible even with the weight of the world increasingly on the side of evil; for every man, as he confronts his life afresh to choose his part, can add his deeds to the right side, and may thus shift the direction of life for all men. The "one greater man," in Michael's teaching, time after time restores us and "regains the blissful seat," not only by his example but by his effect. And finally with the one greatest man the effect is entire redemption. Showing Adam the possibilities still within his reach, Michael encourages him too to become such a "greater man," and to go into his exile confident of his duty and his power.

It will be evident that Michael's instruction of Adam thus corresponds to the whole progress of Dante through the *Commedia*. The sequence and the substance are of course not the same. Dante confronts the unalterable consequences of deed chiefly in *Inferno*, where others are the doers. He takes the three steps of repentance before he enters the purgatorial gate, but has still to make his confession to Beatrice in the Terrestrial Paradise. He gains instruction from past exemplars of right and wrong ways throughout his journey. He learns the full harshness of his coming exile only in the realm of joy. His final assurance is of a community ready to receive him after brief exile. Yet step after step, Adam's progress through Michael's teaching recalls that of Dante.

The lyrical cry of joy with which Adam learns of his eventual redemption is Dantean in tone:

> O goodness infinite, goodness immense!
> That all this good of evil shall produce,
> And evil turn to good; more wonderful
> Than that which by creation first brought forth
> Light out of darkness! full of doubt I stand,
> Whether I should repent me now of sin
> By mee done and occasion'd, or rejoice
> Much more, that much more good thereof shall spring,
> To God more glory, more good will to Men
> From God, and over wrath grace shall abound.
>   (XII.469–478)

Apart from the words "infinite" and "immense," which recall

Dante on the divine goodness (e.g., *Purg.* 3.122; *Par.* 7.109), the closest parallel to Adam's opening lines is the final address to Beatrice in *Paradiso:*

> "O Lady, in whom my hope hath vigour, and
> who for my salvation didst endure to leave
> in Hell thy footprints;
> of all the things which I have seen I recognise
> the grace and might, by thy power and by thine
> excellence.
> Thou hast drawn me from a slave to liberty
> by all those paths, by all those methods by
> which thou hadst the power so to do."
>
> *(Par. 31.79–87)*

The redemptive function that Beatrice has performed for Dante is more exclusively that of Christ in *Paradise Lost*, though in both poems a series of lesser redeemers leads climactically to Christ.

Adam's self-consoling doubt, in the lines just quoted, whether he need now repent at all, resembles Folco's explanation of why the redeemed no longer repent their sins:

> Yet here we repent not, but smile; not at the
> sin, which cometh not again to mind, but at the
> Worth that ordered and provided.
> Here gaze we on the Art that beautifieth its so great
> effect, and here discern the Good which bringeth
> back the world below unto the world above.
>
> *(Par. 9.103–108)*

Michael carefully refrains at this point from reminding Adam of the immense cost of the reparation he has made necessary. He permits Adam to take the same view as Dante's redeemed. Doubtless it is the Christian paradox, not peculiar to Milton's poem or Dante's, that in some sense the sin gave occasion to and displays the beneficence of the divine order. What links

Adam's speech here with Dante is the context, with its sense of pressure from the wretched world, in spite of which the speaker rejoices. The certainty that, however dismal the coming time, all not only will be, but already is well, must accompany Dante into exile and Adam into banishment from Eden. Both are to go forth from their visions to await death with little assurance of joy in this life. Indeed, pleasure is to be recognized as delusive, fame as inconsequential, solitude as the likely share of one who clings to rightness. But comfort can be taken in the ultimate victory and in the present providence that assures it. The earthly future will not be easy, and yet it is not simply to be endured. There is a work to be done in and with the world. Though for both the pilgrim of the *Commedia* and the father of mankind, evil will flourish, and indeed increase, they are both to rejoice in helping to establish ultimate good.

At the end of *Paradise Lost* Adam's relation to life is thus in a measure comparable to Dante's at the end of the *Commedia*. But the instruction of Michael in its urgency, its emphasis on the humbled spirit and the need of grace, its exchanges between questioner and expositor, more nearly resembles the purgatorial climb. Before the fall, Adam's relation to Heaven resembles Dante's in *Paradiso:* he can expect to gain full citizenship there. And yet the instruction of Raphael also—in its use of warning example, its correction of straying impulse, its whole suggestion of alert effort required—more nearly resembles the education given in Purgatory. Paradiso grants Dante his baccalaureate (26.67ff.), but Purgatorio implants the habits that fit him to receive it.

Both of Milton's angelic instructors therefore take more of their method from *Purgatorio* than from *Paradiso*. Michael's explicit preface to the pageant of the future recalls Beatrice introducing the pageant in the Terrestrial Paradise. He names the purpose: from the pageant Adam is

> . . . to learn
> True patience, and to temper joy with fear
> And pious sorrow, equally inur'd
> By moderation either state to bear, . . .
>   . . . and best prepared endure
> Thy mortal passage . . .
>
> (*P.L.* XI.360–366)

Beatrice too names the purpose:

> Therefore to profit the world that liveth ill, fix
> now thine eyes upon the car, and look that thou
> write what thou seest, when returned yonder.
>
> (*Purg.* 32.103–105.)

And Raphael, descending straight from Heaven to make sure that Adam will reach it, recalls Beatrice too. But the specific purpose of Michael, and even of Raphael, is not so much to prepare Adam for participation in ultimate joy as to establish him in the right way of life in this beleaguered world. *Purgatorio* is therefore inevitably more to Milton's purpose. And since the instruction of Raphael and Michael comprises almost half of *Paradise Lost*, *Purgatorio* has the large relation to Milton's poem.

Dante and Milton were both aware of the rashness of venturing into the realms of Hell and Heaven. The two poems have both been called encyclopedias of the learning of their time. But in both perhaps the greatest daring was simply to present education as the central human action, and an organic method of teaching as the substance of poetry. To turn angels, the epic poet of Rome, and Beauty personified into schoolmasters and schoolmistress—small wonder that the *Commedia* and *Paradise Lost* have troubled readers. What is designed to be doctrinal and exemplary is bound to strike many as irksomely doctrinaire. Much depends on what the reader perceives in the doctrine and the example.

Reason and Free Will

Right habit become right impulse is the evident aim of Dante's Purgatory, as right reason directing right choice is that of the instruction Milton's angels provide. Dante is more Aristotelian, Milton more Platonic in his ethic. Whereas Dante elaborates the forming of a habit of choice, Milton stresses its ground; but they agree that if life is to have ethical meaning in the fallen world, reason must know and free will must choose the good.

The position is hardly peculiar to *Paradise Lost* and the *Commedia*, any more than is the humanist ethic to which it belongs. Even the fusion of a humanist ethic with Christian theology is no more a link between Milton and Dante than is the belief in an omnipresent God between Milton and, say, Origen, or the belief that reason and faith are in accord, between Dante and Thomas Aquinas. What does make Dante's position relevant to Milton's is the doctrinal conviction that constantly determines the action of both narrative poems. Auerbach points out that Dante undertook to "reconcile the Thomist system with the mystical ideology of the *cor gentile*" and that the reconciliation was one "only a poet could effect."[1] We may

[1] Erich Auerbach, *Dante: Poet of the Secular World*, tr. Ralph Manheim (Chicago, 1961), p. 71.

see the resemblance between Dante and Milton in the reconcile-
ment each effects between explicit theology and ethics and a
primarily human action, mimetic of recognizable man in
minutest detail and yet inclusive of the broadest generalities
about the scheme of things; and we may say that this reconcile-
ment is of a sort that only the greatest poets could achieve. The
encyclopedic quality, often remarked as evidence of both
poets' learning, is a sign of the large synthesis each attempts
and of the extraordinary power with which each achieves it.
Compared with either Milton or Dante, Homer is a limited
pedagogue and Virgil parochial in his devotions. In the later
poets, not only the broad realm of learning, but the complex
variety of possible human modes of thought and feeling are
caught up in the inclusive scheme and given each its place.

If the doctrines to which we now turn are common enough
property in the European tradition, the narrative presentation
of them in the *Commedia* and *Paradise Lost* is far from common.
Reason and free will, like liberty, equality, fraternity, or the
rights of man, or the law of nature, take their significance from
the details they are applied to. Thus, many who say reason
mean no more than calculation, as Blake objected; and many
who talk at length of free will seem eager only to constrict.
What Dante and Milton call the bidding of reason and the
exercise of a will truly free might shock or terrify Philistines.

Dante and Milton both recognize a problem in man's exercise
of choice. Given a single soul with many faculties, of which
reason is chief (*Purg.* 4.1–6; *P.L.* V.100–102), imperfect man,
with his reason and every lesser faculty damaged, cannot rely
on his own fallible judgment. Given a world awry in which his
very guides may lead him astray, neither can he rely on authorities. The problem would be insoluble if to say that human
reason and authorities are fallible were unequivocal statements.
But fortunately, though reason has its limits and authority its

usurpers, the danger for man has its limits too. We complain chiefly when reason sets limits to our conduct, not because it bids wrong. Few things are so transparent to introspection as that *reason* is not to blame for the "good reasons" we concoct to justify bad choices. And when self-styled authorities mislead, they seldom do more than offer a sanction to the willingly misled. Man, for all his admitted imperfection, has right reason enough, and trustworthy guides enough, if he wants good counsel and right example. No doubt reason cannot fully probe "the secrets of another world" (*P.L.* V.569; *Purg.* 3.34–39; *Par.* 29.73–75); nor can it judge with certainty what this world shows (*Par.* 20.133–135; *P.L.* XI.452ff.), but then it need not. The worth of our lives depends on neither such knowledge nor such judgments.

Milton puts a heavier burden than Dante on right reason, not that he assigns it a higher value but that he sees life as consisting more in conscious choice. Dante takes habit, once established, as relieving man of much of his ethical burden; Milton welcomes alertness as desirable. Even before the fall, the ease of Adam's probable growth is more like Dante's ascent as he approaches the "nido" of the race than as he moves through the heavens to the Empyrean: without the burden of wrong habit, ascent and growth are easy. But for Adam, they are not simply inevitable, as they are in Dante's Paradise. So long as ascent and growth are possible, in Milton's view, descent and decline are also possible. That is the very meaning of free will, and of reason which "also is choice" (*P.L.* III. 106–111).

Thus Raphael declares to Adam in advance of every other admonition,

> That thou art happy, owe to God;
> That thou continu'st such, owe to thyself.
>
> (V.520–521)

And his final admonition is no less plain:

> . . . to stand or fall
> Free in thine own Arbitrement it lies.
> Perfet within, no outward aid require.
> (VIII.640–642)

Despite their resemblance to Virgil's parting words, which "crown and mitre" Dante over himself, Raphael's have almost the opposite import: Dante has been assured that now he cannot err, Adam warned that he must be on guard. Eve makes a natural enough comment on the need for vigilance: "If this be our condition, . . ./ How are we happy, still in fear of harm?" (IX.322–326); then she herself answers, "But harm precedes not sin" (327). Nor does the loss of Eden. Given the free and upright will, prelapsarian man, or Dante after his purgatorial climb, can make right choices without strain. Adam, in fact, goes through a far more elaborate struggle to deceive himself into the wrong choice than he need have made in standing fast—and Eve does too. "No" is more easily said than "Perhaps, after all . . ."

Free will, involved so deeply in the retention or loss of the Miltonic Eden, does not imply great efforts for unfallen man, as it does after the fall, but only a world of choice with what choice entails: different possibilities that have really different consequences. Any alternative way of life would "serve necessity." To be protected from error by the absence of its possibility is to be denied the exercise of self-government. And for both Dante and Milton, liberty was too precious to be eliminated from the universe, even for the sake of certainty. To hold the stars responsible for man—the error Marco Lombardo attacks in *Purgatorio* 16—is but one of many possible versions of determinism; to make God responsible can be another. If man is to be human, not a puppet controlled by the stars or even by God himself, he inevitably has impulses, desires, tendencies within him corresponding to all manner of possible objects without; his selfhood depends on his choice among the various appetites and objects. Thus both Dante and Milton.

Virgil warns in advance that his treatment of the subject will be amended by Beatrice; but in fact nothing in *Paradiso* contravenes his humanist doctrine. He explains the impulsive nature as deserving neither blame nor praise, since it is native to man and in itself morally neutral (*Purg.* 18.55–60). That is distinctly Milton's creed: not the impulse, but reason's voluntary assent or dissent merits praise or blame. Thus when Adam before the fall suggests that nature has failed in him or has lavished excessive beauty on Eve, Raphael answers frowning:

> Accuse not Nature, she hath done her part;
> Do thou but thine, and be not diffident
> Of Wisdom, she deserts thee not, if thou
> Dismiss not her.   (*P.L.* VIII.561–564)

For, as Virgil explains, also innate in man is the power to discriminate among his impulses:

> . . . innate with you is the virtue which giveth counsel, and ought to guard the threshold of assent.
> This is the principle whence is derived the reason of desert in you, according as it garners and winnows good and evil loves.
> Those who in their reasoning went to the foundation, perceived this innate freedom, therefore they left ethics to the world.
> Wherefore, suppose that every love which is kindled within you arises of necessity, the power to arrest it is within you.
>   (*Purg.* 18.62–72)

It is of this "nobile virtù" that Beatrice is to speak, "lo libero arbitrio" (73–74). What she says accords with the teaching of Marco and Virgil; Beatrice simply pronounces free will the greatest of God's benefactions to man:

> The greatest gift God of his largess made at the
>   creation, and the most conformed to his own
>   excellence, and which he most prizeth,
> was the will's liberty, wherewith creatures intelli-
>   gent, both all and each, were and are endowed.
>
> *(Par.* 5.19–24)

Milton gives a like statement to a supremely authoritative voice when he has God himself proclaim it at the Council in Heaven (*P.L.* III.98–128). Thus for both Dante and Milton, man has free will and mind with which to determine his own actions, and this is God's supreme gift to him.

In *Paradise Lost*, the doctrine requires emphasis to make the action meaningful; and the action in turn underscores the doctrine. In the *Commedia*, human choice is both the doctrinal and the mathematical center of the whole. Above all else Dante and Milton tell their readers that we live in a world of inner freedom, and that such freedom constitutes the ground of our humanity.

For both poets it is therefore important to insist that God's foreknowledge implies no limitation on man's will (*Par.* 17.37–42; *P.L.* III.114–119). Dante gives the same emphasis in the brief reference to the fall of Adam in *Purgatorio* as Milton in the elaborate analysis of *Paradise Lost*.

> Per sua diffalta qui dimorò poco;
>   per sua diffalta in pianto ed in affanno
>   cambiò onesto riso e dolce gioco.
> (Through his default, little time he sojourned
>   here; through his default, for tears and sweat
>   he exchanged honest laughter and sweet play.)
>
> *(Purg.* 28.94–96)

The "onesto riso e dolce gioco" as well as "sua diffalta" appears in Milton's handling of the fall. Eve argues that when they work together "Looks intervene and smiles" so that "th' hour of Supper comes unearn'd" (IX.222–225). And Adam, a good Dantean, answers that "smiles from Reason flow,/ To brute deni'd, and are of Love the food,/ Love not the lowest end of human life" (239–241). The smiles that feed love recall Beatrice in sphere after sphere of Paradise. To the New England housewife's argument of Eve, taking work as life's purpose rather than life itself as the purpose of everything else, Adam opposes a Mediterranean sanity: "Not to irksome toil, but to delight/ He made us, and delight to Reason join'd" (242–243).

The perversity that abjures delight as interfering with the earning of supper has its root in nothing so noble as the sense of duty under which it hides. Milton links it with the querulous habits of self-assertiveness, carefully marking Eve's tone from the beginning of the scene. Her insistence that to fear for her is to doubt her "firm Faith and Love," and that to guard her is to assume her incapacity to meet danger, elicits Adam's "fervent" assertion of the doctrine of free will: "within [man] himself/ The danger lies, yet lies within his power" (348–349). Adam's speech sums up more than Dante's doctrine, but it agrees with the *Commedia* in its most important point. His explanation, that

> God left free the Will, for what obeys
> Reason is free, and Reason he made right,
> But bid her well beware, and still erect,
> Lest by some fair appearing good surpris'd
> She dictate false, and misinform the Will
> To do what God expressly hath forbid,
>
> (IX.351–356)

recalls Beatrice's remark on how Dante came to err, "imagini di ben seguendo false" ("pursuing false visions of good,"

Purg. 30.131), and on how the soul is drawn from its proper course, "torto da falso piacere" ("wrenched aside by false-seeming pleasure," *Par.* 1.135). Milton has God himself emphatically state the doctrine when he sends Raphael to forewarn Adam (V.235–237), and Raphael restates it. Ironically enough, his restatement predicts exactly how the fall will occur:

> . . . take heed lest Passion sway
> Thy Judgment to do aught, which else free Will
> Would not admit.   (VIII.635–637)

The idea, ultimately Platonic, that all error is ignorance becomes, as Dante and Milton use it, no excuse, since the ignorance is itself a voluntary abdication of reason, allowing "falso piacere" to misinform the judgment.

Only such an emphasis on free will could justify the argument of either the *Commedia* or *Paradise Lost*. The liberty that Dante goes seeking is primarily freedom of the will, the great initial endowment of mankind, which has been lost by pursuing illusions. In *Paradiso* Adam himself briefly summarizes what went amiss in the fall:

> Or, figliuol mio, non il gustar del legno
>   fu per sè la cagion di tanto esilio,
>   ma solamente il trapassar del segno.
> (Now know, my son, that not the tasting of the
>   tree was in itself the cause of so great exile,
>   but only the transgressing of the mark.)
>   (*Par.* 26.115–117)

"Segno" is the emphatic word in Milton's explanation too, when Adam himself first speaks to Eve of the forbidden tree as "The only sign of our obedience left/ Among so many signs of power and rule" (*P.L.* IV.428–429). In the phrase of both Dante and Milton, the freedom of unfallen man involved his respecting one only restraint. Thus *Paradiso* summarizes the fall:

> Because he endured not for his own good a rein
> upon the power that wills, that man who ne'er
> was born, as he condemned himself, condemned
> his whole offspring.   (*Par.* 7.25–27)

And Milton introduces the action of his poem by referring to our grand parents' transgressing "For one restraint, Lords of the World besides" (*P.L.* I.32).

Although the motives that led to the fall are given in the *Commedia* no such involved treatment as in *Paradise Lost*, in the main Dante and Milton were naturally enough agreed. The central motive was the desire to be as God (*Par.* 7.100–102; *P.L.* III.206); in Eve the defect of credulity played a large part (*Purg.* 32.31–32; *P.L.* IX.643–644,733–734). Dante also suggests in a brief phrase one of the chief themes Milton was to elaborate—Eve's vanity. Newly arrived in the Earthly Paradise, the pilgrim blames Eve for having lost him this home:

> righteous zeal made me reprove Eve's daring,
> who, there where heaven and earth obeyed, a
> woman alone and but then formed, did not
> bear to remain under any veil.
>   (*Purg.* 29.23–27)

Her unwillingness to remain "under a veil" is the motive upon which Satan chiefly plays in *Paradise Lost*:

> . . . one man except,
> Who sees thee? (and what is one?) who shouldst be seen
> A Goddess among Gods . . .   (*P.L.* IX.545–547)

And Dante's phrase suggests, even more, Adam's later words accusing Eve of "longing to be seen/ Though by the Devil himself" (*P.L.* X.877–878). In Milton it is clearly fallen Adam who makes the charge, whereas Dante speaks in his own

241

person, approving what he thought during his pilgrimage. The shift has force: Milton uses an idea like Dante's, but by assigning it to Adam, makes it a symptom of his decay.

Adam's ruling motive in the fall, so emphatically given by Milton as his fear of losing Eve, is not treated at all by Dante. But his greater responsibility is clear in the *Commedia* too: he is the one who explains the fall in *Paradiso* 26, and the final word on the subject names him

> il padre, per lo cui ardito gusto
> l' umana specie tanto amaro gusta
> (that Father because of whose audacious tast-
> ing the human race tasteth such bitterness).
> (*Par.* 32.122–123)

So in *Purgatorio* when Dante sees the symbolic tree despoiled of foliage, the murmur he hears from the whole assembly is "Adamo" (*Purg.* 32.37). Something of the impression that passage made on Milton is perhaps echoed in Adam's horror as he thinks how his descendants will blame him for their woes: "For this we may thank Adam" (*P.L.* X.736).

Milton deliberately lightens the burden of guilt that has traditionally been placed on Eve. As the more responsible of the pair, Adam comes off worse in the fall itself. And afterward his confused attempts at self-exculpation before their judge (*P.L.* X.125–143) contrast badly with Eve's single "abasht" sentence: "The Serpent me beguil'd and I did eat" (162). Milton could have expanded her brief speech from Genesis 3 along with Adam's. Instead he kept it brief to stress her shame, "not before her Judge/ Bold or loquacious." She resembles the humbled Dante answering the accusation of Beatrice in the Earthly Paradise:

> confusion and fear, together mingled, drove forth
> from my mouth a "Yea" such that to understand
> it the eyes were needed. (*Purg.* 31.13–15)

That Eve in the presence of her judge resembles Dante in the presence of Beatrice, may indicate how Milton understood the Beatrice-figure of the *Commedia*. Had he taken her as the mere "proud fair" of the conventional "starv'd lover," he would have thought Dante "best quitted with disdain," his scathing comment on the whole tradition of courtly love (IV.767–770). For the beloved woman ought not, in Milton's view, be put in the role of idol, mother-substitute, mentor, or divine representative; and the relation to her ought not to be dependent. Adam vituperating Eve clearly has the worst of Milton's condemnation, but an Eve responsible for Adam would have pleased him as little. He recognizes in Beatrice a savior-figure; in *Paradise Lost* the Son himself naturally fills that role. Dante's role in the scene he also understands, and shifts largely to Eve. For the clearest parallel to Dante weeping and apologetic before the seemingly relentless Beatrice of *Purgatorio* 31 is Eve, humble and tearful, finally moving Adam to relent, in *Paradise Lost* X. And Milton has not only transferred the humble tears to Eve, he has made them a sign of her superiority at that point to Adam. Joseph Summers, in *The Muse's Method* (pp. 107–111, 176–185), has made the significance amply clear.

Milton's Eve, though the first, is the lesser sinner of the pair; afterward she degenerates less, she finds a right way more quickly, and in fact she begins the whole redemptive process for Adam as well as herself. The part of the Dante-role that Adam plays is less dignified. His efforts at self-exculpation in Book X bring upon him a reproach from the Son as judge that recalls Beatrice addressing Dante:

> what pits didst find athwart thy path, or what
> chains, that thou needs must strip thee of the
> hope of passing onward?
> And what allurements or what advantages were
> displayed to thee in the aspect of the others,
> that thou must needs wander before them?
> (*Purg.* 31.25–30)

When Dante answers,

> Present things with their false pleasure
> turned away my steps soon as your face
> was hidden,   (34–36)

she renews the charge:

> and if the highest pleasure thus failed thee by
> my death, what mortal thing ought then to
> have drawn thee to desire it?   (52–54)

So after Adam's fumbling speech,

> This Woman whom thou mad'st to be my help,
> And gav'st me as thy perfet gift, so good,
> So fit, so acceptable, so Divine,
> That from her hand I could suspect no ill,
> And what she did, whatever in itself,
> Her doing seem'd to justify the deed;
> Shee gave me of the Tree, and I did eat,
> (X.137–143)

the Son demands:

> Was shee thy God, that her thou didst obey
> Before his voice, or was shee made thy guide,
> Superior, or but equal, that to her
> Thou didst resign thy Manhood . . . ?
> (145–148)

Beatrice too remarks on the erring one's supposed manhood
(61–63, 67–69), as Dante notes:

> when by the beard she asked for my face, well
> I knew the venom of the argument.   (74–75)

The central question to the wrongdoer is simply what else was worth his devotion compared with what he knew to be best.

But Beatrice can be reconciled to the pilgrim Dante more quickly than Adam's judge to him. It is a not very original sin that Dante committed, and he has already climbed the penitential mountain, renewing himself, before he is confronted by Beatrice. On the enormity of "Man's First Disobedience," the poet Dante and Milton naturally agree. Reason and free will having permitted the fall, the consequences were inevitable. Naturally too, both connect original sin with man's mortality, and the vicarious atonement with man's restoration. Milton's God decrees, "Die hee or Justice must" except as Christ dies for man (*P.L.* III.210ff.), and Dante gives the familiar theological doctrine a similar emphasis (*Par.* 7.25–33). More surprisingly, God's speech on his irrevocable "high Decree" (*P.L.* III.126ff.) reads like Beatrice's explanatory words to those who witness her tongue-lashing of Dante:

> God's high decree would be broken, if Lethe were
> passed, and such viands were tasted, without some
> scot of penitence that may shed tears.
> (*Purg.* 30.142–145)

The resemblance need not derive from Milton's reading of *Purgatorio;* but probably the whole sequence of Dante's entry into the Earthly Paradise left its impression.

Minor parallels between *Purgatorio* and the treatment of the fall in *Paradise Lost* include Dante's image, "I felt my pinions grow for the flight" (*Purg.* 27.123), and Milton on Adam and Eve's false exhilaration after they eat of the fruit:

Dante and Milton

> They swim in mirth, and fancy that they feel
> Divinity within them breeding wings
> Wherewith to scorn the Earth.
>
> (*P.L.* IX.1009–1011)

Again, when Satan reports his achievement to his followers, he comments that he did it all,

> . . . the more to increase
> Your wonder, with an Apple . . .
> . . . worth your laughter.
>
> (*P.L.* X.486–488)

The collocation of laughter and an apple may recall *Purgatorio* 27, when Virgil "smiled as one does to a child that is won by an apple" (44–45). The sham trees on which the devils compulsively feed (*P.L.* X.547–555) may have been suggested in part by the symbolic trees on the terrace of gluttony (*Purg.* 22.130ff.; 24.103ff.) and in the pageant of history (*Purg.* 33.52–57). The introduction of seasons into postlapsarian Eden (*P.L.* X.651ff.) inverts the emphatic exclusion of weather from Dante's Earthly Paradise (*Purg.* 28.97–102).

But these are minor matters, unlike the correspondences between Beatrice confronting Dante and the Son confronting Adam and Eve in *Paradise Lost* X. The tone of the lady is sterner:

> What thinkest
> thou? Answer me, for the sad memories in
> thee are not yet destroyed by the water.
>
> (31.10–12)

The Son speaks more gently: "Where art thou Adam? . . . Come forth" (*P.L.* X.103ff.). And yet the comment of Beatrice when Dante, duly humbled, has satisfied her that he is contrite, might be a summary of the whole sequence in which Adam and Eve, finally self-condemning, confess their faults, and with their penitence win heaven's renewed favor. In Beatrice's words,

246

> . . . when self-accusation of sin bursts from the
> cheeks in our Court, the grindstone is turned
> back against the edge.   (*Purg.* 31.40–42)

The willingness of Heaven to have its verdicts thus turned
aside is repeated in *Paradiso* 20.94–99: Heaven is in fact eager
to be influenced. So too in *Purgatorio* 6, Virgil answers Dante's
query how "prayer may bend heaven's decree" with the assurance that "fire of love fulfils in one moment the satisfaction"
(28ff.). Milton uses the same idea in the dialogue between
God and the Son (*P.L.* III.80–343), in the colloquy with God
Adam reports (VIII.357ff.), and again in Adam's comment on
the effect of prayer:

> Eve, easily may Faith admit, that all
> The good which we enjoy, from Heav'n descends;
> But that from us aught should ascend to Heav'n
> So prevalent as to concern the mind
> Of God high-blest, or to incline his will,
> Hard to belief may seem; yet this will Prayer,
> Or one short sigh of human breath, up-borne
> Ev'n to the Seat of God.   (XI.141–148)

Prayer, like repentance an act of free will seeking the good,
can change the course of things, adding its effect to the effects
of all other acts. The first effect is in Adam himself:

> For since I sought
> By Prayer th' offended Deity to appease,
> Kneel'd and before him humbl'd all my heart,
> Methought I saw him placable and mild,
> Bending his ear; persuasion in me grew
> That I was heard with favor; peace return'd
> Home to my Breast . . .   (148–154)

Effects in the one who prays entail corresponding effects in
Heaven that hears, just as the action of the fall has entailed a
reaction in Heaven. Dante and Milton both make scorn the
response of Heaven to man's error. In *Paradiso* 26.113, Dante

has Adam refer to "la propria cagion del gran *disdegno*"; in *Paradise Lost* IX.6–9, the "breach/ Disloyal on the part of Man" elicits "On the part of Heav'n/ Now alienated, distance and *distaste*." The desire to make restitution for the evil done itself begins the healing of the breach, according to *Paradise Lost* XI.252–257, and the whole of *Purgatorio* as well as *Paradiso* 4.136–138 and 5.13ff. But what has been shattered is not so easily mended. On the necessity of the vicarious atonement Dante and Milton inevitably agree, seeing it as combining the absolute fulfillment of the demands both of justice and of love (*Par.* 7.25–45,91–99,115–120; *P.L.* III.80–302, 410–411; XII.396–404). But the need remains for man to earn the grace thus offered. Though gratitude itself in some sense cancels debts to God, whether of man or angel (*Par.* 5.46–47; 29.64–66; *P.L.* IV.46–47), though grace is freely given, and even in special measure to some chosen few (*Par.* 20.130–135; *P.L.* III.183–184), man must nonetheless himself take steps toward the proffered gift in order that it may reach him. Pardon must be offered before it can be earned, but it must still be earned.

And man must take his steps with an uncertainty of footing that he himself has caused. The change in man after the fall is emphasized in *Paradiso:*

> Your nature, when it sinned in its totality in its
> first seed, from these dignities, even as from
> Paradise, was parted.   (*Par.* 7.85–87)

So too in *Paradise Lost:*

> Thir Maker's Image, answer'd Michael, then
> Forsook them, when themselves they vilified
> To serve ungovern'd appetite, . . .
> Inductive mainly to the sin of Eve.
>   (XI. 515–519)

The Purgatorial Way

Since thy original lapse, true Liberty
Is lost, which always with right Reason dwells
Twinn'd, and from her hath no dividual being.
(XII.83–85)

Hence for both Dante and Milton the large importance of faith as a confidence amounting to conviction that man's future is assured by the effective atonement of Christ, that all will be well, the breach finally perfectly healed, the universe entirely renewed in peace, joy, and love. The faith defined in *Paradiso* (24.52ff.), and taught by Michael in *Paradise Lost* XII, makes freedom again possible.

Such faith does not cancel the need for reason and choice. As Marco Lombardo and Virgil explain, and as all *Purgatorio* demonstrates, the office of reason is to direct or redirect desire. The three varieties of error analyzed in *Purgatorio* 18, the bad habits of excessive, defective, and misdirected love, are to be avoided or cured by reason guiding the will repeatedly to good habit. Hence, while the acts repeated by the penitents cure the will by instituting right habit, the exempla, hortatory and minatory, of each terrace define for reason the virtue to be aimed at and the vice to be shunned. A variety of maxims, admonitions, and exclamations announce the principles involved in the examples. So with the exempla of Michael's instruction: hortatory or minatory, they illustrate the principles that must henceforth guide Adam. He is neither to love nor to hate his life, seeking neither to prolong nor to abbreviate it, but only to live it well (*P.L.* XI.553–554); he is to observe a Greek moderation, the rule of nothing too much (XI.531); he is to remain undeluded by pleasure (XI.603–604); and so forth. Each illustrative scene serves as exemplum for one or more maxims.

The order of the scenes in *Paradise Lost* XI–XII has nothing obvious in common with the order of *Purgatorio*. Chronology replaces psychology as scheme: Adam beholds the future of mankind, Dante an analysis of human error. But both have as their purpose to rebuild the human soul, and to this end they use like means. An authoritative expounder of the human scene clarifies its meanings, and leads his interlocutor step by step to the point where he can be assured that he now knows what he needs to know in order to go on confident in the adequacy of his reason and his will to make right choices. And however little the chronological sequence of the instructive scenes in *Paradise Lost* owes to *Purgatorio*, Milton's treatment of themes may occasionally derive in part from his reading of the *Commedia*.

The elaborate handling by Michael of the desire for fame in Book XI resembles Dante's similarly complex treatment. In the Purgatorial circle that cures pride, Dante has Oderisi speak at length of the absurd desire for wordly repute:

> O empty glory of human powers! How short
> the time its green endures upon the top, if it
> be not overtaken by rude ages!
>
> (*Purg.* 11.91–93)

Such fame is transitory, and quickly lost with shifts of taste:

> Earthly fame is naught but a breath of wind,
> which now cometh hence and now thence, and
> changes name because it changes direction.
>
> (100–102)

The admonition, appropriate to humbling the "gran tumor" of Dante's pride (119), agrees with *Paradiso* 6.112–117 in making the desire for "onore e fama" at best a diminution of the "vero amore." Later in *Purgatorio* Guido Guinicelli takes up the theme in a condemnation of the fickle public:

> To rumour rather than to truth they turn their
> faces, and thus do fix their opinion ere art or
> reason is listened to by them
>
> (*Purg.* 26.121–123)

Lycidas, with its large debt to the *Commedia*, had likewise spoken of the false fame that grows on mortal soil as mere "rumor," and of the desire for it as the "last infirmity of noble mind," but had allowed the possibility of a true fame to be awarded in Heaven by all-judging Jove—a concept like that of the glory of the redeemed in Dante's *Paradiso*. But Michael in *Paradise Lost* keeps close to the expressed view of the *Commedia* when he asserts that worldly fame has no due relation to merit, and may in fact have an inverse one:

> Thus Fame shall be achiev'd, renown on Earth,
> And what most merits fame in silence hid.
>
> (XI.698–699)

The same grim view is elaborated by the authoritative voice in *Paradise Regained*:

> For what is glory but the blaze of fame,
> The people's praise, if always praise unmixt?
> And what the people but a herd confus'd,
> A miscellaneous rabble, who extol
> Things vulgar, and well weigh'd, scarce worth the praise?
> They praise and they admire they know not what;
> And know not whom, but as one leads the other;
> And what delight to be by such extoll'd,
> To live upon thir tongues and be thir talk,
> Of whom to be disprais'd were no small praise?
>
> (*P.R.* III.47–56)

And yet to be unnamed is an exceptional penalty in both Dante and Milton. *Purgatorio* 14.29–30 declares that "verily 'tis meet that the name of such a vale perish," namelessness being a fit reward of evil. Even in *Inferno*, as we have seen, namelessness is the special doom of the nonentities in Canto 3; and in Canto 32.91–96, to want to be nameless is a sign of deep depravity. The desire to have their earthly fame repaired is constantly, though sometimes mistakenly, assumed in the

Dante and Milton

damned among whom Dante makes his way (*Inf.* 27.57ff.;
28.133ff.; 29.103–104; 31.125–127). And the desire is not
wholly wrong. Virgil plays on Dante's own desire for fame
(*Inf.* 24.47–51). Sapia in *Purgatorio* asks

> And I beseech thee by all thou most desirest, if
> e'er thou tread the land of Tuscany, that thou
> restore my fame among my kinsfolk.
> (*Purg.* 13.148–150)

In *Paradiso* Cunizza introduces Folco as one whose fame remains
and will remain, then comments:

> See if a man should make himself excel, so
> that another life should follow the first!
> (*Par.* 9.41–42)

The fame of such a one is evidently worth aiming at, however
worthless most worldly repute. A like assumption about namelessness and the desirability of fame underlies Raphael's comment on the lesser rebel angels:

> Cancell'd from Heav'n and sacred memory,
> Nameless in dark oblivion let them dwell.
> For strength from Truth divided and from Just,
> Illaudable, naught merits but dispraise
> And ignominy, yet to glory aspires
> Vain-glorious, and through infamy seeks fame:
> Therefore Eternal silence be thir doom.
> (*P.L.* VI.379–385)

Dante derides both the lack of aspiration for renown and the
mistaken zeal for mere reputation; Milton more consistently
distinguishes the desire for esteem on just grounds from mere
desire for fame on any, even the falsest ground. Both recognize
that some concern with repute is natural to man, but that it
can be a distorted concern, and that at best it remains a concern

252

with something short of realities. On the distortion Milton is usually sterner than Dante; but the phrase in *Purgatorio* defining the worthless view of the crowd, "To rumor rather than to truth they turn their faces," comes close to Milton's sustained view. What both poets affirm is that such praise is a substitute for real good. The man of worth does not need it; the less worthy seek it in order to hide from themselves. But so with all the wrongly directed loves examined in *Purgatorio*, and so too with the excesses and defects of love.

It would be easy to find the seven capital sins in *Paradise Lost*, and to find them given treatment comparable to Dante's. But Milton avoids the schematic, shaping even the historical sequence to afford Adam a developing view of the world and man's right relation to it. What Adam and Dante chiefly learn from the curative instruction is to distinguish realities from shams, the genuine from the illusory good.

If both the pilgrim Dante and Adam must start their re-education with the crushed spirit—Dante first symbolically, kneeling to Cato and girded with a reed, later with personal anguish encountering Beatrice's lashing tongue—for both the relief of accepted repentance soon follows. Human mortality, the one immitigable consequence of the fall in the theology that sustains both poems, is, as it happens, mitigated in both. Adam feels at once after his prayer that "the bitterness of death/ Is past, and we shall live" (XI.157–158). And he learns finally from Michael's instruction that "to the faithful Death [is] the Gate of Life" (XII.571). Death as penalty, death as entrance to immortality—both meanings are present in the *Commedia* too. The utterly damned may be dead, and their souls in Hell even before their bodies die, according to *Inferno* 33.121–135. And *Convivio* states the same thesis in prose: "A bad man may rightly be called dead" (IV.vii.106). Yet the pilgrim who must leave Paradiso for the strife-torn

Italy of the year 1300 knows that his death will restore him forever to the joys he has briefly tasted. So in *Paradise Lost* the ghastly figure of Death symbolizes an outward penalty as well as its inward cause; yet man's mortality is his promise of renewed life.

Thus Milton's "mortalist heresy," since it includes man's immortality, however postponed, bears as little on the main issues of *Paradise Lost* as the time spent by the dead in Purgatory. The eventual certainty makes the one delay a prolonged sleep before waking, the other an active preparation for a realm of permanence. Neither poet uses death to terrify his reader; neither expects his reader to associate himself with the realm where Death rules. Rather, both expect him to be roused from the inward death, or slumber too like death, that permits evil to extend the City of Dis in this world, to an exercise of reason and will that may help establish on earth the city patterned on the heavenly. Final death is the end only of the ineducability of Hell. But the *Commedia* and *Paradise Lost* address themselves to the educable.

The Politics of Vision

How, in a world awry, is man to use reason and will to regain his full human stature? Dante and Milton both not only assume, they insist that evil is rampant in the world. The theme recurs throughout the *Commedia*, most startlingly in *Paradiso* where it interrupts the very joy of the redeemed; in *Paradise Lost* it broods over all that Adam sees and hears of mankind's future. Michael's climactic assertion,

> . . . so shall the World go on,
> To good malignant, to bad men benign,
> *(P.L.* XII.537–538)

summarizes what episode after episode has shown, and might be used to summarize much of the *Commedia* as well. Marco's statement in *Purgatorio* (16.121–123), that only three just men are still alive in Lombardy, would need a mere change of place name to serve for virtually every city-state that Dante reviews in the *Commedia*—and for virtually every period of history that Michael reveals to Adam. In Book XI Enoch, the "only righteous in a World perverse," is "therefore hated, therefore so beset/ With Foes for daring single to be just,/ And utter odious Truth" (701–704); and Noah, "the only Son of light/ In a dark Age, against example good,/ Against allurement, custom, and a World/ Offended," is viciously "derided"

(808–817). Their situation is very much what Cacciaguida predicts for Dante among his fellow exiles:

> Of their brutishness their progress shall make
> proof, so that it shall be for thy fair fame to
> have made a party for thyself.
>
> *(Par.* 17.67–69)

And Michael's words to Adam on the kings who will follow David, "Part good, part bad, of bad the longer scroll" *(P.L.* XII.336), translate Thomas Aquinas addressing Dante on kings "che son molti, e i buon son rari" *(Par.* 13.108). Doubtless psychologizing critics would remind us that both Dante and Milton were disappointed in their political hopes. But, as we shall see, both Dante and Milton *place* their certainty of the world's evil, and they do not place it so as to account merely for their own political misfortunes.

First we observe the extent of the assertion. Dante cries out in *Purgatorio,*

> Ah Italy, thou slave, hostel of woe, vessel
> without pilot in a mighty storm, no mistress
> of provinces, but a brothel!   (6.76–78)

And the whole anguished passage that follows, with Rome wailing, "Cesare mio, perchè non m'accompagne?" can be resolved only by the coming, prophesied in the last canto of *Purgatorio,* of "un cinquecento dieci e cinque" sent by God *(Purg.* 33.43–44). In *Paradise Lost,* after the renewal of the world following the flood, Michael simply predicts

> Thus will this latter, as the former World,
> Still tend from bad to worse;
>
> (XII. 105–106)

and again after Christ's life, death, and resurrection, the world will continue the same, "Under her own weight groaning"

(XII.539), with no hope "of respiration to the just,/ And vengeance to the wicked" until the Second Coming (540–551). Whether Milton took the "veltro" of *Inferno* 1 and the "DXV" of *Purgatorio* 33 as Christ returned to judge the world, the interpretation of most early commentators, or as some particular political leader like Can Grande della Scala, following the interpretation of Daniello, or whether he regarded it as a deliberate mystery like his own "two-handed engine" in *Lycidas*, he not only saw Restoration England as fallen into a state like that of Dante's Italy, its particular hope of wise leadership, at least for the time, wholly lost; he also saw the political hope itself, by the very nature of the world, as in some measure delusive. According to Michael's prophecy, only the Second Coming can finally put an end to the recurrent ills of the world.

On a major source of those ills, the confusion of temporal and spiritual power, Milton largely agreed with Dante. For Dante, the trouble arose from the assumption of civil power by a corrupt church; for Milton, it was the assumption of political control, whether by kings, bishops, parliament, or "new presbyter," over areas of life that should be left free. For Dante, the world needed above all an emperor who would end the anarchy of conflicting claims, restoring the rule of law, and a pope who would abjure worldly power, renewing the gospel of Christ. For Milton, the world needed above all a rule of law that would not encroach on conscience. The immediate political remedies envisioned by Dante and Milton were of course not the same; but in his ultimate political position Milton clearly regarded Dante as his ally. On one fact of political life he fully agreed with Dante: evil leadership leads the world astray, but equally an evil world asks for evil leadership.

The Tuscany Guido del Duca describes in *Purgatorio* doubtless deserves the fate he predicts for it at the hands of Rinieri da Calboli's descendant:

> I see thy grandson, who is becoming a hunter of
> those wolves on the bank of the fierce river, and
> strikes them all with terror.
>
> He sells their flesh while yet alive; then slaughters
> them like worn-out cattle: many he deprives of
> life and himself of honour.
>
> *(Purg.* 14.58–63)

In Michael's prophecy Nimrod, also a hunter whose game is
"Men not Beasts" (*P.L.* XII.30), represents all such tyrants.
When Adam "fatherly displeas'd" speaks of his usurpation of
authority over his fellow men, "from God not giv'n" since
"Man over men/ He made not Lord" (69–70), Michael
answers with the central political doctrine of *Paradise Lost*
(XII.79–101). The passage merits examination in detail as
the one avowedly political passage in a poem where on the
whole politics are implicit rather than explicit. Yet time after
time those implications are not to be missed by a reader who
respects the author's intention.

Hell is a tyranny, Heaven a realm of natural law; and Eden
has been designed as a community of merit whose citizens would
hold all things in common, wives and children excepted, like the
friends of the Greek proverb (*P.L.* IV.751–752). Wives and
children are clearly not things, therefore not possessions, and the
"propriety" in them is not property. Indeed, we note in Book IX
how quickly, once Eve and then Adam change from thinking of
each other as persons to regarding each other as possessions,
they fall to using each other as things. Dante's Heaven too is a
community of persons where no questions of property, or even
of exclusiveness, are relevant. All such issues have been fully
resolved by Virgil's explanation in *Purgatorio* (15.49–57). The
good that increases by being shared is no one's property, but
public good.

Misdirected desire all too obviously has public as well as personal consequences. Hence, just as the pageant in the Terrestrial Paradise provides the final instruction of Dante's middle world, the last two, purgatorial books of *Paradise Lost* link the redemptive process with political history and make clear that the full human stature and the full reconquest of lost bliss are possible only in a community, though one far different from any in the known world.

Michael's whole speech on Nimrod's tyranny must be given full weight. The very sequence of arrogance toward man, shown in empire-building, followed by arrogance toward God in attempting the tower of Babel, links Nimrod with Satan. In the introductory explanation of Satan's fall (I.36–40) the sequence is the same: Satan wanted to be better than his equals, "aspiring/ To set himself in Glory above his Peers," and to be equal to his betters: "He trusted to have equall'd the most High." Milton is expressing no complacent doctrine about remaining in the station in life that God has seen fit to assign; rather, he is denouncing the pride that sees other men as inferiors and desires God-like dominion over them. Adam's statement deserves repetition:

> Man over men
> He made not Lord; such title to himself
> Reserving, human left from human free.
> (XII.69–71)

And Michael first comments:

> Justly thou abhorr'st
> That Son, who on the quiet state of men
> Such trouble brought, affecting to subdue
> Rational Liberty.　　(XII.79–82)

Rational liberty is not only the freedom of reason, but the freedom that befits the rational creature, man, the freedom without which he cannot fully exercise reason. Only then does Michael explain how political tyranny takes its rise from the tyranny within:

> Since thy original lapse, true Liberty
> Is lost, which always with right Reason dwells
> Twinn'd, and from her hath no dividual being:
> Reason in man obscur'd, or not obey'd,
> Immediately inordinate desires
> And upstart Passions catch the Government
> From Reason, and to servitude reduce
> Man till then free. Therefore since hee permits
> Within himself unworthy Powers to reign
> Over free Reason, God in Judgment just
> Subjects him from without to violent Lords;
> Who oft as undeservedly enthral
> His outward freedom: Tyranny must be,
> Though to the Tyrant thereby no excuse.
>
> (XII.83–96)

The passage does not justify the imperfections of governments as inevitable since Adam's fall; it recognizes the relation and suggests a curative procedure. In his introduction to the Yale edition of *The Tenure of Kings and Magistrates*, Merritt Y. Hughes resolves the issue thus:

Definitely though Milton accepted Augustine's doctrine of original sin as infecting organized society, he never lost his hope that it might some day realize the divine justice which he once quoted Solomon as saying was the foundation of all thrones, and which he himself identified with "The universall Justice that Aristotle so much praises, containing in it all vertues." (pp. 121–122)

The Platonism of Michael's politics is evident; we do not find in Dante any comparable assertion that the ills of the state are the ills of the individual soul writ large. What we do find is an emphasis on liberty as the desideratum that approximates

Milton's more nearly than any thing in Plato. The very placing of Cato as warden of the Mount suggests that the purgatorial climb is toward political as well as individual freedom. When Dante is both "crowned and mitred" over himself, in Virgil's parting words, he is given symbols of the liberty he went seeking, the liberty proper to a citizen as well as to a soul. The pageant in the Earthly Paradise tells of freedom gained and lost in church and state. Doubtless the author of the *Monarchia* felt no such urgency about civil liberties as the author of *Areopagitica*, but he too saw his time as a "secol selvaggio" (*Purg.* 16.135), and agreed that true liberty "always with right Reason dwells/ Twinn'd." To the view that without right reason in individuals, "Tyranny must be,/ Though to the Tyrant thereby no excuse," Dante countered that the worse the time, the greater the need of good leadership (*Purg.* 16.103–105), whatever may be the opportunity afforded to bad.

The pageant elaborating the relations of church and state sums up a major theme of the *Commedia*, the denunciation of a worldly church. Not even Dostoyevsky's Ivan Karamazov declares more unequivocally that a church that turns itself into a state fails of its own special task. If the proper office of the state is to protect the bodily well-being of its citizens, and the office of the church to guide them in the habits of mind and heart that produce everlasting well-being, the distinction of offices may at times be hard to make. But a church that seeks money, power, realms, and armies, has obviously abrogated its own function and disrupted the due performance of the state's. Dante's condemnation of the erring church is far more severe and insistent than his condemnation of bad kings and princes. For the bad individual ruler passes, but institutions that mistake their function lead generation after generation astray. The pageant of *Purgatorio* 29–33 foretells the emphasis of *Paradiso* 9.127–142; 11.124–139; 17.50–51; 18.118–136;

Dante and Milton

21.124–135; 22.73–96; 27.19–27,40–66,139–148; 29.88–126; 30.139–148. It is remarkable how much readers like T. S. Eliot can write about Dante without so much as mentioning this vein of his poem. Milton was less disingenuous: he gave it due attention, as his citations of Dante show, though he himself in *Paradise Lost* limited the theme to a brief passage in Michael's forecast of church history (XII.508–537). What distinguishes that forecast from the tirades of St. Peter and Beatrice is that Michael denies the church's right to enforce matters of faith, whereas St. Peter and Beatrice deny that a church concerned with force or money is the church at all.

There was ample ground for Milton's finding Dante sympathetic on the matter. The assertion in *Purgatorio* that excommunication does not damn in spite of the clergy, providing the sinner repents, even though he must wait outside Purgatory "thirtyfold for all the time that he hath lived in his presumption" (3.139–140), limits the ecclesiastical claim to control the destiny of souls. And the scene with Adrian V (*Purg.* 19.99ff.) limits the clerical office to this world. Dante, who has knelt not only to angels (*Purg.* 2 and 9) but to Cato as the warden of the Mount (1.51), is forbidden by Adrian himself to kneel to him:

> "What reason," he said, "thus bent thee down?"
> And I to him: "Because of your dignity my
> conscience smote me for standing."
> "Make straight thy legs, uplift thee, brother," he
> answered; "err not, a fellow-servant am I with
> thee and with the others unto one Power.
> If ever thou didst understand that hallowed gospel
> sound which saith, '*Neque nubent*,' well canst
> thou see why thus I speak."
> (*Purg.* 19.130–138)

The pope who learned the right thing from his brief tenure

262

asserts that he stands in the same relation to God as every other soul. The doctrine is Catholic enough, but it is startling doctrine for the one pope except Peter himself with whom Dante reports any speech outside Hell. The point would not have been lost on Milton.

If a good pope found danger in even brief tenure of the office for which evil men so readily competed, the hope of the world cannot rest in officeholders. Milton denounced bishops only so long as they held office; thereafter he considered the ways to remove from the church all would-be controllers of the mind. Perhaps he, like Dante, had no special animus against the idea of papacy or bishopric, but knew that "blind mouths" at any level are likely to gape for power, misusing the service they have undertaken as an opportunity to exalt themselves.

Dante cherishes the hope of a "veltro," a "DXV" who, restoring monarchy to its right function, will cure the world of at least its worst ills.[1] In Michael's prophecies we read no such hope. Perhaps that difference explains why there is nothing in Dante to compare with Adam's description of warmakers as "Death's Ministers, not Men" (XI.676). For Dante too thought peace essential to civic well-being, and made it a main argument for the necessity of a single imperial rule (*Conv.* IV.iv–vi; *Mon.*, passim). But doubtless first the "veltro" would have to chase the she-wolf out of the way. Dante hopes for a power that will end the power of evil; Milton, by the time he wrote *Paradise Lost*, doubted that the earth would ever see such a power.

Their views are closer on what leads to civic broils. Cacciaguida traces the degeneration of Florence to the growth of luxury (*Par.* 15.97ff.); Michael asserts a similar doctrine:

[1] Cf. Auerbach's analysis of the political meaning of the *Commedia* in *Dante: Poet of the Secular World*, tr. Ralph Manheim (Chicago, 1961), pp. 126–133.

"Luxurious wealth" leads to "much blood, and . . . much waste" in war (XI.788–792). So long as men live with the memory of the flood "Fresh in thir minds," and therefore "With some regard to what is just and right," they will lead simple lives and "spend thir days in joy unblam'd" (XII.15–22). But the memory does not stay fresh for long. Again, after the return from Babylon, the Israelites will "for a while/ In mean estate live moderate, till grown/ In wealth and multitude, factious they grow" (XII.350–352). Wealth and multitude leading to faction is precisely Cacciaguida's argument, and Michael's lines on the rise of Nimrod, "Of proud ambitious heart, who not content/ With fair equality, fraternal state," arrogates undeserved dominion and dispossesses "Concord and law of Nature from the Earth" (XII.24–29), might summarize the passage in *Paradiso* 15.

A return to the temperate life of the moderate state would presumably end faction and the civic broils it engenders. But what, short of a cataclysm, can return men to such idyllic politics? The world cannot await the millennium, or even some more immediate deliverance, no matter how certain it is to go on until then without final solutions. Something short of the communion of saints must be attempted by men here and now. And at this point of the political argument, Dante and Milton each offers a paradox. Dante, whose entire *Commedia* reduces earth to at most the threshing-floor of souls, is determined to the very end of his vision that he will speak out to men of the urgent need to set their earthly house in order: almost every voice in Paradise has something to say on what is wrong, what should be done, in the world to which the pilgrim must return. Milton, who insists that earth is the shadow of Heaven, with nothing of the perfect paradigm inimitable here except the ultimate perfection, seemingly renounces all hope of the world's ever being more than briefly set right.

Nothing like Heaven can be achieved on earth, according to Dante, but still the effort to correct every error of earth must be made. A realm very like heaven can be achieved on earth, according to Milton, and yet the effort to achieve it is over and over doomed to fail. Clearly the context of the political doctrine must be taken into account: in *Paradise Lost*, with its synoptic view of the whole human story, to prophesy any ultimate stability in the world's affairs short of Judgment Day would be fatuous. It is not the failure of Milton's political hopes but his knowledge of history that makes the emphasis of Book XII inevitable. But Dante's *Commedia* keeps constantly in view the moment in time at which the pilgrim's voyage into the eternal began. It is not a greater hope that the world can be made right once for all in his own lifetime—or indeed ever, short of Judgment Day—that keeps his eye fixed on what needs to be made right, but a constant awareness that this now is the world men must cope with. If Dante had attempted the story of the fall, or if Milton had attempted a poem on his own time seen in the light of eternity, the political emphasis of the two works might have been more nearly the same.

Even given the difference in focus between the two poems, there is major agreement. Man's search for God involves the effort to know what is just, to behold what is true, and to adhere to that truth in responsible deeds.[2] Such an obligation requires public as well as private commitment. It is likely to entail public disapproval, and yet the man of conviction will ultimately find that, even when he seemed to stand alone, like Abdiel he has had the forces of the universe on his side. And

[2] Neither Dante nor Milton stresses fear, even of God. Dante uses the concept in *Inf.* 3.107–108: "la riva malvagia,/ che attende ciascun uom, che Dio non teme"; Milton suggests the same idea in *P.L.* XII.562: "And love with fear the only God." But clearly it is only God who should be feared, and that fear is simply awe and a zeal to do right.

that is enough—that and the certainty that the world he desires to bring into being is possible, though as yet far off. As each individual man works toward the possible Eden in Milton's terms, or toward the communion of saints in Dante's, he helps to eradicate the blindness and crookedness, to establish liberty as that much more of a possibility in the world. When all Purgatory quakes with rejoicing each time a soul is freed from its sins, it is because all have gained a share of freedom, that being one of the goods that multiply by being shared, as enlightenment and justice multiply, and as power and possession cannot. The politics of freedom are the politics of vision, of "caritas," of joy, of mutual generosity and inclusion, as the politics of power are the politics of exclusion and greed.

Doubtless such truisms are more easily declared than put into action. But even to declare them has a value in a world where they are seldom so much as spoken with enough conviction to counterbalance the repeated banalities of self-justifying illiberality. From Dante and Milton, the declaration has the more value since both men did in fact make the attempt to act upon it. Whatever the defeat of their political hopes, they had earned the right in the *Commedia* and in *Paradise Lost* to do Cacciaguida's bidding: "Make thy entire vision manifest" (*Par.* 17.128). Milton could write with assurance that the prophetic words to Dante would hold for him too:

> . . . if thy voice be grievous at first taste, yet
>   vital nutriment shall it leave thereafter when
>   digested.
> This cry of thine shall do as doth the wind, which
>   smiteth most upon the loftiest summits; and this
>   shall be no little argument of honour.
>
> (*Par.* 17.130–135)

Paradise Lost gave Milton little occasion for such statements; but what there was he took, using the invocation to the Muse

who is own sister of Wisdom to associate himself with the
figure of Abdiel:

> . . . though fall'n on evil days,
> On evil days though fall'n, and evil tongues;
> In darkness, and with dangers compast round,
> And solitude; yet not alone, while thou
> Visit'st my slumbers Nightly, or when Morn
> Purples the East.   (*P.L.* VII.25–30)

In thus linking himself at the center of his poem to the servant
of God who "single . . . maintain'd/ Against revolted multitudes the Cause/ Of Truth" and therefore bore "Universal
reproach," Milton was in effect, if not by intention, linking
himself with Dante. The words of Cacciaguida to his descendant fit Milton too; and the words of Milton's God to Abdiel
fit Dante:

> . . . this was all thy care
> To stand approv'd in sight of God, though Worlds
> Judg'd thee perverse.   (*P.L.* VI.35–37)

The mission prescribed to the prophetic poet at the center of
Paradiso was chosen by the poet of *Paradise Lost:* to offer no
millennial hopes, and yet to show—though in the grimness of
its likely defeats—the right way. And though each expected
to have to be a party by himself, since partisans of all sorts
seek only partial goals, each expected too that because of his
very effort he would be "*not* alone."

The acceptance of immediate defeats with the expectation of
ultimate victory is, after all, more heartening than the certainty
of immediate victory and ultimate defeat. For self-preservation
is not the first law of human nature. The politics of self-
preservation fail to preserve even the basest selves. Perhaps,
indeed, self-transcendence affords the better hope. It is a

process that must, of course, start within, but its bearing on politics is clear. *Purgatorio* takes on its chief political meaning as it dissociates the erring from the error, and *Paradise Lost* as it disentangles Adam from the original sin. At every liberation on the Mount every soul rejoices, as every perceptive reader rejoices at the rescue of Adam and Eve.

VII

The Narrative of Meaning

ON two poems so various as the *Commedia* and *Paradise Lost* no last word can be said. Each lures the commentator into betraying serious limitations of awareness, for both are more than any one study can say about either—books to think with, not merely to think about. To re-experience the mimesis each presents is to experience a growth, a growth that does not necessarily culminate in agreement with the explicit doctrine of either poem. Dante did not convert Milton to Catholicism or to a belief in a divinely ordained Roman empire. And Milton is most unlikely to persuade his reader to share his specific religious or political convictions. But that is not their doctrinal impulse. What the *Commedia* and *Paradise Lost* can effect is a re-examination of values more inclusive and at the same time humbler, closer to the admirations and distastes by which we live.

This is not, of course, the effect upon every reader; nor will any one reader respond in the same degree or precisely the same areas as another. But for those who do respond, both Dante and Milton are civilizing poets. The reader who seeks only to have his own views mirrored, his own thought elaborated, inevitably misses what is there. It was genial of C. S. Lewis, who missed little of what *Paradise Lost* has to offer, to regard Milton with such admiration that he read into him his own doctrine of hierarchy; it is even genial of William

Empson, who misses most of the poem's meanings, to want so much to regard Milton favorably that he reads into him his own tensions about the Christian God. But Lewis found in *Paradise Lost* much more than a re-enforcement of his own convictions; and the same may be hoped even of Empson, in spite of the distortions in his *Milton's God*. Any book on *Paradise Lost*, any book on the *Commedia*, is bound to be limited in comparison with the inclusive vision of either poem.

Milton himself did not attend equally to all the strands of Dante's work. But he surely attended to more than I have shown. Some remaining areas of his debt, probable but not easily documented, warrant further exploration.

First, we need a detailed study of Milton's diction in relation to Dante's. It is likely that his reading of Dante encouraged him to write in the vernacular, and perhaps even to eschew rhyme for his long narrative poem. Dante was surely not the only influence at work here; but his comment in *Convivio* I.x on rhyme as an extrinsic adornment, and his defense of the common tongue as a medium, not only in his book on the subject, but in *Convivio* I. ix–xiii, are among the milestones of critical theory. Sister Margaret Teresa (1938) notes that many of their linguistic inventions are parallel (pp. 160–163), and recently Joseph Raben has demonstrated that Shelley in translating Dante chose to use Milton's phrases.[1] Perhaps E. T. Prince is right to concentrate on Italian poets closer to Milton's time as his possible models, but we need more detailed evidence than Prince gives in *The Italian Element in Milton's Verse*.

Some features of Dante's style have a patent relation to the style of *Paradise Lost*. The special nature of their similes is one

[1] "Milton's Influence on Shelley's Translation of Dante's 'Matilda Gathering Flowers,'" *RES* 14 (1963), 142–156.

example. What Whaler calls the "homologation"[2] of Milton's similes would reward study in comparison with Dante; it is a more notable feature of the *Commedia* than of any other poem before *Paradise Lost*. As Ruth Wallerstein observed in *Studies in Seventeenth-Century Poetic*, such neo-Platonic humanists as Spenser and Milton use sensuous terms, in simile, metaphor, epithet, and descriptive detail to convey moral truth. Dante may well turn out to be Milton's closest model in this practice. What Auerbach writes of Dante's "metaphoric technique"—which evidently is meant to include the simile—that its terms are "not parallel but concordant" (p. 154), holds of Milton's too. Again, the relation of word order to the tensions of meaning links Milton with Dante. As Auerbach puts it, "Dante employs deviation from natural word order more frequently and radically than any other medieval stylist" (p. 165). The detailed study by Christopher Ricks in *Milton's Grand Style* shows the precision of effect similar deviations give to the phrasing of *Paradise Lost*. What Dante had achieved by assimilating Virgilian techniques to the Italian language in developing his own style was not lost on Milton.

One striking feature of Dante's style is the repetition of a phrase—in close sequence for emphasis, or to provide links of meaning between widely separated passages. Three interesting examples of the first kind occur in *Purgatorio* 30, where they mark major events. "Virgilio" is thrice repeated (49–51) in Dante's lament at his companion's disappearance. Beatrice adds a fourth "Virgilio" (55) before the triple "pianger" in her emphatic repetition: "non pianger anco, non pianger ancora:/ chè pianger ti convien per altra spada" (56–57). The

---

[2] See the articles by James Whaler on Milton's similes: *MP* 28 (1931), 313–327; *JEGP* 30 (1931), 327–334; *PMLA* 46 (1931), 1034–1074; *PMLA* 47 (1932), 534–553.

climax of the scene comes with her triple "ben" in the climactic repetition: "Guardami ben: ben son, ben son Beatrice" (73). The repetitions convey an almost Hamlet-like impatience; "di,' di'" (*Purg.* 31.5) is another example. Other repetitions have other emphatic effects: we have spoken elsewhere of St. Peter's in *Paradiso* 27, and of the Eagle's in *Paradiso* 20. The "chiusa chiusa" of *Paradiso* 5.138, the "Ringrazia,/ ringrazia" of *Paradiso* 10.52–53 stress two variants of joyous admiration.

Milton assigns to Satan a special kind of repetition and word play to show his demagogic tendencies. For Satan can hardly address a single person—or even himself, for that matter— without slipping almost immediately into the tone and stylistic devices of mob oratory. Take only the repetitions at the beginning of his first speech to the still-overwhelmed Beelzebub:

> *If* thou beest *he;* But O *how* fall'n! *how* chang'd
> From him, who in the happy Realms of Light
> Cloth'd with transcendent *bright*ness didst outshine
> Myriads though *bright: If he* whom mutual league,
> United thoughts and counsels, *equal* hope,
> And hazard in the Glorious Enterprise,
> *Join'd* with me once, now misery hath *join'd*
> In *equal* ruin. . . .   (I.84ff.)

And so it continues through to the rhetorical parallelism of "since . . . Since . . . In . . . in" in lines 116–119, which enables him to contradict his opening statements: Heaven was not the "happy Realms of Light" at all, but a "Tyranny," and nothing significant has been lost in comparison with the "experience" gained, which assures that their "grand Foe,/ Who now triumphs," will not necessarily triumph for ever. Verbal repetition takes on a demagogic force in Satan's harangues.

With other speakers, the device has other effects. The narrator's own *"with difficulty and labor hard/ . . . with difficulty and labor hee;/ But hee"* (II.1021–1023) suggests the grudging admiration that the Satanic voyage through Chaos evokes. *"Accurst,* and in a *cursed* hour," in the last line of Book II, underscores his grim arrival at the edge of the new universe. Omniscience uses repetition, rhyme, and alliteration with a more straightforward effect in the ironic comment on Satan "whom *no* bounds/ . . . , *no* bars of Hell, *nor* all the chains/ . . . *nor* yet the main Abyss/ . . . can hold" (III.81–84), in the prediction that Satan will try to *"pervert;* and shall *pervert"* man (92), in the declarative reference to "the *sole* Command,/ *Sole* pledge" (94–95), and the interrogatory *"whose* fault?/ *Whose* but his own?" (96–97), through the doctrinal "Freely they *stood* who *stood,* and *fell* who *fell"* (102), echoing the *stood* and *fail'd* of the preceding line, to the longer sweep from *Mercy* to *Mercy* in the three concluding lines (131–134). But the effects Milton, like Dante, achieves through such repetition are too many and various to be elaborated, and owe a great deal to the rhetorical tradition both poets inherited from antiquity.

More striking is their variant of epic repetition to link widely separate parts of the poem. Thus when the line "Brought Death into the World, and all our woe" of the opening invocation is echoed in the renewed invocation to Book IX, "That brought into this World a world of woe,/ Sin and her shadow Death" (11–12), it ties the episode of the fall to the subject initially promised and marks it unmistakably as the central action, the true crisis of the poem. The inversion of Satan's magniloquent "Better to reign in Hell, than serve in Heav'n" (I.263) in Abdiel's "Reign thou in Hell thy Kingdom, let mee serve/ In Heav'n God ever blest" (VI.183–184) strips Satan's line—later chronologically, though it comes earlier in the poem—of its magnetic force. Throughout *Paradise Lost* Milton uses such subtle variants of the stock epic device of repetition to suggest

Dante and Milton

complex meanings. Dante achieves a comparable subtlety when he links the ostensibly admirable Farinata degli Uberti with Lucifer through the phrases "ei *levò le ciglia* un poco in soso" (*Inf*. 10.45) and "contra il suo Fattore *alzò le ciglia*" (34.35), or when Francesca's famous "Amor, che a nullo amato amar perdona" (*Inf*. 5.103) is amended in Virgil's "Amore,/ acceso di virtù, sempre altro accese" (*Purg*. 22.10–11) and in Dante's "il bene, in quanto ben, come s'intende,/ così accende amore" (*Par*. 26.28–29).

And the catching up of earlier phrases in the final canto helps immensely to convey the sense that this is indeed the climax toward which the whole work has been moving.

> Qual è colui che somniando vede,
>   chè dopo il sogno la passione impressa
>   rimane, e l' altro alla mente non riede;
> cotal son io, chè quasi tutta cessa
>   mia visione, ed ancor mi distilla
>   nel cor lo dolce che nacque da essa.
> (As is he who dreaming seeth, and when the dream
>   is gone the impression stamped remaineth, and
>   naught else cometh to the mind again;
> even such am I; for almost wholly faileth me my
>   vision, yet doth the sweetness that was born of it
>   still drop within my heart.)   (*Par*. 33.58–63)

Somniando, vede, sogno, visione, cor, dolce—a glance at a concordance shows variant forms of these key words in key passages of the *Commedia*; "nacque" is rarer, but suggests the whole idea of the journey as a rebirth. And the simile that follows of the melting snow (64), as it echoes the earlier more elaborate simile in *Purgatorio* (30.85–99) of snow and ice melting, which in turn recalls the ice of the last circle of Inferno (Cantos 32–34), proves more conclusively than most commentaries the absolute importance of Beatrice to the final revelation of the *Commedia*. The "stelle" with which each cantica ends needs no comment. Obviously Dante used the device of repetition consciously. Milton surely recognized the conscious device in the *Commedia* and exploited it with like deliberateness.

The mastery with which both Dante and Milton handle language is matched by the assurance with which they pronounce on a vast range of issues. Both the *Commedia* and *Paradise Lost* remind some readers uncomfortably of preaching, and for an obvious reason. In both poems voices of unimpeachable authority speak on a variety of subjects: Virgil, Statius, Beatrice, all the redeemed who address Dante in *Paradiso*; in *Paradist Lost* God, the Son, Uriel, Gabriel, Raphael, Michael—their decisive words are there to carry the poet's convictions. Milton had begun to use the device as early as *Comus*, where the attendant Spirit, afterwards Thyrsis, not only takes part in the action but states its import. When in *Lycidas* he used the authoritative voice first of Apollo and then of St. Peter to resolve issues, he was probably adopting the device from Dante, whose influence appears throughout the entire pattern. Both poets show a delicacy of mind in assigning such speeches. As we have elsewhere observed each declares his own inadequacy to the high task, and attributes all that is right in it to the power that inspires the "sacred song."

Something of his delicate procedure Milton learned from Dante, as we may discover by comparing the hymnology of his angels with Dante's description of the songs in Paradise. Milton carefully works up to direct presentation, using first Dante's technique of indirect reporting. With the first angelic song he starts with narrative summary:

> Thee Father first they sung Omnipotent,
> Immutable, Immortal, Infinite . . .
>
> (III.372–373)

This is very much Dante's way.

> There did they sing, not Bacchus, and not Paean,
> but three Persons in the divine nature, and it
> and the human nature in one Person.
>
> (*Par.* 13.25–27)

> That One and Two and Three who ever liveth
> and reigneth ever in Three and Two and One,
> not circumscribed, but all circumscribing,
> three times was hymned by each one of those
> spirits with such melody as were a fit reward
> to any merit.   (*Par.* 14.28–33)

Only at the end of the hymn does Milton imply that these are the very words, not merely the substance, of what was sung:

> Hail Son of God, Savior of Men, thy Name
> Shall be the copious matter of my Song
> Henceforth, and never shall my Harp thy praise
> Forget, nor from thy Father's praise disjoin.
> Thus they in Heav'n, above the starry Sphere,
> Thir happy hours in joy and hymning spent.
>
> (III.412–417)

Raphael, reporting the hymns of praise at the end of the war in Heaven and at the subsequent seven days' creation, generally uses Dante's technique of summary (VI.885–886; VII.256–260,274–275,449–450), so that when he finally repeats the very words of an angelic song (VII.565–573), the reader is prepared to accept them. Milton himself as narrator gives the very words of such a song only much later in Book X.643–648, by which time the reader no longer questions the propriety. And the avoidance of repetition in dealing with such repeated material as the angels' songs itself recalls Dante's way of varying where repetition seems almost unavoidable, for example in the removal of the seven *P*'s from the pilgrim's forehead.

Dante may have suggested to Milton still more important ways of securing variety, in a still more important area. Renaissance denigrators of the *Commedia* complained that it had only one agent, Dante—or at most three, if we allow Virgil and Beatrice roles in the human action. Commentators on *Paradise Lost* have also complained of the paucity of human agents. Adam and Eve present only two—or at best, according to Addison, four—personae. A more sympathetic critic of the *Commedia* such as Auerbach recognizes in the action a mimesis of the entire gamut of human ethos. And Adam and Eve, we may submit, each possess a nature of such range, before as well as after the fall, that to list their attitudes comes as near exhausting the humanly possible as to list the attitudes of Dante's other world. The varieties in ethos of Milton's Hell and Heaven are themselves human varieties, as we have elsewhere noted. Perhaps to name some aspects of the mimetic range of Adam and Eve may indicate what multitudes they contain.

Newborn Adam begins as a Pindaric athlete rejoicing in his powers; becomes a classical philosopher seeking the first cause; shows a conviction like the Psalmist's that the realm of nature can best declare its maker; turns mystic in beholding God; enacts a Biblical disputation with God that proves his divine origin; experiences, in the trance in which his inner eye beholds Eve's genesis, what will later seem to the poet Keats a parable of the relation between imagination and reality; turns lover, husband, even uxorious husband, almost courtly lover—this all on his first day in life, narrated by him in little more than three hundred lines (VIII.253–559). Eve has almost as crowded a natal day. From self-admiring infant to devoted wife, she moves in one swift rush up a ladder of love that strikingly combines a prophetic Freudian teaching with the ancient lore of Plato. From narcissism to the capacity for devotion, from doting on a shadowy fair appearance to recognition of the reality of wisdom, "which alone is truly fair," Eve's progress during her first day in life is a remarkable achievement, especially as she recounts it in little more than fifty lines (IV.449–491), all modulated with her bridal reminiscences of how she and her husband first met. Something of the tenderness normal people feel for the young and happy permeates Milton's tone in these speeches for Eve and Adam. Even the narrative voice in *Paradise Lost* has a wide mimetic range, as Anne Davidson Ferry demonstrates.[3]

Adam and Eve, as they appear in Book IV in all the dignity of their mutual love, represent far more than a dream of amorous felicity. Eve thinks herself more highly favored by God in having been given Adam, while he was given only her; Adam rejoices in his care for this "likeness," this "fit help," this "other self" answering exactly to his "heart's desire," as he will phrase it to Raphael in Book X. They are as married a couple as Tolstoy's Natasha and Pierre at the end of *War and Peace*, or Kitty and Levin at the end of *Anna Karenina*, without the downgrading of Eros or the near-bourgeois complacency that regularly mars Tolstoy's presentation of married happiness. They are married enough to welcome the stranger Raphael and delight in his prolonged visit.

Then with her first words in Book IX Eve becomes in rapid succession a slightly self-righteous Major Barbara, an Ibsen's Nora reinterpreted by Strindberg, a stubborn Rosamond Vincy, a triumphant Lucrezia del Sarto, and at noon with one swift plunge a Pamela who takes the bait, a Cleopatra determined to hold her Antony, a Helen consciously alluring, a Lady Macbeth prescribing ambitious crimes, a Jocasta certain that trouble can be dismissed as mere superstition, a Clytemnestra sodden with victory, and a shrewish, railing Dame Alisoun. Or take Adam in Book X from his shabby self-exculpation in the manner al-

[3] *Milton's Epic Voice* (Cambridge, Mass., 1963).

most of Tito Melema, his self-defensive twistings in the manner almost of Jason, through his prolonged Hamlet-like despair and misogyny, to his pity as of an undemented Othello, and his Lear-like recognition of his own need of forgiveness. The narrative skill with which Milton through a few strokes reveals a whole ethos in dialogue, deed, attitude, and gesture, without for a moment losing Eve's or Adam's essential self-consistency —no poet but Dante had ever achieved a comparable swiftness. And Dante assigns each ethos in his rapid sequence to a separate person, except as he shows a deliberate and steady change in himself.

One last remark: Both poems owe much of their compelling force to the inclusive circuit by which at their end they reach a beginning. No reader can arrive at the last lines of the *Commedia* without feeling that everything has been gone through and yet that everything is about to begin—in Heaven itself with the vast audience of the "candida rosa" ready, as it were, for the curtain to rise, and on earth for Dante returning to live his prophesied life and transcribe his vision. No one can reach the closing lines of *Paradise Lost* without feeling that everything is over, Eden lost, and all history until Doomsday foreseen, and yet that everything is about to begin—for Adam and Eve as they venture into "the World . . . all before them," and for mankind as the human story commences. It is the myth of Sisyphus with a tremendous difference: everything that is about to occur and to recur has gained a significance that only the greatest poets can enable us to see.

Appendixes

A Table of Milton's References to Dante before *Paradise Lost*[1]

Year	Work and line number	Work cited	Noted by
1626	On . . . Ely, 53–58	? Paradiso	Hughes, *Minor Poems*, p. 47n.
1629	Nativity Ode, 173–180	? Par. 17.31–33	Plumptre, II,98n.
?1630	Elegia VII, 84	? Inf. 20.29–36	Hughes, p. 60n.
1631	Epitaph . . . Winchester, 61–70	? Par. 32.7–10	Hanford
?1631	Il Penseroso	? Dante's life	Plumptre, II, 348
?1632–	Arcades, 56–58	? Purg. 24.145–147	Todd
1633	84–86	? Inf. 4.118	Todd
?1633	On Time, 18	? Par. 33	Hughes, p. 80n.
	At a Solemn Musick 6	? Purg. 8.13–15	
		? Par. 12.7–9	
1634	Comus, 1ff., 15–17	? Inf. 2.52ff.,91–93 9.82–84	
	138–140	? Purg. 9.2.	Todd
	450ff.	? Vita Nuova	Herford, pp. 202–203
	602–604	? Inf. 3.52–54	Toynbee
	893–894	? Inf. 4.118	Kellett, p. 136
1637	Lycidas	? Paradiso	P. E. More; Hughes, p. 119
	71	? Inf. 3.46; 24.46ff.	Plumptre, I, 15n., 121n.
	80–84	? Par. 6.112–117	Hughes, p. 122n.
	110–111	? Inf. 13; 27.103–104	Todd; Toynbee
		? Purg. 9.117–118	
		? Par. 27.49	
	113–131	? Inf. 19.90;	Kuhns, pp. 2–3
		? Par. 27.19–63	
		? Par. 29.106–107	Toynbee; Plumptre, II, 171n.

[1] The dates of Milton's minor poems are as given by Hughes in *John Milton: The Complete Poems and Major Prose*. Page references to Hughes are also to this edition, except in the first entry.

Year	Work and line number	Work cited	Noted by
	120	? Inf. 6.93	
	130–131	? Par. 22.13–17	
	168	? Purg. 2.15	E. Moore, III, 84n.
	171	? Purg. 9.4	E. Moore, III, 84n.
	180	? Par. 31.4–5	
1638	Letter to Buommattei	Dante	
1641	Of Reformation, Yale I, 558–559	Inf. 19.115–117; Par. 20.55	
1642	Church-Government, Yale I, 812ff.	? end of Vita Nuova ? Purg. 19.7–33	Kuhns, p. 4
	Apology . . . Smectymnuus, Yale I, 890	The "renowner of Beatrice"	
1646	Sonnet XIII to Lawes	Purg. 2.76–119	
1647	Letter to Dati	Dante	
1653	Translation of Psalm 2	? Dante's terza rima	Hughes, p. 161
1654	Defensio Secunda, Columbia VIII, 225ff.	? Epistle VII	Herford, p. 213
?1655	Sonnet XIX, 14	? Par. 28.110	Hughes, p. 168n.
?1655	Sonnet XXIII	? The "donna angelicata" of Dante	Hughes, p. 170n.
1659	Means . . . Hirelings, Columbia VI, 48	? Inf. 19.115–117	Hughes, p. 858n.
	Commonplace Book		(For all data see
? after 1639	Fol. 12	Inf. 7.25,37–48, 52–54	Hanford, "Chronology," and Mohl, Yale I.)
	Fol. 16	Inf. 13	
	Fol. 70	Inf. 3.34–49,52–63	
	Fol. 111	Par. 8.140ff.	
	Fol. 160	Inf. 11.109ff.; and comment of Bernardino Daniello da Lucca	
	Fol. 182	Monarchia; and Boccaccio's Vita di Dante	
	Fol. 191	Convivio, IV, canzone	
? after 1647	Fol. 197	Purg. 16.106–112, 127–129	

APPENDIX C

Comments on the Relation of Milton and Dante, in Chronological Sequence

FRANÇOIS MARIE AROUET DE VOLTAIRE. Essay on Milton, ed. and tr. Desmond Flower. Cambridge, 1954. First published London, 1727.

JONATHAN RICHARDSON. *Paradise Lost* Explained. London, 1734. See Toynbee, I, 201–202.

ANTONIO CONTI. "Giudizio sopra la *Divina Commedia.*" First published 1739. Poesie e Prose 4.II, 228–230. Venice, 1759.

HENRY JOHN TODD. The Poetical Works of John Milton. London, 1801.

HENRY FRANCIS CARY. Letter to Anna Seward. August 16, 1806. See Toynbee, I, 473–474.

FRANÇOIS AUGUSTE CHATEAUBRIAND. Génie du Christianisme, II, 10,56,262,282–294. Lyon, 1809.

WILLIAM HAZLITT. The Round Table. London, 1817. See Collected Works. I, 37. London, 1930–1934.

SAMUEL TAYLOR COLERIDGE. Lectures on Dante. 1818. See Toynbee, I, 622–623,626.

"Dante's *Divine Comedy*, and Cary's Translation." The North American Review 8 (1819), 342–347.

PERCY BYSSHE SHELLEY. Defence of Poetry. 1821.

JOHN KEBLE. Quarterly Review 32 (1825), 229. See Toynbee, II, 436.

THOMAS BABINGTON MACAULAY. "Essay on Milton," originally in Edinburgh Review 42 (1825), 31–64. See Milton and Machiavelli. London, 1868.

Dante and Milton

"JANUS." Article, Edinburgh Literary Almanack (1826), 180–183. See Toynbee, II, 457–458.

"Todd's edition of Milton." Quarterly Review 36 (1827), 49–54. See Toynbee, II, 471–476.

HENRY STEBBING. Life of Dante, I, 69–71. London, ?1831. See Toynbee, II, 543.

"Stebbing's Italian Poets." The Monthly Review (1831), 295–305.

"Wright's Translation of the *Inferno* of Dante." Edinburgh Review 57 (1833), 412–434.

JAMES RUSSELL LOWELL. Letter to G. B. Loring. Dec. 22, 1837. New Letters of J. R. Lowell, ed. M. A. De Wolfe Howe. New York, 1932.

THOMAS CARLYLE. Lectures 5 and 8. May 14 and 25, 1838. Lectures on the History of Literature. See Toynbee, II, 488,494.

"A Triad of Great Poets." Tait's Edinburgh Magazine 20 (1853), 513–525, 577–587,641–650.

FÉLICITÉ DE LAMENNAIS. Introduction, *L'Enfer: La Divine Comédie*, I, by Dante Alighieri, pp. lxvii–lxxxv. Paris, 1855.

ALPHONSE DE LAMARTINE. "Milton." Oeuvres Complètes, XXXVI, 3–35. Paris, 1860–1866.

ARTHUR HENRY HALLAM. Remains, p. 140. Boston, 1863.

HENRY HALLAM. Introduction to the Literature of Europe in 15th, 16th, 17th Centuries, IV, 236–239. London, 1864.

JOHN ADDINGTON SYMONDS. An Introduction to the Study of Dante, London, 1872.

WALTER SAVAGE LANDOR. "Southey and Landor." Conversations, 3rd Series. Works, IV, 427–528. London, 1876.

MATTHEW ARNOLD. "Byron." Essays in Criticism, 2nd Series, pp. 163–204. London, 1881.

E. H. PLUMPTRE, tr. The Commedia and Canzoniere of Dante Alighiere. 2v. London, 1886–1887.

JAMES RUSSELL LOWELL. Letter to Charles Eliot Norton. Sept. 24, 1889. Letters of James Russell Lowell, ed. Charles Eliot Norton, II, 386.

Appendix C

JAMES RUSSELL LOWELL. "Study in Modern Languages" and "Milton's *Areopagitica.*" Latest Literary Essays and Addresses. Prose Works, VII, 106,137. Boston, 1892.

HERMANN OELSNER. The Influence of Dante on Modern Thought, pp. 75, 92–93, 117. London, 1895.

S. HUMPHREYS GURTEEN. The Epic of the Fall of Man: . . . Caedmon, Dante, Milton, pp. 305–308, 311–318, 322, 365–367, 376, 378–383. London, 1896.

ADOLF KAHLE. "Der Teufel in der Poesie." Die Gegenwart 50 (1896), 182–184.

OSCAR KUHNS. "Dante's Influence on Milton." MLN 13 (1898), 1–12.

EDWARD MOORE. Studies in Dante, III and IV. Oxford, 1903 and 1917.

KENNETH C. M. SILLS. "References to Dante in Seventeenth-Century English Literature." MP 3 (1905–1906), 99–116.

J. S. P. TATLOCK. "Milton's *Sin* and *Death.*" MLN 21 (1906), 239–240.

CHARLES G. OSGOOD. "Milton's Sphere of Fortune." MLN 22 (1907), 140–141.

ETTORE ALLODOLI. Giovanni Milton e l'Italia, pp. 17–18, 79–80. Prato, 1907.

W. J. COURTHOPE. "A Consideration of Macaulay's Comparison of Dante and Milton." Proceedings of the British Academy 3 (1907–1908), 258–274.

EDWARD HENRY PEMBER. "On the Conception and Treatment of Satan in *Paradise Lost* and the *Inferno.*" Milton Memorial Lectures, 1908, ed. Percy W. Ames, pp. 59–82. London, 1909.

GEORGE E. SAINTSBURY. "Milton and the Grand Style." Milton Memorial Lectures, 1908, pp. 83–107. London, 1909.

ALFRED AUSTIN. "Milton and Dante: A Comparison and a Contrast." The Quarterly Review 210 (1909), 157–170.

PAGET TOYNBEE. Dante in English Literature. London, 1909.

GEORGE E. SAINTSBURY. "Milton." CHEL VII (1911), 95–138.

C. L. BARNES. "Parallels in Dante and Milton." Manchester Quarterly 36 (1917), 8–29.

OLIN H. MOORE. "The Infernal Council." MP. 16 (1918), 169–193.

Dante and Milton

WILLIAM HALLER. "Order and Progress in *Paradise Lost*." PMLA 35 (1920), 218–225.

JEFFERSON B. FLETCHER. "The Comedy of Dante." SP 18 (1921), 392–411.

ALICE GALIMBERTI. Dante nel Pensiero Inglese, pp. 55–71. Florence, 1921.

PAGET TOYNBEE. Britain's Tribute to Dante in Literature and Art, pp. x, 13–15. London, 1921.

J. H. HANFORD. "The Chronology of Milton's Private Studies." PMLA 36 (1921), 251–314.

STOCKTON AXSON. "Dante and English Literature." Rice Institute Pamphlet 8 (1921), 216–245.

THOMAS NELSON PAGE. Dante and His Influence, pp. 132, 136, 140, 144–148, 169, 171. New York, 1922.

MARY BRADFORD WHITING. "Dante's Beatrice and Milton's Eve." Fortnightly Review 113 (1923), 475–483.

ANTERO MEOZZI. "Paralleli Danteschi." Il Giornale Dantesco 26 (1923), 121–127.

C. H. HERFORD. "Dante and Milton." Bulletin of the John Rylands Library 8 (1924), 191–235.

MICHELE RENZULLI. Dante nella Letteratura Inglese, pp. 45–53. Florence, 1925.

E. E. KELLETT. Reconsiderations, pp. 105–146. Cambridge, 1928.

SISTER MARGARET TERESA. The Influence of Dante's *Paradiso* upon Milton. Unpublished doctoral dissertation, Cornell University, 1938.

KENNETH MCKENZIE. "Echoes of Dante in Milton's *Lycidas*." Italica 20 (1943), 121–126.

F. P. WILSON. A Supplement to Toynbee's Dante in English Literature, pp. 50–62. London, 1946.

WILLIAM J. GRACE. "Orthodoxy and Aesthetic Method in *Paradise Lost* and the *Divine Comedy*." Comparative Literature 1 (1949), 173–187.

WERNER P. FRIEDRICH. Dante's Fame Abroad, 1350–1850, pp. 9–10, 201–210. Rome, 1950.

Appendix C

Ruth Mohl, ed. Milton's *Commonplace Book*. Yale Milton, I, 344–359. New Haven, 1953.

J. B. Broadbent. "Milton's Hell." ELH 21 (1954), 161–192.

W. B. C. Watkins. An Anatomy of Milton's Verse, pp. 35, 44, 48–49, 62, 83, 85. Baton Rouge, 1955.

Harris Francis Fletcher. The Intellectual Development of John Milton. 2v. Urbana, Ill., 1956, 1961.

Dorothy Sayers. "Dante and Milton." Further Papers on Dante, pp. 148–152. London, 1957.

J. B. Broadbent. Some Graver Subject. London, 1960.

John M. Steadman. "Milton and Mazzoni: The Genre of the *Divina Commedia*." HLQ 23 (1960), 107–122.

Don Cameron Allen. "Milton and the Descent to Light." JEGP 60 (1961), 630.

John Arthos. Dante, Michelangelo, and Milton. London, 1963.

APPENDIX D

The Proems of *Paradise Lost* and the *Commedia*

1. The sanctity of the power invoked	P.L. I.6	Purg. 1.8
		Purg. 29.37
2. The inspiring power invoked as having formerly aided others	P.L. I.6–12	Inf. 32.10–12
3. The aid of more than one power, or one power under more than one name, invoked	P.L. I.6, 17	Inf. 2.7–8
4. The height of the undertaking	P.L. I.14–15	Purg. 1.7,9
	23–24	Purg. 9.70–72
5. The novelty of the undertaking	P.L. I.16	Purg. 29.40–42
	III.21	Par. 2.7
6. The need of illumination for the undertaking	P.L. I.22–23	Par. 18.82,85–86
7. Light invoked that the realm of light may be properly sung	P.L. III.1	Par. 30.97–99
	51–55	Par. 33.67–72
8. Light as God's emanation	P.L. III.1–6	Par. 33.67–69
		(cf. Par. 13.52–57, and 19.64–65)
9. Joy at having finished with the infernal part of the poem	P.L. III.13–16	Purg. 1.1–3
10. The notes appropriate to Hell	P.L. III.17–18	Inf. 32. 1–2
11. Only the inspiring power enabled the poet to sing of deepest Hell	P.L. III.19–21	Inf. 32.4–8,10
12. The difficulty of the poet's theme	P.L. III.21	Inf. 32. 1–12
		Purg. 29.42
		Par. 1.13–17
13. A collocation of dawn, light, the joy of light, the Muses, the affliction of sightlessness	P.L. III.22–28	Purg. 1.8–18
14. The sacredness of the song	P.L. III.29	Par. 25.1
15. The poet linked with ancient prototypes	P.L. III.33–36	Inf. 4.88–90,94–102

16. Poetic inspiration asked in recompense for trials endured	P.L. III.40–55	Purg. 29.37–39 Par. 25.1–6
17. The subject invisible to mortal sight	P.L. III.55	Par. 1.5–6
18. Urania invoked by name	P.L. VII.1–2	Purg. 29.40–41
19. The divine muse associated with the adjective "Pegasean"	P.L. VII.2–4	Par. 18.82
20. The inadequacy of the pagan muse to the present theme	P.L. VII.5–7	Par. 23.55–59
21. A shift from earlier invocation to direct prayer for heavenly help with new theme	P.L. VII.5–10 37–39	Par. 30.97–99 Par. 33.67–72
22. Heavenly aid has enabled the poet to write thus far	P.L. VII.12–15	Par. 25.1–3
23. Conscious division of the poem into parts	P.L. VII.21	Inf. 20.1–3 Purg. 1.4 Purg. 33.139–141
24. Distinction of terrestrial and supraterrestrial parts; need of additional inspiration	P.L. VII.23	Par. 1.16–18,91–93, 139–141 Par. 22.112–114,121–123
25. A possible change of tone associated with evil unjustly suffered	P.L. VII.24–28	Par. 25.4–8
26. The fewness of the fit audience; the unfit dismissed	P.L. VII.31–33	Par. 2.1–15
27. Conscious shift of tone	P.L. IX.1–6	Purg. 1.7–9 Par. 1.13–27 Par. 23.55–63
28. Heavenly aid dictates the poem	P.L. IX.21–23	Par. 25.1–3 (cf. Par. 17.127–138, and Par. 27.64–66)
29. Since the inspiring power dictates, the versifying comes easily	P.L. IX.23–24	Purg. 24.52–54,58–59
30. The amount of the poet's life that has gone into the making of the poem	P.L. IX.25–26	Par. 25.1–3
31. The matter and the inspiring power, not the poet's self, give to the poem its worth	P.L. IX.42–47	Par. 1.22–27

Index of Names and Titles

[The Index includes proper names and titles, except for Dante, Milton the *Commedia*, *Inferno*, *Purgatorio*, *Paradiso*, and *Paradise Lost*, which are omitted since they occur *passim*.]

Index of Names and Titles

Index of Names and Titles

Index of Names and Titles

M